SOUTHERN BAPTISTS

&

AMERICAN EVANGELICALS

THE CONVERSATION CONTINUES

EDITED BY
DAVID S. DOCKERY

BROADMAN
&HOLMAN
PUBLISHERS

Nashville, Tennessee

© Copyright • 1993 Broadman & Holman Publishers
All Rights Reserved
4260-41
ISBN: 0-8054-6041-1
Dewey Decimal Classification: 230
Subject Headings: DOCTRINAL THEOLOGY
Library of Congress Catalog Number: 93-11780
Printed in the United States of America

Portions of this volume previously appeared in:

George Marsden, *Evangelicals and Modern America* (Grand Rapids: Eerdmans, 1984).

David Lotz, ed., *Altered Landscapes: Christianity in America 1935-85* (Grand Rapids: Eerdmans, 1989).

Donald Dayton and Robert K. Johnston, eds., *The Variety of Evangelicals* (Knoxville: University of Tennessee Press, 1991).

Library of Congress-in-Publication Data

Southern Baptists and American evangelicals / David S. Dockery, Editor.
　　p. cm.
　　Includes bibliographical references and index.
　　ISBN 0-8054-6041-1
　　1. Southern Baptist Convention—Relations—Evangelicalism.
　　2. Evangelicalism—Relations—Southern Baptist Convention.
　　3. Southern Baptist Convention—Doctrines.
　　4. Evangelicalism--United States. I. Dockery, David S.
　　BX6462.7.S68 1993
　　286' .132—dc20

　　　　　　　　　　　　　　　　　　　　　　　93-11780
　　　　　　　　　　　　　　　　　　　　　　　CIP

To

Jonathan, Benjamin, and Timothy
with thanksgiving for the continuous
joy you provide and with hope that
God might give you ongoing appreciation
for your Baptist and evangelical heritage

CONTRIBUTORS

Daniel L. Akin, Assistant Professor of Church History, Southeastern Baptist Theological Seminary, Wake Forest, NC

Joel A. Carpenter, Program Director, The Pew Charitable Trusts, Philadelphia, Pennsylvania, and formerly Director of the Institute for the Study of American Evangelicals, Wheaton, IL

David F. D'Amico, Billy Graham Professor of Evangelism, Southern Baptist Theological Seminary, Louisville, KY

David S. Dockery, Vice President for Academic Administration and Dean, School of Theology, Southern Baptist Theological Seminary, Louisville, KY

James Leo Garrett, Jr., Professor of Systematic and Historical Theology, Southwestern Baptist Theological Seminary, Fort Worth, TX

Stanley J. Grenz, Professor of Theology, Carey Hall, Regent College, Vancouver, British Columbia

E. Glenn Hinson, Professor of Church History, Baptist Theological Seminary at Richmond, Richmond, VA

Robert K. Johnston, Provost and Professor of Theology, Fuller Theological Seminary, Pasadena, CA

Bill Leonard, Professor of Religion, Samford University, Birmingham, AL

H. Leon McBeth, Professor of Church History, Southwestern Baptist Theological Seminary, Fort Worth, TX

George M. Marsden, Professor of the History of Christianity in America, The Divinity School, Duke University, Durham, NC

Richard R. Melick, Jr., President, Criswell College, Dallas, TX

R. Albert Mohler, Jr., President, Southern Baptist Theological Seminary, Louisville, KY

Richard Mouw, President and Professor of Christian Philosophy and Ethics, Fuller Theological Seminary, Pasadena, CA

John P. Newport, Retired Provost and Academic Vice-President, Southwestern Baptist Theological Seminary, Fort Worth, TX

Mark A. Noll, Professor of Church History, Wheaton College, Wheaton, IL

James Emery White, Pastor, Mecklenburg Community Church, Charlotte, NC

TABLE OF CONTENTS

Contents

PREFACE

Are Southern Baptists "Evangelicals"? James Leo Garrett, Jr. and E. Glenn Hinson raised this significant question in 1983 by issuing a book with this question as its title. The Mercer University Press publication focused on the relationship between Southern Baptists and American evangelicals. This present volume, as indicated by both the title and subtitle, continues and expands that conversation. Most of this work began as presentations during the 1989 and 1990 Denominational Heritage Conferences and the annual pastor's conferences at The Southern Baptist Theological Seminary in Louisville, Kentucky.

The questions addressed in those conference sessions and in this book have largely been brought about by the changing face of the Southern Baptist Convention over the past ten to fifteen years. During these years Southern Baptists have been intentionally self-conscious of their theology, re-examining questions regarding identity, heritage, beliefs, and relationships to other traditions within American Christianity. Groups like Southern Baptists tend to think more functionally and practically rather than analytically, stressing precedent more than logic in defense of its ways. Thus, attempts at classification tend to move beyond the groups' explicit statements of its own beliefs, practices, and principles.

For many years Southern Baptist have primarily talked to themselves and have been cut off, either consciously or unconsciously, from both the ecumenical wing and the evangelical wing of Christendom. The conversation that has taken place among Southern Baptists academicians has largely been carried on with mainline and ecumenical denominations. For a variety of reasons, however, Southern Baptists failed to do the same with the broader evangelical world. As Russell Chandler has noted in *Racing Toward 2001*, the mainline has moved to the sideline.[1]

Thus it has become imperative for Southern Baptists to engage the evangelical world. Yet, for many answering the question, "Are Southern Baptists 'evangelicals'?" it's difficult, if not impossible, due to the lack of

---

[1] Russell Chandler, *Racing Toward 2001* (Grand Rapids: Zondervan, 1992), 151-58.

familiarity with the American evangelical movement. As Russell Dilday has noted:

> Now the time is right for Southern Baptists to broaden the cooperancy which is so characteristic of our internal relationships and include in our cooperation a larger segment of like-minded believers in other groups, particularly in the evangelical world. Without diluting our denominational distinctives, or leaping carelessly into ecumenical alliances, we can find ways to work together and draw strength from our evangelical "cousins."[2]

A mistaken tendency to equate American evangelicalism with American fundamentalism has unfortunately existed among some Southern Baptists. This tendency continues in a few of the essays in this book. Hopefully, this volume will help Southern Baptists better understand evangelicals—who they are, what they believe, what they practice. Likewise, we pray that the larger evangelical community might learn more about the identity and practices of the largest Protestant denomination in the United States. We trust that each community might better understand its own identity and heritage as we move forward together into the twenty-first century.

The book is divided into four sections, with contributions from some of the finest Southern Baptist and Evangelical scholars in this country. Part One: "Searching for Identity" includes essays by George M. Marsden, Robert K. Johnston, Stanley J. Grenz, and H. Leon McBeth. Part Two: "In Dialogue" contains essays by Joel A. Carpenter, John P. Newport, Richard R. Melick, Jr., and David S. Dockery. Part Three: "Beliefs and Practices" advances the conversation with chapters by Richard Mouw, Stan Grenz, Bill Leonard, Daniel L. Akin, and David F. D'Amico. In addition to a fitting conclusion by R. Albert Mohler, Jr., Part Four: "Further Reflections" by E. Glenn Hinson and James Leo Garrett, Jr., brings the present conversation to a close with the two people who started the discussion a decade ago.

I am honored to edit a volume that brings together the works of such outstanding theologians and historians. To each of these participants I express my deep appreciation. Also, I am extremely appreciative of the vision of the previous administration of The Southern Baptist Theological Seminary, specifically President Roy Honeycutt, Dr. Willis Bennett, and Dr. Larry McSwain, for designing the initial conferences and for their encouragement and direction provided for me in preparing

---

[2] Russell Dilday, "From the President," *Southwestern News* 51 (November/December 1992), 3.

Preface

this volume. Words of thanks are also due Jane Jones and the editors at Broadman & Holman Publishers for their editorial work. Perhaps the most significant contribution to this project came from the support of the Pew Charitable Trusts. We hope the positive results of the conferences and this book will enable them to continue their participation in similar ventures in the future. Finally, as always, I am particularly grateful to my wife and three sons for their continued support of my labors with this project.

Soli Deo Gloria
David S. Dockery

FOREWORD

Mark A. Noll, Wheaton College

Southern Baptists and American Evangelicals is a very important book on a vitally important subject. For several decades the Southern Baptist Convention has been the largest Protestant denomination in the United States; yet only in the very recent past have Southern Baptists reached out meaningfully beyond the geographic and cultural boundaries of their hereditary Southern enclaves. As they begin to make such moves outward, the implications for Christianity as a whole in the United States are great. What their impact on others will be hinges in considerable measure on how Southern Baptists will get along with other Christian traditions. Of those traditions, the ones that are closest in belief and religious practice to the Southern Baptists are those groups known as "evangelicals."

This book, as an exploration of Southern Baptist-evangelical relations, is a logical first step toward defining, interpreting, and assessing a whole set of relationships in which the Southern Baptist presence is almost certain to grow in the years to come. To be sure, others have attempted to address the questions of Southern Baptists in relationship to evangelicals.[1] This volume, by the breadth of its coverage and by enlisting both evangelicals and Southern Baptists, makes a singular advance. It is not exactly a coherent book, but first attempts at systematic analysis rarely are. Still, its lively explorations in what might be called cross-cultural religious analysis yield a wealth of insight on several closely-connected questions: How do Southern Baptists look to Yankee evangelicals and non-SBC Baptists? How do Southern Baptists regard evangelicals? How do Southern Baptists look upon their own educational, theological, and evangelistic life in light of new possibilities for contact with evangelicals and other kinds of Christians? How can conditions among Southern Baptists and among evangelicals be studied comparatively for the better health and well-being of both? These important

---

[1]See especially James Leo Garrett, Jr., E. Glenn Hinson, and James E. Tull, *Are Southern Baptists "Evangelicals"?* (Macon, GA: Mercer University Press, 1983).

x

questions receive varied and thought-provoking analysis in the pages that follow.

The book performs several valuable services, not least of which is to illustrate how important questions of definition are in explorations of this sort. Many of the contributors stress the many strands among evangelicals; and a few note that the term "Southern Baptist" shelters widely varying types of Christian life and service. For further explorations aimed at clarifying relationships, identifying common concerns, overcoming prejudices, and enlisting cooperating partners, even more work of this kind is required. Better historical understanding, to which several of the chapters contribute, constitutes a major asset in improving relations across lines established by cultural and denominational traditions. So also do more self-conscious efforts at defining the relative place of doctrine, piety, and ecclesiastical habits within evangelical and Southern Baptist groups. Again the book is exemplary for containing several efforts of this sort.

It also highlights what might be called agenda for further exploration between evangelicals and Southern Baptists. From the side that I know best, as a Yankee evangelical with a great deal of respect for, but only limited understanding of, the Southern Baptists, the book points to several matters that evangelicals may want to probe as they continue these kinds of edifying discussions.

Most evangelicals with a historical sense will have no difficulty recognizing Southern Baptists as belonging somewhere on their own family tree. (For example, the First and Second Great Awakenings of the periods 1740-1760 and 1790-1820 stimulated the growth of evangelical Congregationalists, Presbyterians, and Baptists in the North as well as the Baptist churches in the South that would one day form the Southern Baptist Convention.) At the same time, categories of analysis that Northern evangelicals take for granted do not always work when studying Southern Baptists. Thus, in Northern evangelicalism the difference between independent or congregational churches and churches linked by strong denominational connections is relatively clear. Those distinctions do not seem to apply to Southern Baptists who, at least from a Northern perspective, seem to talk like strict congregationalists and act like strict denominationalists. Similarly, the place of creedal statements is not always clear in the North, but problems tend to center on how to interpret confessional statements as sentiments and opinions change over time. Looking South, however, Northern evangelicals can be easily confused by the way in which Southern Baptists again seem to say one thing and do another. They say they are not creedal, yet documents looking suspiciously like confessions of faith have in fact operated as they have always operated in the history of Christianity—to define who or what should be in and out. These are matters that further discussions like this book should help to clarify, both to show Northerners the internal logic of Southern Baptist practice and to push Southern Baptists to greater efforts at communicating the essence of their faith.

Another issue that evangelicals might hope their discussions with Southern Baptists could stimulate is the matter of "Southern-ness." Although Southern Baptists have in fact become a fully national denomination with vigorous mission work that has carried them around the globe, they still seem from the North to incorporate tremendous amounts of simple regionalism into their expressions of faith. For example, Southern Baptist styles of education, proclivities for populist politicking, defenses of the spirituality of the church, or continuation of ardently localist (that is, Landmark) ecclesiology all seem as much a product of Southern culture as of biblical or theological reasoning. Analyzing Baptist geography reinforces the cultural specificity of Southern Baptist regionalism.[2] So, as Southern Baptists move further out from that Southern base and that Southern heritage, it will be useful for other evangelicals to learn from them how they wish to redirect that rootedness in the South.

Along the same lines, Northern evangelicals want their Southern Baptist counterparts to reflect on the differences of Baptists in other areas of the world. As the experiences of Stanley Grenz as a North American Baptist are not the same as experiences of Southern Baptists, so too Baptist life in Canada, in Scotland, in other European countries,

---

[2]The Southern-ness of the Southern Baptist Convention is suggested graphically by the maps produced by the Glenmary Research Center that chart the county-by-county distribution of American denominations. On the 1974 map (reporting data from 1971), only the South is red (the Baptist's color), but it is very, very red. Keeping in mind that the Baptists reported in such compilations extend beyond Southern Baptists, the concentration of Baptists in the South (with all that such a concentration implies about the relationship of churches to culture) is still extraordinarily striking. Thus, in at least ninety-eight percent of the counties in Alabama, Arkansas, Georgia, and Mississippi, Baptists made up the largest group of church members and at least a quarter of all church members. At least eighty percent of the counties in Oklahoma, South Carolina, North Carolina, Tennessee, Florida, Kentucky, and Missouri contained the same preponderance of Baptists, as did at least 50% of the counties in Texas, Virginia, Louisiana, and around thirty percent of the counties in West Virginia and New Mexico. The only other two states to have more than two counties where Baptists were the largest denomination with at least a quarter of the church members were Illinois and Indiana, where respectively, twenty percent and nine percent of the counties were so populated (and these counties were all in the southern parts of these two states). Thus, eighteen southern and border states accounted for virtually all of the counties in the United States where Baptists were the largest denomination. (There were only thirteen counties in the other thirty-two states in which Baptists were the largest denomination.)

Foreword

or in Third-World regions reveals different patterns than those found among Southern Baptists.[3] From Baptists who are not "established" in the sense that Southern Baptists have served, in Bill Leonard's phrase, as "the Catholic church of the South," it might be possible to learn a great deal about what is more generally Baptistic in their own makeup and more specifically a result of a Southern heritage.

Finally, evangelicals will ask Southern Baptists not to oversimplify the question of who the evangelicals are, as one or two of the essays in this book seem to do. It is no more helpful to think of one group, one person, one style of doctrine or religious practice, or one statement of faith standing for evangelicals than it would be for others to do the same for Southern Baptists. There are only three things to keep in mind when looking at evangelicals in general. They are diverse. They are diverse. They are diverse.[4]

My agenda of instruction from Southern Baptists to evangelicals is shorter. I do not see the world from inside the Southern Baptist framework. The temptation for stereotyping must be stoutly resisted, especially for those who have had only limited contact with Southern Baptists. Also to be resisted is a temptation most strongly felt among Northern evangelicals who have themselves been nurtured in doctrinally or culturally self-conscious strands of the faith. To superficial vision, Southern Baptists can look like an intuitive or even anti-intellectual bunch. While strands of anti-intellectualism are as present among Southern Baptists as among all varieties of Protestant pietists in America, it is also true that Southern Baptists have nurtured dignified and serious theological traditions which have only recently begun to be studied as worthy subjects in their own right.[5] In addition, Southern Baptists will want outsiders to remember that their current contention between so-called moderates and so-called fundamentalists is much more involved than at first appears.

"Fundamentalists" include some red-neck Attilas, but also a large number of thoughtful theologians as well as many who hold their convic-

---

[3]Especially useful for Southern Baptists might be comparisons with Baptist traditions in North Atlantic, English-speaking regions where Baptists have been small minorities, more or less marginalized by comparison with other religious traditions. See, for example, the materials catalogued in Philip G. A. Griffin-Allwood, George A. Rawlyk, and Jarold K. Zeman, *Baptists in Canada, 1760-1990: A Bibliography of Selected Printed Resources in English* (Hantsport, Nova Scotia: Lancelot Press, 1989); and the essays in D. W. Bebbington, ed. *The Baptists in Scotland: A History* (Glasgow: The Baptist Union of Scotland, 1989).

[4]See especially Donald W. Dayton and Robert K. Johnston, eds., *The Variety of Evangelicals* (Knoxville: University of Tennessee Press, 1991).

[5]See, for example, the several essays on Southern Baptists in Timothy George and David S. Dockery, *Baptist Theologians* (Nashville: Broadman, 1990).

tions with due moderation. "Moderates" include a few theological liberals, but many more individuals who might be called "confessional conservatives" or even simply "evangelicals" if they were in another denomination. It would, thus, behoove evangelicals not to quickly pick sides nor to rush to judgment in what is not only a momentous struggle for Southern Baptists, but one fraught with widest implications for the future of evangelicals as a whole.

Finally, several essays by Southern Baptists make the very convincing argument that while Southern Baptists are surely evangelicals in a broad sense of the term, they have every right to be considered "hyphenated evangelicals," "denominational evangelicals," or "Baptists first and evangelicals second." If evangelicalism is really a nominal mosaic, rather than a coherent organic entity, then evangelicals should be among the first to recognize the mingled loyalties that many varieties of evangelicals display—both to the particular traditions of their own denominations and to the more general beliefs and practices that have defined evangelicals since the mid-eighteenth century.[6] The Yankee contributors to this book do recognize this reality, but its full consequences can be explained adequately only by Southern Baptists themselves.

This book will doubtless provide much stimulation for further conversation across far-flung borders, but its first and most immediate contribution is its own chapters. Readers will have different favorites among the essays, but I found three of them especially compelling: Joel Carpenter's warm appreciation as a Northerner for Southern Baptist strengths along with what seem to him to be some pretty quirky distinctives; Stanley Grenz's historical and systematic definitions that carefully unpack the nature of Baptist allegiances to both denominational distinctives and broader evangelical patterns; and Albert Mohler's challenging assessment of how questions of identity for both Southern Baptists and evangelicals more generally are also questions of integrity. What a reader's favorite essays are, however, is much less important than the overall impact of the book. In a word, it is a treasure for all those who would know more about the strategically important relations between Southern Baptists and what I am very glad to call "other evangelicals."

---

[6]An excellent recent effort to define evangelicalism in such generic terms has been provided by David W. Bebbington, an English historian who is a member of a Baptist church in Scotland, in his survey, *Evangelicalism in Modern Britain: A History from the 1730s to the 1980s* (London: Unwin Hyman, 1989). Bebbington, especially pp. 3-17, identifies the general evangelical traditions as marked by a reliance on Scripture, a consistent moral activism, an abiding concern for evangelicalism, and a variably expressed "crucicentrism" (focus on the cross as the key to atonement).

INTRODUCTION

David S. Dockery and James Emery White

Martin Marty has noted that to look at American religion and overlook evangelicalism "would be comparable to scanning the American physical landscape and missing the Rocky Mountains."[1] As a result Southern Baptists have often asked themselves if *they* are evangelicals. Many outside observers would label Southern Baptists the "Evangelical denomination," yet early on in the conversation, Foy Valentine responded, "Southern Baptists are not evangelicals. That's a Yankee word."[2] Most Southern Baptists, however, would say they *are* Evangelicals, representing the largest denomination within the growing ranks of American evangelicalism. This volume addresses such questions by examining the following issues: (1) the identity of American evangelicals; (2) relationships between Southern Baptists and American evangelicals; (3) their common beliefs and practices; and (4) future trends among Southern Baptists.

For the past several years the Southern Baptist Convention (SBC) has been embroiled in a heated controversy concerning denominational polity and theological truth. Some leaders think a movement in the SBC toward a more consistent evangelicalism would be very positive, while others think it would be detrimental to the life and tradition of the denomination. Such differences of opinion evidence the enormous diversity in the Southern Baptist Convention.

Yet such diversity belies other dynamics relevant to the issue, namely that many Southern Baptists simply do not understand the broad evangelical movement in North America. Likewise, many evangelicals are confused by the size and complexity of the SBC. This book is an initial attempt to move both groups in the direction of increased understanding and cooperation. The goal is not to produce a final word on the

---

[1] Martin E. Marty, *A Nation of Behavers* (Chicago: The University of Chicago Press, 1976), 80.
[2] Quoted in Kenneth L. Woodward, et al., "The Evangelicals," *Newsweek* 25 (October 1976), 76.

1

discussion, but to encourage an ongoing conversation. The first movement toward a dialogue of such nature came from Professors E. Glenn Hinson and James Leo Garrett, Jr., in *Are Southern Baptists "Evangelicals"?*[3] The conclusion of this volume offers Hinson and Garrett an opportunity for further reflection on their earlier conversation.

Several essays in this volume originated during the denominational heritage conferences at The Southern Baptist Theological Seminary in 1989 and 1990. Before moving to these essays we will look at two introductory matters: (1) a brief overview of the Southern Baptist Convention; and (2) a survey of the American evangelical movement.

The Southern Baptist Convention: An Introduction

The Southern Baptist Convention is comprised of fifteen million baptized believers in over forty thousand churches in all fifty states of the United States. It is the largest Protestant denomination in America.

The Convention was organized on May 8, 1845, in Augusta, Georgia.[4] The SBC separated from both the American Baptist Home Mission Society and the General Missionary Convention of the Baptist Denomination in the United States for Foreign Missions (known as the Triennial Convention). The issues leading to the division were: (1) the nature of denominational structure; and (2) the question regarding missionary activity and slavery.

The Southern Baptist Structure

A heavy emphasis on evangelistic and missionary activity has helped form the Convention into one of the most aggressive missionary bodies in American Christianity. Most members in the SBC affirm biblical authority, the necessity of salvation by grace through faith, baptism by immersion, and an ecclesiology grounded in the Free Church tradition. These issues are outlined in the *Baptist Faith and Message* (1925, 1963), the official confessional statement of the Southern Baptist Convention.

Southern Baptists have refused formal alignment with the National Association of Evangelicals, the National Council of Churches, and the World Council of Churches. The SBC, however, took the lead in bringing together several diverse Baptist groups from around the globe to form the Baptist World Alliance in 1905.

---

[3] James Leo Garrett, Jr., E. Glenn Hinson, and James E. Tull, *Are Southern Baptists "Evangelicals"?* (Macon, GA: Mercer University Press, 1983).

[4] For a more detailed history, see H. Leon McBeth, *The Baptist Heritage: Four Centuries of Baptist Witness* (Nashville: Broadman, 1987).

The work of the Convention is delegated to four boards, seven commissions, and six seminaries. The four boards include two mission boards which oversee the work of nearly eight thousand missionaries (the Foreign Mission Board and the Home Mission Board). The Baptist Sunday School Board, the nation's largest Christian publishing house, publishes pieces of literature each year including Bibles, books, hymnals, quarterly Bible Study materials and Discipleship Training lessons, and numerous periodicals (from the well-known *Home Life* to the new *Growing Churches*). The Baptist Sunday School Board also houses departments relating to all dimensions of pastoral ministry and the life of the church. The Annuity Board is responsible for a wide range of financial concerns related to churches and ministers.

The seven commissions are as follows: the Brotherhood Commission (a missions organization for men and boys), the Stewardship Commission, the Christian Life Commission, the Education Commission, the American Seminary Commission, the Historical Commission, and the Radio and Television Commission. The Convention is responsible for the oversight of six seminaries which have an enrollment of over ten thousand students, including three of the largest seminaries in the world: The Southern Baptist Theological Seminary in Louisville, Kentucky; Southwestern Baptist Theological Seminary in Fort Worth, Texas; and New Orleans Baptist Theological Seminary in New Orleans, Louisiana. Other seminaries include Golden Gate Baptist Theological Seminary in Mill Valley, California; Midwestern Baptist Theological Seminary in Kansas City, Missouri; and Southeastern Baptist Theological Seminary in Wake Forest, North Carolina. State conventions are responsible for more than fifty colleges and universities and their 160,000 students, including relationships with such nationally known institutions as Baylor University and Samford University.

One of the most difficult things to understand about the SBC for those outside the Convention is its complex structure. At the center of the SBC structure is the local church. The national and state conventions, denominational boards, commissions, agencies, and institutions are nothing more than the result of the cooperation of individual Baptist churches. The belief in the autonomy of the local church is both cherished and carefully guarded in Southern Baptist life. Local congregations relate to local associations, to state conventions and to the national convention. Congregations send messengers to make decisions and elect officers who appoint trustees for boards, commissions, and schools at the associational, state, and national levels.[5] In addition to the colleges mentioned earlier, state conventions sponsor hospitals, orphanages, retreat centers, retirement homes/communities, and other mission and benevolent programs. The national convention has no authority over the local churches. The relationship between the churches and the state and national conventions is voluntary. The SBC depends on voluntary cooperation and financial support, without which the SBC could not function. The heart of this cooperative support is called the Cooperative Program, the name given to the pooling and distribution of the monies donated to the Convention's activities.

The SBC has been somewhat separated from the rest of American Christianity throughout its history for a host of reasons. The tendency toward sectionalism in the Southern Baptist Convention as well as the SBC's inability to separate itself from Southern culture have been leading reasons for this isolation. Southern Baptists have also tended toward parochialism and self-sufficiency. Thus the SBC has not generally related well to American evangelicals or the rest of American Christianity.

The Southern Baptist Controversy

Even more difficult to grasp for those outside of the Southern Baptist Convention is the controversy over the nature of Scripture that has plagued the denomination for the past several years. The SBC has not been alone in this controversy, however, for there are similar debates taking place in Christianity at-large.

Among Southern Baptists, there are at least four different groups represented in the controversy over the nature of Scripture: (1) fundamentalists, (2) conservatives, (3) moderates, and (4) liberals.[6] As this controversy is decisive for understanding the current context within which the SBC operates, the following is an extended analysis of the doctrine of Scripture in each of these groups, noting other theological or social commitments that inform the beliefs and agendas of the various groups.[7]

---

[5] Information on denominational reports and decisions is available yearly with the publication of the *SBC Annual*.

[6] In other places these have been called: (1) militant inerrantists, (2) irenic inerrantists, (3) non-inerrantists, and (4) liberals. Some Baptist state papers have adopted the terms: (1) agenda inerrantists, (2) non-agenda inerrantists, (3) non-agenda moderates, and (4) agenda moderates.

[7] The major issue involved in the SBC controversy centers around biblical inerrancy. For now it should be observed that groups one and two affirm inerrancy. Some in the third group may hold to inerrancy though they often shy away from the use of the term for political and denominational reasons rather than theological ones. Others in the third group and all in the fourth group would reject the concept of biblical inerrancy. See David S. Dockery, *The Doctrine of the Bible* (Nashville: Convention, 1991) for a brief analysis of various approaches to the concept of inerrancy.

Fundamentalists

Fundamentalism in the SBC is closely related to the unique phenomenon in American Christianity in the areas of theological conviction and social agenda. SBC fundamentalists, however, are not generally as militant or separatistic as other bodies of American fundamentalism. In the SBC, fundamentalists include different groupings and theological structures. Among these differences, there are two major groupings: (1) a mystical-pietistic body that emphasizes evangelism and missions, and (2) a more scholastic theological group that often stresses the importance of dispensational theology. Recognizing these significant differences, they should still be treated as one group because in theory their doctrine of Scripture is virtually identical.[8]

The fundamentalist doctrine of Scripture emphasizes the Godward side of inspiration, sometimes seemingly ignoring the human writers. The prophetic model, "thus says the Lord," becomes the paradigm through which all of Scripture is seen. Revelation is understood in propositional terms and the concept of inspiration borders on dictation. The dictation theory places the emphasis upon God's actual dictation of His word to the human writers. It is sometimes uncritically affirmed that the Bible is the writing solely of the living God. Each sentence is dictated by God's Holy Spirit. In the Bible we find God speaking; it is no human voice we hear, but God's.[9] This reflects a docetic tendency that de-emphasizes the human nature of Scripture.[10]

Fundamentalists affirm the full and absolute inerrancy of Scripture, which stresses not only the truthfulness of Scripture, but its precise accuracy as well. In order for this to be maintained, a philosophical framework is sometimes superimposed on the text, whereby literary features and genre differences are diminished in importance as the entire Bible is

---

[8] "Landmarkist ecclesiology" can often be added to these characteristics to produce diverse theological emphases. In practice the more pietistic group can almost function without Scripture because of its reliance upon a mystical relationship with God. While in theory they proclaim the doctrine of absolute inerrancy coupled with a literal interpretation of Scripture, in practice Scripture tends to function on another level, the mystical level or level of the Spirit.

[9] This statement is not representative of W. A. Criswell's more balanced, overall view of Scripture. Nevertheless, these are his affirmations in *Why I Preach the Bible Is Literally True* (Nashville: Broadman, 1969). A more careful statement of the long-time pastor's positions can be found in *Bibliology* (Grand Rapids: Zondervan, 1982).

[10] While working with the prophetic paradigm, we do not find the denial of the human aspect of Scripture in the Princeton theology of C. Hodge, B. B. Warfield, and A. A. Hodge. See the classic work B. B. Warfield, *The Inspiration and Authority of the Bible* (Philadelphia: Presbyterian and Reformed, 1948); see also "The Real Problem of Inspiration," in *The Living God*, ed. Millard J. Erickson (Grand Rapids: Baker, 1973), 177-291.

read as a set of propositional statements, each expressing divine affirmation. Likewise, in their approach to biblical interpretation, historical-critical methods are strongly rejected. Problem passages, such as apparent discrepancies or conflicting accounts, are often explained as errors in the transmission of manuscripts or are eliminated through a harmonization approach to the biblical text. There is a stress on the overall unity of Scripture and a virtual ignoring of the variety and development within the Bible.[11]

Conservative Evangelicals

For nearly fifty years, there has existed a growing movement in conservative Protestantism in Europe and America known as Evangelicalism that is distinct from fundamentalism. Among Southern Baptists, there are many who identify with this movement and affirm its basic theological convictions while functioning in a Baptist context.

Concerning the doctrine of Scripture, evangelicals affirm that revelation is both personal and propositional. While emphasizing propositional revelation, evangelicals are careful to maintain that Scripture's literary diversity is more than a historic accident or decorative device; it is a vehicle for imaginative thought and creative expression about things difficult to grasp.[12] Commands, promises, parables, analogies, metaphors, symbols, and poetry cannot be forced into propositional form without loss.[13] This recognition of literary diversity brings a healthy realization of the human aspect in Scripture, thus balancing the divine-human authorship of the Bible. Evangelicals maintain that the Bible attests to its own inspiration which can be characterized as plenary (meaning all of Scripture is inspired) and concursive (meaning inspiration includes both human and divine aspects). While evangelicals affirm verbal inspiration, they remain cognizant of contemporary linguistic theory that suggests that meaning is at the sentence level and beyond.

Based upon plenary inspiration of Scripture, an evangelical view infers the inerrancy of Scripture which stresses that what the Bible

---

[11] This approach is without a doubt confessed (sometimes consciously and sometimes unconsciously) by many Southern Baptist laypeople, evangelists, and pastors. While we have simplified and generalized for the sake of brevity, an articulation of this approach can be found in the writings of former Southern Baptist John R. Rice, *Our God-Breathed Book—the Bible* (Murfreesboro: Sword of the Lord, 1969).

[12] See the goundbreaking discussion by Kevin J. VanHoozer, "The Semantics of Biblical Literature: Truth and Scripture's Diverse Literary Forms," *Hermeneutics, Authority and Canon*, ed. D.A. Carson and J.D. Woodbridge (Grand Rapids: Zondervan, 1986).

[13] Arthur Holmes, "Ordinary Language Analysis and Theological Method," *Bulletin of the Evangelical Society* 11:3 (1968), 33.

affirms is completely true.[14] Evangelicals attempt to be sensitive to the diversity and development in Holy Scripture, recognizing different literary genres while seeking to determine the original meaning of Scripture.[15] Harmonization is accepted as a legitimate means of handling the diversity in the biblical text, but not at the expense of running roughshod over the context and forcing the Bible to say what it does not say.[16] Because the Bible is a divine-human book, the interpretive tools of literary and historical criticism are employed with care and faith-oriented presuppositions.

Moderate Evangelicals

Moderates in the SBC include representatives from different theological strands entailing neoevangelicalism, neo-orthodoxy, and neoliberalism, as well as new aesthetic and narrative theologies.[17] This group would generally identify with the larger "Mainline" movement in Protestantism. Moderates in the SBC prefer to think of themselves as "denominational loyalists," though current controversy surrounding the Cooperative Program and the rise of the "Cooperative Baptist Fellowship" calls this label into question (many moderates are withdrawing their financial support from the Cooperative Program and designating their funds for other Baptist causes). Many moderates would accept the term "evangelical," some with and some without a theological commitment to biblical inerrancy. Such would be true of laypeople, pastors, and theologians who stand in the tradition of Karl Barth and Emil Brunner.

Moderates generally see Scripture as a witness to God's revelation and prefer the term infallibility instead of inerrancy. When moderates employ the term inerrancy in reference to Scripture, it is generally limited to doctrinal matters. They understand inspiration in a dynamic fashion by which the Holy Spirit directs the writers/redactors to the concepts they should have and then allows for great freedom to express these

---

[14] This concept is superbly articulated by Paul D. Feinberg, "The Meaning of Inerrancy," Inerrancy, ed. Norman L. Geisler (Grand Rapids: Zondervan, 1979), 367-404. On the authors' positions, see David S. Dockery, The Doctrine of the Bible (Nashville: Convention Press, 1991), and James Emery White, "Foundations for Biblical Interpretation," in The Holman Bible Introduction (Nashville: Holman, forthcoming).

[15] J. I. Packer, "Infallible Scripture and the Role of Hermeneutics," Scripture and Truth, ed. D. A. Carson and J. D. Woolbridge (Grand Rapids: Zondervan, 1983), 325-356.

[16] Most evangelicals would take issue with Harold Lindsell's now infamous harmonizations in The Battle for the Bible (Grand Rapids: Zondervan, 1974), 174-176. The finest treatment of this subject is found in Craig L. Blomberg, "The Legitimacy and Limits of Harmonization," Hermeneutics, Authority and Canon, 135-174.

[17] See the descriptions in Lonnie D. Kliever, The Shattered Spectrum: A Survey of Contemporary Theology (Atlanta: John Knox, 1981).

ideas in their own styles through their own personalities and with their own choice of words in a way consistent with and characteristic of their own situation and contexts. Some have creatively expanded the view, looking beyond the human author's role to see the place of the community in the composition of Scripture.

For moderates, Scripture is characteristically understood in light of the central message of salvation. There is an emphasis on Scripture's infallibility in its ability to accomplish its purposes because it will not deceive humanity about matters of salvation. Most moderates would identify with the posture of Dutch theologian G. C. Berkouwer, who states, "The purpose of the God-breathed Scripture is not at all to provide a scientific gnosis in order to convey and increase human knowledge and wisdom, but to witness of the salvation of God unto faith."[18] Scripture is thus understood as a functional and living instrument serving God for the proclamation of the salvation message to its readers.[19]

Liberals

This group is most difficult to describe. While there is much talk about "liberalism" in the SBC, there is little that identifies with the classical liberalism of the nineteenth century, though there are representatives of the more radical theologies of the twentieth century: existentialism, process thought, and some liberation and feminist theologies.[20]

Characterizing a view of Scripture among these diverse theologies is nearly impossible. A common agreement would be the de-emphasis of the divine nature of Scripture and an elevation of the human dynamic. Inspiration involves the Spirit's working within the human writers to raise their religious insight and express themselves with eloquent language. These theologies generally posit that inspiration lifts the authors beyond their normal abilities to express themselves creatively. People reflecting these diverse theologies read the Bible from a subjective, reader-oriented approach and typically disallow objective readings of Scripture.[21] Inspi-

---

[18] G. C. Berkouwer, *Holy Scripture* (Grand Rapids: Eerdmans, 1975), 180-183. Inerrantists would ask how Scripture can be trusted in non-verifiable areas of salvation and ethics if Scripture is doubted in verifiable matters.

[19] Ibid., 330-333.

[20] For descriptions of these viewpoints, see David H. Kelsey, *The Uses of Scripture in Recent Theology* (Philadelphia: Fortress, 1975).

[21] An example of this hermeneutic is found in the creative work of Elizabeth Schussler Fiorenza, *In Memory of Her: A Feminist Theological Reconstruction of Christian Origins* (New York: Crossroad, 1983).

ration, authority, and interpretation are quite often intimately bound together in these approaches.[22]

While all four groups, and many other subsections among these, are present in Southern Baptist life, it is our observation that the SBC is composed primarily of conservative and moderate evangelicals. Of the two groups usually mentioned in the controversy, conservatives would be composed of fundamentalists and conservative evangelicals while moderates would include moderate evangelicals and liberals (including both the "Cooperative Baptist Fellowship" and the "Baptist Alliance"). It would be wrong to deny the representation of fundamentalists and liberals, as is attested to by their obvious vocal presence, but these are not in the majority.

Generally, SBC fundamentalists are not as separatistic as the rest of American fundamentalism, nor are SBC liberals as radical as most of American liberalism. Yet, when one reads the accounts in the newspapers and listens to the speeches at various meetings, the labels "fundamentalist" and "liberal" dominate. This causes confusion as opposing groups are ridiculed by forcing extreme caricatures.

It can be said that the majority of Southern Baptists believe in the Bible and affirm that it is in some sense God's word: it is inspired, authoritative, and can be trusted in salvific matters. If there is much common ground, one might ask, why the decade of controversy and what are the major issues involved in the differences? The controversy has been fueled by political and personal differences, but the focal point has been the affirmation or denial of the doctrine of inerrancy. As was seen by our descriptive summaries, there are also differences in the understanding of revelation, inspiration, interpretation, and the extent of the Bible's authority.

American Evangelicalism: A Description

To understand modern American evangelicalism, it is imperative to understand its formative influences. The meaning of the term "evangelical" has evolved over time to the point that its contemporary usage in the United States is a referent to theologically conservative Protestants as well as a small but increasing number of Roman Catholics. The word itself comes from the Greek word "euangelion," which is used in the New Testament to represent the "gospel," or "good news" of the life and ministry of Jesus Christ. "Evangelical" was not a self-conscious term that the church of the first century used, but was seized by certain groups of

---

[22] See the fuller summaries in Donald K. McKim, *What Christians Believe About the Bible* (Nashville: Thomas Nelson, 1985), 95-152.

Protestants during the Protestant Reformation to distinguish themselves from Roman Catholics.[23] Three historical events take prominence: the Protestant Reformation of the sixteenth century, eighteenth-century evangelical revivals, and the controversy between fundamentalists and modernists of the late nineteenth and early twentieth centuries. The latter of these three formative influences is given the most attention, for it was American fundamentalism's clash with modernists that gave direct birth to contemporary American evangelicalism.[24]

The Protestant Reformation of the Sixteenth Century

The Protestant Reformation of the sixteenth century, especially English Puritanism, can be seen as a formative influence on contemporary American evangelicalism.[25] The Reformers denied starting a new church, and much of what the Reformers and American evangelicals believe about God, Jesus Christ, humanity, sin, and the eternal world is owed to the Catholic tradition from which they eventually separated.[26]

Evangelicals do, however, join in the Reformation restatement of the gospel.[27] While giving no challenge to the orthodox tradition of early Christianity, the Reformers rejected the medieval doctrines regarding sal-

---

[23] For a good discussion on the use of the term in secular Greek, the Old Testament, and the New Testament, see U. Becker, "Gospel, Evangelize, Evangelist," *The New International Dictionary of New Testament Theology*, Vol. 2, ed. Colin Brown (Grand Rapids: Regency Reference Library, 1986), 107-115; also note Gerhard Friedrich's discussion in "euangelizomai, euangelion, proeuangelizomai, euangelistes" in Theological Dictionary of the New Testament, Vol. II, ed. Gerhard Kittel, trans. Geoffrey W. Bromiley (Grand Rapids: Eerdmans, 1964), 707-737.

[24] That evangelicalism has been shaped by these three significant periods of modern Christianity is discussed at length by Bruce L. Shelley in "Evangelicalism," *Dictionary of Christianity in America*, ed. Daniel G. Reid, Robert D. Linder, Bruce L. Shelley, Harry S. Stout (Downers Grove: InterVarsity, 1990), 413; this brief article is one of the best general introductions available regarding the history and shape of American evangelicalism in a brief article format. For an extended discussion of the history and background of American evangelicalism, see James Emery White, "The Concept of Truth in Contemporary American Evangelical Theology," Ph.D. dissertation, May 1991, The Southern Baptist Theological Seminary, Louisville, Kentucky, to be published as *The Ultimate Question: What is Truth? The Evangelical Response* (Nashville: Broadman).

[25] Perhaps the most accessible introduction to the history of the Reformation is Roland H. Bainton's *The Reformation of the Sixteenth Century* (Boston: Beacon, 1952 and 1985).

[26] An excellent introduction to the theological underpinnings of the Reformation is found in Timothy George's *Theology of the Reformers* (Nashville: Broadman, 1988), which examines Reformation thought through the lens of four major reformers of the sixteenth century: Martin Luther, Huldrych Zwingli, John Calvin, and Menno Simons.

[27] On this, see Bernard L. Ramm's *The Evangelical Heritage* (Waco: Word Books, 1973), especially chapter 2, "Evangelical Theology Belongs to Reformation Theology," 23-40.

vation and the church.[28] Four major distinctions can be observed between the Reformers and their Catholic heritage that evangelicals continue to share. The first distinction concerned the issue of salvation (soteriology). The Catholic tradition asserted that justification comes through a combination of faith and good works. The Reformers countered that justification is through faith in Christ alone. The second point of tension was the issue of religious authority. The Roman Church insisted that religious authority is a sacred institution established by Jesus Christ on Peter and his successors (the bishops of Rome). Reformation doctrine held that all truth necessary for faith and behavior is found in one source, the Bible (the written word of God). A third area of disagreement was the doctrine of the church (ecclesiology). Catholic theology at the time of the Reformation held that the true church is that sacred hierarchial and priestly institution that Jesus Christ founded on Peter, the first pope, and on the apostles, the first bishops. The theology of the Reformers did not understand the true church as a sacred hierarchy, but as a community of faith in which all true believers share the priestly task. The final major area of division was over the subject of Christian living. The monastic way of life was thoroughly entrenched in Catholic practice and thought. The Reformers understood the essence of Christian living as serving God in one's calling (whether it be in secular or ecclesiastical life). These four Reformation understandings remain in the mainstream of contemporary American evangelical theology.[29]

Eighteenth-Century Evangelical Revivals

During the seventeenth century the vigorous defense of the gospel in the Protestant Reformation was replaced by an "unyielding spirit of Protestant orthodoxy."[30] Throughout Northern Europe, Protestant-

---

[28] It is to be noted that these distinctives were those present at the time of the Protestant Reformation. The many changes which have resulted from Vatican II have significantly modified many of the theological disagreements that existed during the sixteenth century; on Vatican II, see Austin Flannery, ed., *Vatican Council II: The Conciliar and Postconciliar Documents,* 1981 ed. (Grand Rapids: Eerdmans, 1975); Austin Flannery, *Vatican II: More Postconciliar Documents* (Grand Rapids: Eerdmans, 1982); an excellent overview and study of post-Vatican II Catholic doctrine can be found in Richard P. McBrien's *Catholicism,* study ed. (San Francisco: Harper and Row, 1981). Nonetheless, these distinctions explain why the term "evangelical" was used at the time of the Reformation to designate such individuals as Lutherans and their attempt to renew the church on the grounds of the authoritative Word of God, and why still later it was applied collectively to Lutheran and Reformed communities in Germany; see Shelley, "Evangelicalism," *Dictionary of Christianity in America,* 414, who discusses the use of the term "evangelical" by the Reformers.

[29] See Richard Mouw, "Theological and Ethical Dimensions of American Evangelicals" in this volume.

[30] Shelley, "Evangelicalism," *Dictionary of Christianity in America,* 414.

ism was accepted, but it had lost much of its vibrancy. A series of renewal movements changed the face of traditional Protestantism and gave a new meaning to the term evangelical: that of being "born again."[31]

The first of these revivals was a movement in Germany termed Pietism, which stressed a sincere faith through Bible study, prayer, and the nurture and fellowship of the church as a supportive community of faith.[32] In Northern Germany Pietism expanded through a refugee group from Moravia called the Moravian Brethren under the leadership of Count Nicholas von Zinzendorf.[33] In other areas of Europe, Pietism merged with the Anabaptist tradition to create the Mennonite and German Brethren traditions of faith.[34] One of the greatest contributions Pietism made to evangelicalism was through its influence on John Wesley, who became the most prominent spokesman for England's great spiritual awakening.[35]

The American colonial counterpart to the Methodist revival in the British Isles has become known as the Great Awakening. This event was chronicled and led by one of America's most brilliant minds, Jonathan Edwards, but it soon spread beyond the confines of his parish

---

[31] The phrase "born again" was not an invention of eighteenth century revivalism. Its introduction dates back to Jesus' words as recorded in the third chapter of the gospel of John in the New Testament with use in the Reformation period as well as the German pietistic era. As a phrase denoting spiritual regeneration, and thus prone to a broad and imprecise usage in general discourse, "born again" has generally come to mean "any Christian who exhibits intensity or overt self-identification or a keen sense of divine presence, or one who attributes causation to God for events in personal life or in the historical and natural processes," C. D. Weaver, "Born Again," *Dictionary of Christianity in America,* 177; perhaps the single best introduction to eighteenth century evangelical revivalism is William G. McLoughlin's *Revivals, Awakenings, and Reform: An Essay on Religion and Social Change in America, 1607-1977* (Chicago and London: The University of Chicago Press, 1978).

[32] Jacob Spener's *Pia Desideria,* ed. and trans. Theodore G. Toppert (Philadelphia: Fortress, 1964), was clearly the book which established the program for Pietism; F. Ernest Stoeffler is the individual who has given the most attention to the subject of Pietism in recent years: *The Rise of Evangelical Pietism* (Leiden: Brill, 1965); *German Pietism During the Eighteenth Century* (Leiden: Brill, 1973); and as editor, *Continental Pietism and Early American Christianity* (Grand Rapids: Eerdmans, 1976).

[33] For the impact this brought to America, see John R. Weinlick's "Moravianism in the American Colonies" in *Continental Pietism,* 123-163.

[34] A good introduction to the Anabaptist tradition can be found in *Spiritual and Anabaptist Writers: Documents Illustrative of the Radical Reformation,* ed. George Hunston Williams and Angel M. Mergal, The Library of Christian Classics (Philadelphia: Westminster, 1957); see also Martin Schrag, "The Impact of Pietism upon the Mennonites in Early American Christianity," *Continental Pietism,* 74-122.

[35] On Wesley, see Stanley Ayling's *John Wesley* (London: Collins, 1979); A. C. Outler, ed., *John Wesley* (New York: Oxford University Press, 1964).

ministry.[36] Appearing first in the 1720s as a series of regional awakenings under the preaching ministry of George Whitefield (a friend of
John Wesley), these regional revivals coalesced into a Great Awakening
that arguably lasted until the American Revolution.[37] Other preachers
of influence during the Great Awakening include Theodore Frelinghuy-
sen and Gilbert Tennant. As Harry S. Stout has noted, these revivals
"mark the beginning of popular evangelicalism in the American
churches."[38] This had a decisive impact on American religion, for the

> Great Awakening, by increasing piety, increased proportionately dis-
> satisfaction with rigid and especially political control of spiritual
> affairs. Pietism is invariably associated with that which is voluntary
> and personal, as it is antagonistic toward that which is compulsory
> and cultural—in the name of Christ.[39]

This evangelical call for an immediate and instantaneous conversion to Christ continued throughout the nineteenth century in camp
meetings, revivals, and classrooms all across America.[40] Perhaps most
noteworthy were the camp meetings led by James McGready in Kentucky and Tennessee. The nineteenth century witnessed the development of Christian missions that raised the issue of how parachurch
missions should relate to established churches and denominations.[41] The
leadership of such evangelicals as Timothy Dwight (President of Yale),
revivalist Charles Finney at Oberlin, and circuit-riding preacher Peter
Cartwright helped to install evangelical Christianity as the dominant faith

---

[36] See Jonathan Edwards' "A Faithful Narrative" (1737), "Distinguishing Marks of a
Work of the Spirit of God" (1741) and "Some Thoughts Concerning the Present Revival"
(1742) in The Works of Jonathan Edwards, Vol. 4 (New Haven: Yale University Press,
1957), which offer excellent primary sources regarding the Great Awakening. See also
Richard L. Bushman, ed., The Great Awakening: Documents on the Revival of Religion,
1740-1745 (Chapel Hill: Institute of Early American History and Culture/University of
North Carolina Press, 1969/1989); Edwin S. Gaustad, The Great Awakening in New
England (New York: Harper and Row, 1957); Perry Miller and Alan Heimer, ed. The
Great Awakening: Documents Illustrating the Crisis and its Consequences (Indianapo-
lis: Bobbs-Merrill, 1967); and Perry Miller, Jonathan Edwards (New York: William Sloane,
1949).

[37] On Whitefield, see Arnold A. Dallimore, George Whitefield: The Life and Times
of the Great Evangelist of the Eighteenth Century Revival, 2 vols., Amer. ed. (Westchester, IL: Cornerstone Books, 1980); and Harry S. Stout, The Divine Dramatist: George
Whitefield and the Rise of Modern Evangelicalism (Grand Rapids: Eerdmans, 1991).

[38] Stout, "Great Awakening," Dictionary of Christianity in America, 494.

[39] Gaustad, Great Awakening, 110.

[40] Shelley, "Evangelicalism," Dictionary of Christianity in America, 414. See also
Nathan O. Hatch, The Democratization of American Christianity (New Haven: Yale University Press, 1989).

[41] See Joel A. Carpenter and Wilbert B. Shenk, ed., Earthen Vessels: American
Evangelicals and Foreign Missions, 1880-1980 (Grand Rapids: Eerdmans, 1990).

in America before the Civil War.[42] It is difficult to underestimate the influence of American evangelicalism upon nineteenth-century America. For example, William G. McLoughlin contends that evangelical religion

> lay behind the concept of rugged individualism in business enterprise, laissez faire in economic theory, constitutional democracy in political thought, the Protestant ethic in morality, and the millennial hope in the manifest destiny of white, Anglo-Saxon, Protestant America to lead the world to its latter-day glory.[43]

During the critical years between the Civil War and World War I, evangelicalism was removed as the dominant religious perspective of American society, largely due to the clash between fundamentalists and modernists during the nineteenth and early twentieth centuries. The seeds for this controversy were sown by the questions created in the nineteenth-century context. How were people to combine intellectual rigor with personal religious experience? In particular, what should be the Christian's response to the rise of biblical criticism? On the scientific landscape, what of Darwin? Could there be such a thing as theistic evolution? Traditional Christian faith and the modern world were on a collision course that set the state for the rise of American fundamentalism.

American Fundamentalism

The term "fundamentalist" or "fundamentalism" was probably first coined by Curtis Lee Laws in the Baptist paper, *The Watchman-Examiner*, in 1920.[44] According to Laws, fundamentalists were those who were ready "to do battle for the Fundamentals."[45]

---

[42] Shelley, "Evangelicalism," *Dictionary of Christianity in American*, 415; Sydney Ahlstom calls this the "golden age of democratic evangelicalism" and writes that "evangelical Protestant churches, with their message and methods tuned to the patriotic aspirations of a young nation, reached their high point of cultural influence," *Religious History*, 387.

[43] William G. McLoughlin, "Introduction," in *The American Evangelicals, 1800-1900: An Anthology*, ed. William G. McLoughlin (Gloucester, Mass.: Peter Smith, 1976), 1.

[44] Curtis Lee Laws, "Convention Side Lights," *The Watchman-Examiner*, July 1, 1920, a name which perhaps drew on the publication of *The Fundamentals* (Los Angeles, CA: The Bible Institute of Los Angeles, 1917), a series of 12 volumes which intended to put forth the orthodox Christian faith; the best collection of primary sources concerning American fundamentalism can be found in *Fundamentalism in American Religion 1880-1950*, ed. Joel A. Carpenter with advisory ed. Donald W. Dayton, George M. Marsden, Mark A. Noll, and Grant Wacker, a 45-volume facsimile series reproducing all major primary sources in relation to the history of American fundamentalism (New York: Garland Publishing). The single best introduction to fundamentalism remains George Marsden's *Fundamentalism and American Culture: The Shaping of Twentieth-Century Evangelicalism, 1870-1925* (Oxford: Oxford University Press, 1980).

[45] Ibid.

Origins of Fundamentalism

The origins of fundamentalism have been filled with as much diversity and disagreement as fundamentalism itself. Stewart Cole and Norman Furniss explored the origins of fundamentalism in terms of a reaction to modernity.[46] Ernest Sandeen explored a more theological basis for understanding fundamentalism.[47] For Sandeen millennialism and Princeton Theology were the catalysts of fundamentalism.[48] Under individuals such as J. Nelson Darby and events like the Niagara Bible Conferences (most notably the 1878 Conference), dispensational, pretribulation, premillennial theology was spread. Throughout the second half of the nineteenth century there was a plethora of prophetic conferences that spread millennialist ideas.

Princeton Theology, Sandeen's second catalyst, was born in Princeton Theological Seminary under Archibald Alexander and Charles Hodge and their students, Archibald Alexander Hodge, B. B. Warfield, and J. Gresham Machen. Machen's *Christianity and Liberalism* continues to serve as an excellent, persuasive introduction to Princeton Theology.[49] Together they argued for the infallibility of Scripture and a rationalistic system of thought, largely based on Thomas Reid and the philosophical school of Scottish Common Sense Realism.[50]

---

[46] Stewart Cole, *The History of Fundamentalism* (1931; Hamden, Conn.: Archon Books, 1963); Norman Furniss, *The Fundamentalist Controversy, 1918-1931* (New Haven: Yale University Press, 1954).

[47] Ernest Sandeen, *The Roots of Fundamentalism* (Grand Rapids: Baker Book House, 1970).

[48] Millennialism is characterized by the belief that a period of unprecedented peace and righteousness will reign upon the earth, usually associated with the return of Christ; Postmillennialists believe that the present age will be gradually transformed into the millennium through natural means, such as religious revival and social reform. Premillennialists believe that the golden age will come only after the current age is destroyed through supernatural means, such as the Second Coming of Christ; see Timothy Weber, "Millenarian Movements," *Dictionary of Christianity in America*, 738-739; see also Leonard I. Sweet, "Millennialism in America: Recent Studies," *Theological Studies* 40 (September 1979), 510-531. Sandeen writes that millennialism gave life and shape to the fundamentalist movement and should not be understood apart from the history of millennialism; see *Roots*, xix.

[49] J. Gresham Machen, *Christianity and Liberalism* (1923; Grand Rapids: Eerdmans, 1987). For other representatives of Princeton Theology, see Benjamin B. Warfield's *The Inspiration and Authority of the Bible* (Phillipsburg, N.J.: Presbyterian and Reformed, 1948); Charles Hodge, *Systematic Theology*, 3 (Grand Rapids: Eerdmans, reprinted September 1989); a good introduction to Princeton Theology is found in *The Princeton Theology, 1812-1921*, ed. Mark A. Noll (Grand Rapids: Baker, 1983).

[50] Scottish Common Sense philosophy is part of what Henry May in *The Enlightenment in America* (New York: Oxford University Press, 1976), xvi and 307-362, called the "didactic" category of the Enlightenment, which opposed both skepticism and revolution but wanted to save from what it saw as the debacle of the Enlightenment the intelligible universe, clear and certain moral judgments, and progress. Thus Locke, Newton, Montesquieu, science, progress, intellectual freedom, and republicanism were good, but Voltaire,

C. Allyn Russell explored a different thesis, arguing that the energy behind fundamentalism was Protestant Liberalism.[51] Russell's work was helpful in exemplifying the theological differences between the leaders of fundamentalism, thus tempering Sandeen's contention that there was a theological unanimity that undergirded and energized the entire movement.

George Marsden argues for four main streams that fed into fundamentalism: (1) the revivalistic empire of D. L. Moody (and revivalism in general); (2) the onslaught of modernity, breeding an ambivalence toward culture; (3) the holiness movements (especially the British-born Keswich movement); and (4) with Sandeen, pretribulational, premillennial, dispensationalist theology, although Marsden doubts that "premillennialism was really the organizing principle."[52] Perhaps the best conclusion is that of Bill J. Leonard, who notes that the study of fundamentalism "reveals the complexity and diversity of the movement," and therefore concludes that premillennialism and Princeton Theology "were but elements of an even broader base which included revivalism, moralism, individualism, and a strong reaction to modernism."[53]

Theology of Fundamentalism

Three areas can be examined to determine the theology of fundamentalism.[54] First, the Presbyterian General Assembly in 1910 produced what has become known as the "Five Points" of fundamentalism: the deity of Christ; His virgin birth and miracles; the inspiration and infallibility of Scripture; Christ's penal death for our sins; and His physical resurrection and personal return.[55] These five areas were considered by the fundamentalists to be under direct attack from the secular society and

---

Hume, Rousseau, religious skepticism, frantic innovation, undisciplined emotions, and the French Revolution were bad. These distinctions had to be made through rational argument and not just through appeals to biblical or other authority. May argues that the "didactic" Enlightenment was part of a significant "counter-Enlightenment" and was the primary mode in which the Enlightenment was assimilated by the American culture of the nineteenth century.

[51] C. Allyn Russell, *Voices of American Fundamentalism* (Philadelphia: Westminster Press, 1976), 1.

[52] Marsden, *Fundamentalism*, 5.

[53] Leonard, "The Origin and Character of Fundamentalism," *Review and Expositor,* 14.

[54] Many areas beyond these three can be examined for insight into the theology of the American fundamentalist movement, such as the annual Niagara Bible Conferences which began in 1876; therefore, these three are cited merely as representative examples.

[55] Marsden, *Fundamentalism*, 117; J. I. Packer, *"Fundamentalism" and the Word of God* (Grand Rapids: Eerdmans, 1958), 28.

from within the contemporary church.[56] The second source for fundamentalist theology is the *Scofield Reference Bible* (published in 1909). Selling over two million copies, this annotated "study Bible" is blatantly pretribulational, premillennial, and dispensational. Sandeen has called this work "perhaps the most influential single publication in millennial and fundamentalist historiography."[57] Finally, a series of twelve volumes published between 1910 and 1915 called *The Fundamentals* both represented and shaped fundamentalist theology.[58] Written by an impressive team of American and British scholars, these volumes were mailed free of charge to pastors, teachers, Sunday School workers, and laypersons across the United States. Over one-third of the essays defended Scripture, and the vast majority had the theme of the authority of God in Scripture over and against the authority of science. Though not overtly involved in the controversy, Southern Baptist E. Y. Mullins contributed to the volumes.

Fundamentalist Clash with Modernists

Fundamentalism became increasingly militant in the years surrounding World War II.[59] Three major concerns occupied the fundamentalists during this time.[60] The first concern was the influx of millions of immigrants and their various world views after World War I. Many of these were professing Roman Catholics, Lutherans, and Jews, none of whom shared the Puritan and revivalistic traditions of America and American evangelicalism. In three decades these immigrants changed the nature of religious life in America. The second concern that occupied fundamentalists was the radical shift in contemporary thought. The Scopes trial typified such conflicts as the "city" versus the "country," progress versus supposed ignorance, and most certainly modernism ver-

---

[56] Walter A. Elwell, *Evangelical Dictionary of Theology* (Grand Rapids: Baker Book House, 1984), 433.

[57] Sandeen, *Roots*, 222.

[58] Recently re-published as *The Fundamentals: The Famous Sourcebook of Foundational Biblical Truths*, ed. R. A. Torrey, et. al., updated by Charles L. Feinberg, et al., with biographical introductions by Warren W. Wiersbe (Grand Rapids: Kregel, 1990); originally published with Charles Erdman as editor as *The Fundamentals* (Los Angeles, CA: The Bible Institute of Los Angeles, 1917). This project was funded by Lyman and Milton Stewart.

[59] Marsden, *Fundamentalism*, 141.

[60] These three concerns are common in regard to discussing the history of fundamentalism, as noted by Shelley's article on "Evangelicalism" in *Dictionary of Christianity in America*, 413-416.

sus fundamentalism.[61] Although Darwin's *Origin of Species* (1859) did not directly challenge Christianity, popular speculation about the book's doctrine of evolution tended to discount the traditional explanation of the origin of life and the personal God behind the universe. Men and women began to think in terms of process, progress, and evolution as opposed to creation, miracles, and new birth.[62] The third concern of the fundamentalists was higher criticism.[63] For fundamentalists, higher criticism undermined the idea that the Bible was special revelation, left the Christian minister bereft of a supernatural gospel, and provided little basis for the evangelical experience of the new birth.[64] It has therefore been suggested that a "systematic theology of biblical authority which defended the common evangelical faith in the infallibility of the Bible had to be created."[65]

---

[61] The Scopes trial, as it has become known, revolved around a teacher who was charged and found guilty of violating the Tennessee anti-evolution law. Though fundamentalists "won" on the issue of evolution, some contend that their movement as a whole earned nothing but ridicule. This interpretation is based largely as a result of William Jennings Bryan allowing himself to be cross-examined by Scopes' attorney Clarence Darrow, one of the most gifted attorneys in the nation, and being unable to defend the Bible on the most simplistic points. Marsden has written in *Fundamentalism*, 184, that the trial brought an "outpouring of derision. The rural setting . . . stamped the entire movement with an indelible image," that of the anti-intellectual Southern farmer. This is not to say that the national response (including the media) to the Scopes trial at the time of the trial did not side with the fundamentalist perspective.

[62] Shelley, "Evangelicalism," *Dictionary of Christianity in America*, 415; on Darwin's theories, see *The Origin of Species by Natural Selection*, Vol. 49, ed. Robert Maynard Hutchins (Chicago: Encyclopedia Britannica, Inc., 1952), where the summation of his argument is presented on pp. 230-243, and *The Descent of Man and Selection in Relation to Sex* in *The Great Books of the Western World*, Vol. 49, ed. Robert Maynard Hutchins (Chicago: Encyclopedia Britannica, Inc., 1952).

[63] Higher criticism is the term used to describe the study of Scripture from the standpoint of literature, as opposed to "lower criticism," which deals with the text of Scripture and its transmission. Higher criticism thus has three main concerns: (1) detecting the presence of underlying literary sources in a work; (2) identifying the literary types that make up the composition; and (3) conjecturing on matters of authorship and date, see R. K. Harrison, "Higher Criticism," *Evangelical Dictionary of Theology*, 511-512; an excellent introduction to the area of biblical criticism can be found in Richard N. Soulen's *Handbook of Biblical Criticism*, 2nd ed. (Atlanta: John Knox, 1981).

[64] See Timothy Weber's article, "The Two-Edged Sword: The Fundamentalist Use of the Bible" in *The Bible in America*, ed. Nathan O. Hatch and Mark A. Noll (Oxford: Oxford University Press, 1982).

[65] Sandeen, *Roots*, 106; this view has been rejected by evangelical scholars such as John Woodbridge and Randall H. Balmer; see "The Princetonians and Biblical Authority: An Assessment of the Ernest Sandeen Proposal," *Scripture and Truth*, 151-279; Woodbridge and Balmer contend that a systematic theology of biblical authority stressing inerrancy of the original manuscripts was relatively commonplace by 1850 and far from an invention of Princeton theologians.

Fundamentalist Retreat into Institutionalization

After the 1920s, fundamentalism entered into a period which is perhaps best termed a "retreat into institutionalization."[66] Rather than engage culture, they retreated and sought areas where they could control doctrine, education, and morals. This often involved withdrawing from denominations in order to form their own alliances.[67] Such educational institutions as Dallas Theological Seminary were founded as a result of this philosophy.[68]

Birth of Contemporary American Evangelicalism

Many fundamentalists grew uneasy with the denominational separatism, social and cultural irresponsibility, and anti-intellectual stance that pervaded the years of controversy with the modernists.[69] These individuals branched off and formed the movement that is now known as con-

---

[66] The retreat was hastened by the winsome appeal to tolerance from the modernist camp, as found in Harry Emerson Fosdick's sermon, "Shall the Fundamentalists Win?", *The Annals of America,* Vol. 14 (Chicago: Encyclopedia Britannica, 1976), 325-330. Marsden writes in *Fundamentalism,* 180, that the ideal of tolerance was regarded as almost sacred in most American churches, thus making this response to fundamentalism powerfully compelling. This mood against fundamentalism was aided greatly by the publication of Shailer Matthews' *The Faith of Modernism* (1924), an answer to J. Gresham Machen's *Christianity and Liberalism* (1923), and Sinclair Lewis' popular *Elmer Gantry* (1927) which parodied a fundamentalist preacher.

[67] Harold Lindsell argues that the reason the fundamentalists left the major denominations is that they lost control of their ecclesiastical machinery to the moderates; see his *The Battle for the Bible* (Grand Rapids: Zondervan, 1976), 85. It can be said that by the 1930s, fundamentalists were "either outside the mainline structures or powerless minorities within them," Richard F. Lovelace, *Dynamics of Spiritual Life* (Downers Grove: Inter-Varsity, 1979), 314. Another major impetus to the move was the dispensationalist theory of the inevitable apostasy of the church, typified by A. C. Gaebelein who as early as 1914 understood the doctrine of separation from the world as necessitating separation from the "worldly" church; see "The Present Day Apostasy," *The Coming and Kingdom of Christ: A Stenographic Report of the Prophetic Bible Conference Held at the Moody Bible Institute of Chicago Feb. 24-27, 1914* (Chicago, 1914), 154, as quoted by Marsden, *Fundamentalism,* 127.

[68] On this organizational regrouping, see Joel A. Carpenter, "Fundamentalist Institutions and the Rise of Evangelical Protestantism, 1929-1942," *Church History* 49 (March 1980), 62-75.

[69] See Mark A. Noll, *Between Faith and Criticism: Evangelicals, Scholarship, and the Bible in America* (San Francisco: Harper and Row, 1986), 91-121; Shelley, "Evangelicalism," *Dictionary of Christianity in America,* 415.

temporary American evangelicalism.[70] Carl F.H. Henry wrote *The Uneasy Conscience of Fundamentalism* in 1947 which warned of these excesses; nevertheless Henry still equated fundamentalism with evangelicalism. Later, in *Evangelical Responsibility in Contemporary Theology* (1957), Henry defined himself as an evangelical and associated fundamentalism with a narrow-spirited polemicism.[71] Others who followed this new mindset and became significant leaders were evangelist Billy Graham, Harold Ockenga, E. J. Carnell, and Bernard Ramm.[72] The formation of the National Association of Evangelicals in 1942, Fuller Theological Seminary in 1947, and *Christianity Today* magazine in 1956 helped to distinguish the two movements. Perhaps most decisive in the rise of evangelicalism as a distinct movement from fundamentalism was Billy Graham's 1957 New York City crusade. Fundamentalists criticized Graham as a result of his efforts to gain broad ecumenical support

---

[70] A selection of the many works which give good general introductions and surveys of the history and thought of contemporary American evangelicalism would include the following: Randall Balmer, *Mine Eyes Have Seen the Glory: A Journey into the Evangelical Subculture in America* (New York and Oxford: Oxford University Press, 1989); Donald Dayton and Robert K. Johnston, eds. *The Variety of American Evangelicalism* (Downers Grove: InterVarsity, 1991); Carol Flake, *Redemptorama: Culture, Politics, and the New Evangelicalism* (New York: Penguin, 1984); Douglas W. Frank, *Less than Conquerors: How Evangelicals Entered the Twentieth Century* (Grand Rapids: William B. Eerdmans, 1986); James Davison Hunter, *American Evangelicalism: Conservative Religion and Quandary of Modernity* (New Brunswick, NJ: Rutgers University Press, 1983); James Davison Hunter, *Evangelicalism: The Coming Generation* (Chicago and London: The University of Chicago Press, 1987); George Marsden, ed., *Evangelicalism and Modern America* (Grand Rapids: Eerdmans, 1984); George Marsden, *Reforming Fundamentalism: Fuller Seminary and the New Evangelicalism* (Grand Rapids: William B. Eerdmans, 1987); George Marsden, *Understanding Fundamentalism and Evangelicalism* (Grand Rapids: Eerdmans, 1991); Ronald Nash, *The New Evangelicalism* (Grand Rapids: Zondervan, 1963); Ronald Nash, *Evangelicals in America: Who They Are, What They Believe* (Nashville: Abingdon, 1987); Richard Quebedeaux, *The Young Evangelicals: The Story of the Emergence of a New Generation of Evangelicals* (San Francisco: Harper and Row, 1974); Leonard I. Sweet, ed. *The Evangelical Tradition in America* (Macon: Mercer University Press, 1984), note especially Sweet's article, "The Evangelical Tradition in America," 1-86, which presents what is perhaps the best historiographical essay on Evangelicalism to date; William W. Wells, *Welcome to the Family: An Introduction to Evangelical Christianity* (Downers Grove: InterVarsity, 1979); David F. Wells and John D. Woodbridge, eds., *The Evangelicals: What They Believe, Who They Are, Where They Are Changing* (Nashville: Abingdon, 1975).

[71] See Gabriel Fackre, "Carl F. H. Henry," *A Handbook of Christian Theologians*, enlarged ed., ed. Dean G. Peerman and Martin E. Marty (Nashville: Abingdon, 1984), 589, note 8.

[72] An excellent introduction to these and other leaders of contemporary American evangelicalism can be found in William Martin's biography of the life of Billy Graham, *A Prophet with Honor: The Billy Graham Story* (New York: William Morrow and Company, 1991). Indeed, this volume serves as one of the best introductions available to American evangelicalism.

for this crusade. For example, Graham accepted the sponsorship of the local Protestant Council of Churches. From this point forward the movement tended toward fragmentation in that fundamentalists separated themselves from evangelicals.[73] During the 1960s a related movement, the charismatic movement, added new vitality to American Evangelicalism.[74]

These "new Evangelicals" avoided the negative reaction of fundamentalism. With scientists and secularists not as confident as they had been in the previous century, the nation as a whole was looking for stability and authority. It was time for the Word of God to be announced with authority. Ockenga provided the strategy and Henry, Carnell, and Ramm provided the theological, ethical, and apologetical substance. They emphasized that the true authority of the Bible is primarily a faith affirmation rather than a theological dictate.

This new coalition gained national attention in 1976 when Jimmy Carter, a Southern Baptist and professed "born-again" evangelical, was elected President of the United States. *Newsweek* magazine declared 1976 "The Year of the Evangelical."[75] Books such as Donald Bloesch's *The Evangelical Renaissance* (1973) and Dean M. Kelley's *Why Conservative Churches Are Growing* (1972) typified the evangelical triumph in America.

This newfound prominence led to the desire among certain evangelicals to shape contemporary culture and values, largely through the political realm.[76] The late 1970s saw the formation of a "Christian Right," or conservative Christian political activity that became associated with contemporary American evangelicalism. These groups organized evangelicals to support the 1980 election of Ronald Reagan to the presidency of the United States and to lend their voices to a host of issues,

---

[73] This split is discussed by Butler Farley Porter, Jr., "Billy Graham and the End of Evangelical Unity" (Ph.D. dissertation, University of Florida, 1976). See also William Martin's treatment of this period in Graham's life in *A Prophet with Honor*.

[74] For an introductory level discussion of the charismatic involvement in American Evangelicalism, see Ronald N. Nash, *Evangelicals in America*, 76-83; the cautious but sincere acceptance of charismatics by non-charismatic evangelicals is exhibited by J. I. Packer's article, "Is the Charismatic Renewal, Seen in Many Churches Today, from God?," in the Christianity Today Series, *Tough Questions Christians Ask*, ed. David Neff (Wheaton: Victor Press/Christianity Today, Inc., 1989), 49-62; see also John R. W. Stott, *Baptist and Fullness: The Work of the Holy Spirit Today* (Downers Grove: InterVarsity, 1975).

[75] Kenneth L. Woodward with John Barnes in Texas, Laurie Lisle in New York and bureau reports, "Born Again: The Year of the Evangelical," *Newsweek* (October 25, 1976), 68-78.

[76] On this, see Garry Wills, *Under God: Religion and American Politics* (New York: Simon and Schuster, 1990).

including school prayer, tuition tax credits, and the reversal of Supreme Court decisions such as "Roe v. Wade" which legalized abortion.

Two concerns fueled this politicization: first, there was an obsession, bordering on paranoia, with what was called "secular humanism." Popularized as a tremendous threat to the continuing existence of Christianity by such evangelical leaders as Francis A. Schaeffer, secular humanism was generally defined as the idea that humanity does not answer to any higher authority than humanity itself.[77] The second concern that brought many evangelicals into the public arena was the vision of a "Christian America," perhaps popularized most widely by evangelical authors Peter Marshall and David Manuel in *The Light and the Glory* (1977).[78] Marshall and Manuel held that America was founded as a Christian nation and flourished under the benevolent hand of divine providence, arguing further that America's blessings will remain only as long as America is faithful to God as a nation.[79] A team of evangelical historians attempted to lay this thesis to rest, but it is far from diminished as a popular framework for viewing American history among contemporary American evangelicals.[80]

Contemporary American Evangelicalism

Rooted and shaped in the Reformation of the sixteenth century, the eighteenth-century evangelical revivals, and most recently in the controversy between fundamentalists and modernists, contemporary American evangelicalism has a rich and varied history that has made definition problematic. It can be concluded from the previous historical analysis that contemporary American evangelicalism has gained its theology from the Reformation, its spirituality and commitment to evangelism from eighteenth-century revivalism, and its concern for orthodoxy and

---

[77] Two works by Francis Schaeffer emphasized the danger of secular humanism in particular and heightened this interest among Evangelicals, *How Should We Then Live: The Rise and Decline of Western Thought and Culture* (Old Tappan, NJ: Fleming H. Revell, 1976), and *A Christian Manifesto* (Westchester, IL: Crossway, 1981); see also the contribution to this concern among evangelicals from Tim LaHaye, *The Battle for the Mind* (Old Tappan, NJ: Fleming H. Revell, 1980).

[78] Peter Marshall and David Manuel have since written a sequel to *The Light and the Glory* (Old Tappan, NJ: Fleming H. Revell, 1977) titled *From Sea to Shining Sea* (Old Tappan, NJ: Fleming H. Revell, 1986); the enormously popular writings of Francis A. Schaeffer, especially *A Christian Manifesto*, should be included in regard to the promotion of this thesis.

[79] The idea of "choseness" and special "blessing" from God has been a constant theme throughout the history of the United States, thus far from an evangelical innovation; on this, see Conrad Cherry, ed., *God's New Israel: Religious Interpretations of American Destiny* (Englewood Cliffs, NJ: Prentice-Hall, Inc., 1971).

[80] Mark A. Noll, Nathan O. Hatch, and George M. Marsden, *The Search for Christian America*, expanded ed. (Colorado Springs: Helmers and Howard, 1989).

intellectual engagement from the clash between fundamentalists and modernists in the early part of the twentieth century. The present generation of evangelicals has continued the pattern established by the previous generation while showing more concern with social responsibility, hermeneutics, and unity in the church.

George Marsden does an admirable job of pulling the many diverse threads together in his essay "The Evangelical Denomination," which offers the following three-fold understanding of contemporary American Evangelicalism: a single phenomenon which involves the senses of (1) a conceptual unity that designates a grouping of Christians who fit a certain definition;[81] (2) an organic movement with some common traditions and experiences tending in some common directions; and (3) a transdenominational community with complicated infrastructures of institutions and persons who identify with evangelicalism.[82] It is in this sense that most of the authors in this work will use the terms evangelical and evangelicalism.[83]

The current state of American evangelicalism is therefore best described as a "mosaic" or "kaleidoscope."[84] The major participants in the mosaic would include the following: (1) evangelical denominations;[85] and (2) parachurch organizations,[86] which current estimates list at up to

---

[81] For example, evangelical Christians typically emphasize the Reformation doctrine of the final authority of Scripture; the real, historical character of God's saving work recorded in Scripture; eternal salvation only through personal trust in Christ; the importance of evangelism and missions; and the importance of a spiritually transformed life.

[82] George M. Marsden, "The Evangelical Denomination" in *Evangelicalism in Modern America*, vii-xix.

[83] It is to be noted that there have been some objections to the self-conscious use of the term "Evangelical" for one particular group within Christianity due to the rich, biblical history of the term. One such plaintiff has been Martin E. Marty, who, in his own words, has "only grudgingly yielded them their chosen designation" out of "sociological necessity"; see *Nation of Behavers*, 88; Donald W. Dayton, noting the variety within contemporary American evangelicalism, advocates "giving up the word entirely;" see "An Interview with Donald W. Dayton," *Faith and Thought* 1 (Spring 1983), 25.

[84] Timothy L. Smith, "The Evangelical Kaleidoscope and the Call to Christian Unity," *Christian Scholar's Review* 15/2 (1986), 125-140; see Marsden, *Evangelicalism*, "Introduction: The Evangelical Denomination," viii and 175, note 3.

[85] Bruce L. Shelley has identified at least seven evangelical traditions in his article "Evangelicalism" in *Dictionary of Christianity in America*, 416: (1) evangelicals in the Reformation tradition, primarily Lutheran and Reformed Christians; (2) Wesleyan evangelicals, such as the Church of the Nazarene; (3) Pentecostal and charismatic evangelicals, such as the Assemblies of God; (4) Black evangelicals with their own distinctive witness to the gospel; (5) the counter-culture churches (sometimes called Peace Churches), such as the evangelical Quakers and Mennonites; (6) several traditionally white Southern denominations, such as the Southern Baptists; (7) the spiritual heirs of fundamentalism found in independent churches and many parachurch agencies.

[86] Maurice Smith in his article "Parachurch Movements," *Missions USA* (October-December 1984), 145-149, has determined five types of parachurch groups: (1) tertiary organizations which promote a particular belief, such as Pentecostalism by the Full Gospel

twenty thousand separate groups in America alone, including four of the ten largest Protestant missionary organizations in terms of staff and finances.[87] Parachurch organizations should be further categorized, thus creating the additional groupings: (3) the "Electronic Church";[88] (4) evangelical mission organizations;[89] (5) evangelical publishing companies;[90] and (6) evangelical colleges and seminaries.[91]

While organizational unity may be problematic as a result of the many denominations and parachurch organizations within the evangeli-

---

Businessman's Fellowship; (2) theme or role-oriented organizations which work with a particular theme, such as American Bible Society, Bread for the World, and Gideons International; (3) evangelistic or missionary organizations such as Campus Crusade for Christ and the hundreds of missionary organizations; (4) media-oriented groups which make up what is often called the "Electronic Church"; and (5) spiritual growth centers, in which he places a number of Christian, sub-Christian, and/or non-Christian groups, including New Age organizations. This aspect of evangelicalism must not be overlooked, for as Ronald Nash has written, "nowhere is Evangelicalism's transdenominational character more apparent than in its many parachurch organizations," *Evangelicals*, 30.

[87]See Jerry White, *The Church and the Parachurch: An Uneasy Marriage* (Portland: Multnomah Press, 1983); Samuel Wilson and John Siewart, eds., *Mission Handbook: North American Protestant Missions Overseas*, 13th ed. (Monrovia, CA: Missions Advanced Research and Communications Center, 1986), 601-603; Ron Wilson, "Parachurch: Becoming Part of the Body," *Christianity Today* 24 (September 19, 1980), 18; J. Alan Youngren, "Parachurch Proliferation: The Frontier Spirit Caught in Traffic," *Christianity Today* 25 (November 6, 1981), 6.

[88]For example, the Christian Broadcasting Network (CBN) which, according to a 1984 University of Pennsylvania study, is in thirty million homes with thirteen million individuals watching Christian television regularly; see Richard N. Ostling, "Evangelical Publishing and Broadcasting," *Evangelicalism*, ed. Marsden, 46-55; see also Stewart M. Hoover, *Mass Media Religion: The Social Sources of the Electronic Church* (Newbury Park: Sage Publications, 1988); Quentin J. Schultze, ed., *American Evangelicals and the Mass Media Religion: The Social Sources of the Electronic Church* (Newbury Park: Sage Publications, 1988), and Quentin J. Schultze, ed., *American Evangelicals and the Mass Media* (Grand Rapids: Academie/Zondervan, 1990).

[89]For example, the Wycliffe Bible Translators; see Nash, *Evangelicals*, 33-34; one of the first products of the National Association of Evangelicals was the Evangelical Foreign Missionary Association.

[90]Examples of evangelical publishers would include Zondervan, Word, Tyndale, Baker, and InterVarsity; as of 1986, there were 3,500 members of the Christian Booksellers Association; major evangelical periodicals include *Christianity Today* and *Moody Monthly*. Naisbitt and Aburdene report in *Megatrends 2000* (New York: William Morrow, 1990), 292, that in 1987 alone sales among Christian booksellers topped 1.5 billion dollars

[91]Denominational evangelical colleges and seminaries include Calvin College (The Christian Reformed Church), Trinity College, Trinity Evangelical Divinity School (The Evangelical Free Church), and Bethel College and Seminary (Baptist General Conference); non-denominational colleges and seminaries include Wheaton College, Gordon College and Gordon-Conwell Theological Seminary, Fuller Theological Seminary, Dallas Theological Seminary, and Westminster Theological Seminary. The fastest growing school is Jerry Falwell's Liberty University (formerly Liberty Baptist College) in Lynchburg, Virginia; see William C. Ringenberg, *The Christian College: A History of Protestant Higher Education in America* (Grand Rapids: Eerdmans Christian University Press, 1984).

cal mosaic, theological unity has been sought among evangelicals. For example, unity has been advanced through such efforts as the covenant signed by approximately three thousand evangelicals who gathered at Lausanne, Switzerland, in July 1974, for the Lausanne Congress on World Evangelization. The most recent effort was in May, 1989, when a gathering of evangelicals resulted in a series of "Evangelical Affirmations."[92] Other affirmations of unity have been posited in "The Chicago Call" and "The Chicago Statement on Biblical Inerrancy," two documents put forth by groups of leading evangelicals in an effort to sharpen evangelical identity and foster evangelical unity.[93]

American evangelicalism is presently a very diverse movement with a fascinating history. Some of the finest evangelical historians and theologians, Joel Carpenter, George Marsden, Stanley Grenz, Richard Mouw, and Robert Johnston, help us better understand this movement in their essays in this volume.

Southern Baptists have not generally been a part of the developments within American evangelicalism. Yet in some ways, our history runs parallel to the evangelical world. In other ways, we are sixty years behind the evangelicals as we go through our own version of the "Modernist-Fundamentalist" controversy.

Southern Baptists can learn from evangelicalism's periods of stability and growth. Southern Baptists can learn to place simultaneous emphases on understanding the Bible *and* our world. A balanced concern for biblical authority and hermeneutical and social responsibility is needed. SBC denominational commitment, theological traditions, ethical responsibility, and Christian experience must be re-examined in light of a renewed commitment to biblical authority. It is the hope of this volume and many of its contributors that as the conversation continues between Southern Baptists and American evangelicals, a growing understanding and spirit of cooperation would emerge that would propel the spread of the gospel throughout the world.

---

[92] The affirmations put forth by this conference, including the various papers which were presented during the gathering, can be found in *Evangelical Affirmations*, eds. Kenneth S. Kantzer and Carl F. H. Henry (Grand Rapids: Academie/Zondervan, 1990).

[93] The "Chicago Call," representing eight themes in its final form, was the result of a gathering in Chicago, Illinois, of forty-five evangelicals in May of 1977. A much larger group of evangelicals put forth "The Chicago Statement on Biblical Inerrancy," under the organizational title, "The International Council on Biblical Inerrancy," which first met in October of 1978. The "Chicago Statement" can be found in Ronald Youngblood, ed., *Evangelicals and Inerrancy* (Nashville: Thomas Nelson, 1984), 230-239. The "Chicago Call" can be found in *The Orthodox Evangelicals: Who They Are and What They Are Saying*, eds. Robert E. Webber and Donald G. Bloesch (Nashville: Thomas Nelson, 1978).

PART I

Searching
———————— for ————————
Identity

1

Contemporary
———— American ————
Evangelicalism[*]

George M. Marsden

Defining Evangelicalism

The first problem in talking about evangelicalism is that of definition. Before presenting some long, involved, nuanced definitions, let me
give you some short, easy, and un-nuanced ones. What is an evangelical? An evangelical is someone who likes Billy Graham. What's the difference between an evangelical and a fundamentalist? I have two: A
fundamentalist is someone who is more conservative than you are. Or,
alternatively, a fundamentalist is an evangelical who wants to fight about
something. What is a fundamentalist Southern Baptist? A fundamentalist
Southern Baptist is someone who both likes Billy Graham and wants to
fight about something.

Southern Baptists sometimes raise the question of whether they
are evangelicals. Most other people do not raise this question because
either they do not know what an evangelical is or they do know and
think it is obvious that many Southern Baptists qualify. If we look carefully enough at the issue of defining evangelicalism, however, we can
understand the ambiguities that cause some disagreement over this issue.

---

[*] This essay was prepared as a lecture at The Southern Baptist Theological Seminary,
Louisville, Kentucky, in April 1989, and still bears some of the informal marks of that ori-
gin. For documentation see "The Evangelical Denomination," the introduction to *Evangel-
icalism and Modern America*, ed. George M. Marsden (Grand Rapids: William B.
Eerdmans, 1984), some of which is paraphrased in the first section of the present essay.
Also see "Unity and Diversity in the Evangelical Resurgence," in David W. Lotz, et al., eds.
Altered Landscapes: Christianity in America, 1935-1985 (Grand Rapids: William B.
Eerdmans, 1989), from which a substantial portion of the second section of the present
essay is borrowed, with permission.

We can also help locate Southern Baptists in the larger evangelical context.

We all often speak of evangelicalism as though it were one entity. In fact, however, it is a collection of diverse groups. Timothy L. Smith, a perceptive evangelical historian, has long been pointing out the diversity within evangelicalism. Smith, at one time, spoke of the "evangelical mosaic." A mosaic is made up of many disconnected pieces and can be properly viewed as a collection of those pieces. It also has an overall pattern. Smith, however, has been more eager to emphasize the disunity than I am. Recently, he has been using the image of the kaleidoscope—which suggests that the overall pattern is more random and chaotic.

Smith's point is that we find evangelicals in bewildering varieties; many have very little in common. On the one hand, we have African-American Pentecostals and on another strict separatist fundamentalists, such as at Bob Jones University, who condemn Pentecostals and shun blacks. Then we have peace churches, especially in the Mennonite-Anabaptist tradition, who would differ sharply with the nationalism and militarism of much of evangelicalism. Further, we have ethnic groups who are theologically conservative and technically evangelical in doctrine, but also are defined by confessional traditions, such as the Missouri Synod Lutheran or the Christian Reformed Church. Still another type of evangelicals are the restorationists, such as the Christian Church of the Churches of Christ. Another version of evangelicalism is found in the pietist and Methodist traditions, as in the Good News renewal movement in the United Methodist Church. Then there are separatist holiness groups, such as the Nazarenes or the Salvation Army. Pentecostal groups also come in many varieties, both black and white. African-American Christians have their own varieties of most major American traditions: Baptists, Methodists, and Pentecostals. Then, of course, there are Southern Baptists, who do not associate much with any of the above.

So how can we possibly talk about evangelicalism as one movement? To clarify the issue we must realize that there are two primary ways of talking about evangelicalism, a broad one and a narrow one. The broad approach refers to people who can be classified as evangelical. The narrow view refers to people who would call themselves evangelical.

The broad approach simply defines an evangelical as a Christian who fits a certain definition or profile—an evangelical is a person who subscribes to certain evangelical views. These basic views would include things like (1) the Reformation doctrine of the final authority of Scripture—a high view of the authority of Scripture and of its trustworthiness—though not necessarily involving inerrancy; (2) belief in the real, historical character of God's saving work recorded in Scripture; (3) eternal salvation only through faith in the atoning work of Christ; (4) the importance of evangelism and missions—since that is the kindest thing you can do for other persons; and (5) the importance of a spiritually transformed life—a trait that all other Christian groups share.

One way of looking at evangelicalism that has depended heavily on this definitional approach is the opinion survey. Pollsters deal best with abstractions and must remove their topics to operational definitions. So in recent years they have developed various sets of questions that will identify evangelicals. They have found perhaps fifty million evangelicals in the United States. This approach does not deal very well with the problem of the way in which evangelical beliefs merge with American folk piety. It also lumps all types of evangelicals together and finds that the typical evangelical is a poor Southern woman.

This heavy-handed approach does, however, tell us something. It tells us that, despite all the varieties of evangelicalism we have mentioned, most of them are connected by a common heritage that produces common traits. All reflect the sixteenth-century Reformation effort to get back to the pure Scriptures as the only ultimate authority and to confine salvation to a God-given faith in Christ, unencumbered by presumptuous human authority. During the next centuries these emphases were renewed and modified in a variety of ways, often parallel or interconnected, by groups such as the Puritans, Pietists, Methodists, Baptists, restorationists, African-American Christians, holiness groups, Pentecostals, and others.

As a result, many evangelical groups, now separate, have common roots and similar emphases. Most of these groups, for instance, participated in nineteenth-century revivalism, and share common hymnody, techniques of evangelism, styles of prayer and Bible study, worship, and standards for behavior.

Such varieties of evangelicals also have much in common because of the shared cultural experiences of being American. All, for instance, have been shaped to some extent by the experience of living in a democratic society that favors optimistic views of human nature, the importance of choosing for oneself, lay participation, and simple popular approaches. American materialism has also provided a common environment for most evangelicals.

All these evangelical groups have also faced similar challenges in twentieth-century America. All have had to deal with the questions of modernism and higher criticism. All have had to deal with the questions of the authority of the Bible in the modern age. All have had to take strong stands to preserve the traditional supernaturalist dimension of their heritages. All have had to promote evangelistic programs to survive and grow. So there is a common evangelical movement, even though it has many disconnected branches. In this sense it is appropriate. This usage simply refers to people who would call themselves evangelicals— what I call "card-carrying evangelicals." Evangelicals are by this definition those people who view themselves as part of a transdenominational evangelical movement. This movement functions almost as a denomination or as a religious affiliation of which people consider themselves to be a part.

The key question is, where do people see their primary religious identity? For most of the varieties of evangelicals whom I listed earlier, their primary identity is with their denomination. For instance, very few African-American Christians would think of themselves as evangelicals. Their primary identity is with their denomination—or perhaps to a more transdenominational black church. Missouri Synod Lutherans, although evangelicals in the broad sense, think of themselves first of all as confessional Lutherans and are not greatly interested in other groups. The same applies to most Southern Baptists. Their overriding group loyalty is to the Southern Baptist Convention.

On the other hand, card-carrying evangelicals are those who also have a strong identity with the transdenominational movement. Billy Graham and Harold Lindsell happen to be Southern Baptists, but their real allegiance is to a broader evangelical movement. Of course, it is also not unusual to have a dual identity. Some people have true denominational loyalty but are also loyal to the transdenominational movement.

This transdenominational evangelicalism goes back to the transatlantic revivalism of the eighteenth and nineteenth centuries. In addition to the formation of the specific denominations, this era saw the emergence of a self-conscious evangelical movement for revivalism and for social reform. Almost always this movement has had a leading evangelist as a prominent public figure—starting with George Whitefield in the eighteenth century, Charles Finney in the early nineteenth, then Dwight L. Moody, Billy Sunday, and lately Billy Graham. This transdenominational movement tended to lean in a Reformed direction with a disproportionate number of Baptists and Presbyterians. It has, however, always included some others, especially those from holiness groups who also saw themselves as part of the wider evangelical movement working for national revival and reform. This transdenominational movement has always seen itself as a national (and international) movement, working first of all for revival but also to mobilize and unite the various other evangelical subgroups.

We can better understand the current state of evangelicalism in contemporary America if we look at how such card-carrying transdenominational evangelicalism has developed in this century and how it has related to more denominationally-oriented evangelicals.

Evangelicalism in Twentieth-Century America

In 1900 the vast majority of American Protestants would have been classified as evangelicals. However, in the next thirty years this broad evangelical coalition broke into two major parts—liberal or inclusivist evangelicalism and fundamentalism. During the 1920s fundamentalism was the term that designated those who wanted to preserve the essentials of the traditional evangelical faith and were willing to fight for it. Fundamentalism at that time was a somewhat broader coalition than it has become since. In the 1920s fundamentalist meant basically what "conservative evangelical" means today.

By the 1930s evangelicalism was not a term much used anywhere in American religious life. Since both sides had claimed the word "evangelical," it was no longer of much use to either. Actually, most American Protestants, clergy as well as laypeople, were neither strictly fundamentalists nor modernists, but somewhere in-between. The fundamentalist/modernist wars, however, had forced many such moderates to choose sides. In the North most clergy had lined up on the side of tolerance of modernism and most laypersons did not want a fight. In the South, most of both were willing to hold the line with the fundamentalists, although the Methodists chose tolerance and merged with the Northern church in 1939.

The Northern white Protestant churches were in the meantime going through a time of realignment. Fundamentalists were relocating and building their own networks of separate institutions. A small but influential minority of fundamentalists left the major denominations to found purer alternatives. Uncounted numbers of others left to join or found independent local Bible churches or forsook a more liberal denomination for a smaller, more conservative one. Most fundamentalists, nonetheless, remained quietly within the major denominations, hoping to work within existing structures, especially through conservative local churches. At the same time they increasingly gave their support to a growing network of transdenominational fundamentalist evangelistic agencies.

Fundamentalism embodied two paradoxical impulses that its advocates always had difficulty reconciling. On the one hand, what distinguished fundamentalism most from earlier evangelicalism was its militancy against modernist theology and cultural change. Metaphors of warfare dominated their thinking, and the rhetoric of "no compromise" often precipitated denominational showdowns. Once it became apparent after 1925, however, that fundamentalists could not control the major Northern denominations, the logic of their no-compromise positions pointed toward separatism. Dispensational premillennial interpretations of history that had spread widely among fundamentalists supported this separatist tendency. Dispensationalism taught the apostasy of the major churches of "Christendom" as part of a steady cultural degeneration during the present "church age." By the 1930s, the strictest fundamentalists increasingly proclaimed the duty of ecclesiastical separatism.

Fundamentalism, however, also incorporated a positive impulse that often worked at cross-purposes with this negativism. Antedating fundamentalist anti-modernism was the evangelical revivalist tradition out of which it had grown. This movement's overriding preoccupation was the saving of souls. Any responsible means to promote this end was approved.

This prior agenda to win America and the world for Christ worked against the fundamentalist impulses to controversy and to separation. To evangelize effectively, many thought it would be best to retain their positions in the respected denominations. Also, since the movement had the ongoing goal of transdenominational evangelicalism of ultimately saving America, how could that be done if the movement were confined to the marginal separatist group? Furthermore, it might be better not constantly to engage in ugly controversies that might scare off prospective converts. So they emphasized the positive.

This positive strategy meant only a halfway separatism of most fundamentalists from the denominational mainstream. While some fundamentalists built new institutions that were strictly separatist, others built institutions that were in practice separate, but in theory had not repudiated the mainstream. During the 1930s the lines between these two kinds of separatism were not always clear. Some leading fundamentalists insisted on repudiating old-line denominations. Others, equally prominent, stayed in. In the South, of course, staying in was less of a problem for Baptists and Presbyterians, who remained predominantly conservative. On the other hand, some Southern Baptists (the predecessors of the Jerry Falwell types) followed J. Frank Norris and separated. In general the situation was fluid, so that for most in the transdenominational coalition, separatism was not yet a test of the faith.

In this ecclesiastically unsettled atmosphere, fundamentalists moved ahead by building their own network of largely evangelistic agencies. Radio ministries were a particularly effective way to build up ministries that, consistent with long-standing revivalist practice, ignored denominational considerations. By the early 1940s Charles E. Fuller of "The Old-Fashioned Revival Hour," had gained one of the largest radio audiences in the country.

By the early 1940s fundamentalists, typically working through recently formed organizations, were seeing signs of revival on a number of fronts. The most successful of the new organizations was Youth for Christ. During World War II youth evangelists such as Percy Crawford and Jack Wyrtzen sponsored remarkably successful mass rallies in American cities, notably New York and Chicago. In 1945 Youth for Christ International was organized to consolidate a considerable revival. During its first year Youth for Christ sponsored nearly nine hundred rallies nationwide with a total of about one million constituents. The new organization chose a young graduate of Wheaton College, Billy Graham, as its first full-time evangelist. By the end of the decade, Graham carried the revival movement to massive national success.

Graham's base was a network of positive fundamentalists who had been organizing for such a revival throughout the 1940s. The most apparent institutional manifestation of this network was the National Association of Evangelicals, founded in 1942 as a loose affiliation of diverse evangelical denominations and individuals, primarily to promote evangelism. Harold John Ockenga, a former student of the scholarly J. Gresham Machen and pastor of the Park Street Congregational Church in Boston, became the chief organizer of the NAE and also headed a number of other important agencies founded during the next two decades. He and Charles Fuller in 1947 founded Fuller Theological Seminary, which became a formidable West Coast base for the renewal movements. At the center of these organizations were a group of people, predominantly Baptist and Presbyterian, most of whom had connections with institutions such as Wheaton College, Moody Bible Institute, Dallas Theological Seminary, Gordon College and Seminary in Boston, and those followers of Machen who were not strict separatists.

This group built up a broader constituency, as illustrated in the NAE, that by 1947 included thirty small denominations, representing 1,300,000 members. Southern Baptists flirted with the NAE in the 1940s but then stayed out. The NAE leadership reflected the more-or-less mainstream heritage of Northern fundamentalism. Many of its leaders, such as Ockenga, still belonged to major denominations. Working from this broad fundamentalist base, they were also bringing in some evangelical groups that had been on the periphery of the earlier fundamentalist movement.

This positive fundamentalism was emerging as what would soon be called a "new evangelicalism." National revival was the goal. In the late 1940s new evangelical leaders were talking in terms that at the time seemed grandiose—about a national revival, about "winning America" or as Carl F. H. Henry put it, even "remaking the modern mind." They were picking up the old nineteenth-century agenda of a transdenominational evangelical movement. They saw themselves as standing in the tradition of Dwight L. Moody, Charles Finney, Jonathan Edwards, and George Whitefield. If positive evangelicals simply organized and built substantial institutions, they thought they could still be a formidable force in American culture and a challenge to the dominant trends toward secularism in the West.

During the 1950s, the spectacular success of Billy Graham gave the transdenominational evangelical program some plausibility. Graham's vast popular appeal gave him virtual independence—so that his organization could function as a denomination. This cultivation of wider national influence also meant a break with the more separatist fundamentalists. Separatists saw doctrinal purity as an overriding issue and viewed the new evangelicalism as being too willing to compromise with mainline Protestantism.

The showdown came in 1957 when Billy Graham was holding a crusade in New York. Unlike in his earlier crusades, Graham had accepted sponsorship from the New York local Council of Churches. This was the last straw for the strict separatists, such as John R. Rice and Bob Jones. They denounced Graham and broke with him. Since that time we have been able to make a distinction—at least in the North—between those who call themselves fundamentalists and insist on ecclesiastical separatism as a test of the faith and evangelicals who might cooperate with mainline Protestants (that is, those belonging to the National Council of Churches) on a limited basis.

The Graham coalition continued to try to build a unified transdenominational evangelicalism. In 1956 they founded a serious journal, *Christianity Today*, under the editorship of Carl F. H. Henry. Modeled after *Christian Century*, it soon had a larger circulation. Perhaps the high-water mark in their efforts to be the organizers of a culturally significant and coherent evangelistic coalition came in 1967 with their sponsorship of the World Congress on Evangelism, a notable display of unity among most of the major evangelical leaders from America and throughout the world. The Congress pointed to a dimension of the American evangelical coalition that had been important since the nineteenth century, it being part of a wider trans-Atlantic movement with major missionary ties.

By 1967, however, it was beginning to become clear that American evangelicalism was not a single coalition with unified and recognized leadership. Part of the reason for this was an internal crisis. The core ex-fundamentalist movement that the new evangelicals hoped to speak for was splitting apart. The political issues of the 1960s were becoming sources of sharp dissensions. During the 1940s and 1950s neoevangelical spokespersons had called for an evangelical social program but they had assumed it would be a Christianized version of Republicanism. By the 1960s their movement and a growing number of colleges associated with it were producing a second generation that was calling for more progressive political stances. Vietnam polarized everyone over these issues, and arch-conservatives such as J. Howard Pew (who financed many of the enterprises) demanded that evangelicals take unreservedly pro-nationalist, pro-capitalist positions. Carl F. H. Henry, who was solidly Republican nonetheless lost his job at *Christianity Today* partly over his unwillingness to be sufficiently militant. He was replaced in 1968 by Harold Lindsell, who proved ready to provide Christianized versions of the rhetoric of Spiro Agnew during the Nixon era.

This militantly conservative political stance of the evangelical "establishment" sparked a direct reaction on the left. In 1971 dissident students at Trinity Evangelical Divinity School (then the intellectual center for "establishment evangelicalism") organized The People's Christian Coalition and founded an underground newspaper, *The Post-American*. Later this became *Sojourners*, published by the radical evangelical Sojourner's Community in Washington, D. C. Senator Mark Hatfield of Oregon became the best-known supporter of this movement. During the 1970s a spectrum of well-represented evangelical political stances emerged. By now articulate evangelical groups championed women's equality, pacifism, and progressive versions of social justice. A conservative old guard advocated opposite views. Evangelical social-political involvement, for which neoevangelical leaders had called in the 1940s and 1950s, now indeed emerged, but as a major source of division.

At the same time the parallel issue of biblical inerrancy erupted. Although the new evangelicals had attempted to reform fundamentalism, an important element in this "establishment" party had never wanted to break with fundamentalist militancy. "Inerrancy," a real concern in its own right, also served as a symbol of a number of other things. Progressive evangelicals usually were relatively sensitive to the relationship of historical context to understanding the absolute claims of the gospel. This stance opened the door for more progressive applications of the social implications of the gospel. It also opened them to non-destructive aspects of historical criticism. In their view, the inerrancy of Scripture usually implied a wooden hermeneutic that tended to interpret the Bible simply as a set of true propositions without taking into account the original biblical standards of meaning. Conservatives, on the other hand, reasoned that inaccuracies in the original Scriptures would be unworthy of God and undermine biblical authority. Conservatives on this issue were unlikely to have made even modest concessions to the relativist tendencies of progressive modern thought.

By the 1970s, two major conservative denominations, the Southern Baptist Convention and the Missouri Synod Lutheran Church, were embroiled in deep controversies over inerrancy. In 1976 *Christianity Today* editor Harold Lindsell successfully revived inerrancy as a major issue in transdenominational evangelicalism, suggesting in his much-discussed *The Battle for the Bible* that those who denied inerrancy were not evangelicals at all. The transdenominational movement to reform fundamentalism was thus irreparably split over a combination of political and doctrinal issues. The "new evangelicals" were so divided among themselves that the term lost its meaning. By the late 1970s, no one, not even Billy Graham, could claim to stand at the center of so divided a coalition.

In addition to these negative forces dividing the movement stood positive ones related to evangelical success. As evangelicalism in the late 1970s reemerged into prominence in American public life, the movement produced spin-offs that shone more brightly than the fragmenting ex-fundamentalism that once provided a center of transdenominational leadership. One of these was the rise of the Moral Majority, coming from the unexpected quarter of separatist fundamentalism. Jerry Falwell became a reformer of fundamentalism. His role in some ways paralleled that of Graham and his new evangelical cohorts of the 1950s. "Neofundamentalism" is an appropriate term for Falwell's movement. While holding to the fundamentalist heritage of ecclesiastical separatism (and hence remaining distant from Graham), Falwell tried to bring fundamentalists back toward the center of American life, especially through political action. Politics meant making alliances. Stricter fundamentalists, such as Bob Jones, III condemned Falwell as a pseudo-fundamentalist, because of his cooperation with non-fundamentalists. Falwell, nonetheless, proved that the fundamentalist militant and simple style suited the political mood of the era and could mobilize many Americans. While internal divisions immobilized the evangelical "establishment," Falwell took over the program of its right wing and mobilized with fundamentalist decisiveness.

The Moral Majority rode the Reagan wave to success, a strategy apparent from their almost uncritical endorsement of the new president's domestic and foreign policies. The administration, in turn, gave little serious attention to the distinct agenda of the new religious right, including family issues, especially anti-abortion, and school issues, such as school prayer and the mandated teaching of "creation-science."

Neither the Moral Majority nor the now-old neoevangelicals could claim to speak for all evangelicals. Those who aspired to build a unified transdenominational movement kept running into denominationalism. These divisions, in turn, were compounded by regional and social differences. For instance, major African-American denominations that fit the definitions of evangelical participated very little in any of these inter-evangelical activities.

Evangelical growth in recent decades also disrupted efforts to build greater evangelical unity. For instance, the growth of the Southern Baptist Convention and its rise to national prominence shifted the center of gravity of evangelicals. Southern Baptists were not sure whether they were evangelicals since they did not participate strongly in trans-evangelical enterprises. On the other hand, their common heritage was apparent in that they were split over exactly the same issues that divided the evangelical establishment in the North.

Another factor that shifted the center of gravity was the growth of the charismatic and Pentecostal movements. As a movement of transdenominational evangelicalism, the charismatic movements in the 1970s and 1980s overwhelmed the old-new evangelicalism of Billy Graham and his Reformed-leaning friends. At the same time the older separatist Pentecostal denominations were growing rapidly, especially abroad, thus establishing themselves as a major force in evangelicalism. By 1979, 19 percent of all Americans identified themselves as charismatic or Pentecostal. Furthermore, 18 percent of all American Catholics said they were charismatic. This added still another new and entirely unanticipated variation in the evangelical evolution.

We need only mention the giant television ministries that have provided some of the most bizarre variations in the evangelical evolution. Part of the reason that the movement is not susceptible to effective transdenominational unification is that it is structured along the lines of the free-enterprise system. This trait is connected with the typically low American view of the church. Accordingly, much of American evangelicalism is built around competing empires, each focused on one personality. Unless some extraordinarily attractive personality emerges, none of these is likely to draw evangelicalism together. Charismatic Pat Robertson's efforts to forge a larger unity in the 1988 presidential campaign ultimately did no better than Jerry Falwell's earlier efforts.

Evangelicalism Today

So let me draw a few conclusions about the state of evangelicalism today.

First, as has always been the case, evangelicalism is a strange mix of a perceptible unity and of a bewildering diversity that resists transdenominational efforts to mobilize the whole. In this sense it is truly like a mosaic, both united and divided. Only sub-groups with the most similar traditions are likely to be mobilized effectively for wider action.

Second, traditional evangelical divisions are now compounded by theological currents that are cutting across older lines. Perhaps the most important of these divisions is that which divides the charismatic Pentecostals from the non-charismatic evangelicals.

Third, the other major dividing line reflects a growing divide between liberal and conservative cultures in America during the past quarter century. Two cultures representing two differing moral and epistemological outlooks are both growing in American life. Another way to put it is that in the past quarter century a resurgent conservative culture has challenged the old liberal establishment, while during the same era liberalism has become more aggressively permissive on many moral issues.

In the evangelical churches the re-emergence of the conservative culture is particularly strong. What is confusing about this development is that it combines some important doctrinal questions with some American cultural traditions. The clearest example is the odd combination of biblical inerrancy with American nationalism and militarism. One might think that those who insist ardently on "the Bible alone" as an authority would be most critical of human authorities such as national governments. The opposite seems to be the case. During the latter part of the Reagan era a prominent champion of inerrancy preached a series of sermons on television on the importance of the Strategic Defense Initiative ("Star Wars"). Such emphases on cultural-political issues, which serve as virtual articles of faith, are complicating the evangelical scene and making it difficult to discuss the doctrinal concerns on their own merits.

Finally, and perhaps most importantly, is the question of whether while much fanfare accompanies the battles between liberals and conservatives, the evangelical challenge to the secular culture will be sustained. Evangelicalism has always been a combination of Christian and American traditions. At what point do accommodations to popular American outlooks undermine the faith? This is particularly a problem in the late-twentieth century when we face the combination of two major forces. One is all-pervasive media that are shaping everybody's values. The second is an evangelicalism that is largely market driven and dependent on popular appeal. To what extent will these combined forces reshape the dominant evangelicalism in the direction of telling people simply what they want to hear? To what extent will evangelicalism become an endorsement of American views of the autonomy of the self and of the rights of everyone to have whatever they want—whether it is health, success, or material prosperity? These dangers seem to me to be particularly great in almost every part of the movement.

As a historian I can conclude by saying that the situation is indeed alarming. The pressures to conform the Christian message to various American norms—of either the right or the left—sometimes seem almost overwhelming. On the other hand, I can add the small comfort that the church has survived challenges in the past that have been just as severe. Think of the state of the church at the time of Augustine when the survival of civilization as he knew it was threatened. Which is worse: to be destroyed by rock music videos or by Attila the Hun? Perhaps it is always the case that the church itself is a wreck—a bewildering mix of the ridiculous and the sublime. The tares will grow with the wheat.

Looking at the state of the church seems to me to be edifying in the same way that it is edifying to look honestly at the state of one's own heart. Things are a mess and a bundle of contradictions. Yet such an honest look should impel us not only to analyze the situation as best we can and to lay our feeble plans for improvement, but also to trust more in the grace of God who saves us and the church despite our best efforts.

2

Varieties
——— of ———
American Evangelicalism

Robert K. Johnston

There are three indisputable facts about the evangelical tradition in America. First, it is important. Second, it is understudied. Third, it is diverse.[1]

Whether one speaks of an evangelical kaleidoscope, an evangelical mosaic, an evangelical umbrella, or less metaphorically, an evangelical movement, scholars of American evangelicalism struggle to express its present diversity and scope. Cullen Murphy is more colorful than most when he speaks of the "vast tent of evangelical faith," viewing it as a twelve-ring circus with acts performed by "peace-church" conservatives, Arminian conservatives, Wesleyans, Baptists, conservative Calvinists, immigrant churches, pietist churches, Adventists, black Pentecostals, white Pentecostals, black evangelicals, and fundamentalists.[2] The Roman Catholic missiologist Thomas Stransky finds American evangelicalism "a confusing conglomeration." He writes:

What a wide variety of traditions! They come from within the mainline churches (Episcopalian, Presbyterian, Methodist); those Reformation churches with strict interpretations of their confessions (Missouri Synod Lutherans, Christian Reformed); the "peace" churches (Brethren, Mennonite, Friends); the more conservative wing of the Restora-

---

[1] Leonard I. Sweet, "The Evangelical Tradition in America," in *The Evangelical Tradition in America*, ed. Leonard I. Sweet (Macon, GA.: Mercer University Press, 1984), 1.

[2] Cullen Murphy, "Protestantism and the Evangelicals," *Wilson Quarterly* 5 (August 1981), 105-116.

40

tion movement (Campbellites); the "Holiness"tradition (Wesleyan Methodists); Baptists, the fundamentalist groups... Pentecostals, most black churches . . . No wonder it is difficult to reach a description in which all of the above would recognize themselves![3]

Fundamentalists at times have tried to equate the limits of evangelicalism with the limits of their own movement; but the data will not support the equation. Black evangelicals have as little to do with fundamentalism as do the holiness denominations. Pentecostals still are scorned by many fundamentalists. (Think of Jerry Falwell's problems with his constituency when he assumed control of the PTL Club.) Mennonites and Lutherans want to distance themselves from fundamentalists, and the list could be continued. As Joel Carpenter points out, "fundamentalists are evangelicals, but not all evangelicals (are) fundamentalists."[4]

Others attempt to give definitions of the American evangelical that are narrow. Some would limit the term evangelical to those who are descendants of American revivalism. (But what then of the Christian Reformed Church?) Others would stress human faith and active obedience. (But what of the Lutherans?) Or, conversely, they would focus on God's initiating grace. (But what of the Restoration churches?) Many would equate evangelicalism with a commitment to biblical inerrancy or Baconian epistemology. Others would center on premillennialism and dispensationalism. Some would limit the category of evangelicals to those who oppose modern thought. Others would define evangelicalism according to a Reformed perspective. (The most frequently quoted example of this latter stance is John Gerstner's summary concerning the supposed "Pelagianism" of Charles Finney: "To this extent Finney, the greatest of nineteenth-century evangelists, became the greatest of nineteenth-century foes of evangelicalism.[5])

In seeking to move beyond such imperialistic and/or reductive definitions of evangelicalism, William Abraham calls into question the very function of labels themselves. Rather than viewing labels as referential or descriptive, he would have us recognize their prescriptive character.[6] Thus understood, the term evangelical should be judged "an essentially

[3] Thomas Stransky, "A Look at Evangelical Protestantism," *Theology, News and Notes* 35 (March 1988), 24.

[4] Joel Carpenter, "The Fundamentalist Leaven and the Rise of an Evangelical United Front," in *Sweet, Evangelical Tradition in America*, 26. Compare George M. Marsden, "Evangelical and Fundamental Christianity," in *The Encyclopedia of Religion*, ed. M. Eliade (New York: MacMillan, 1987), 5:195.

[5] John H. Gertsner, "Theological Boundaries: The Reformed Perspective," in *The Evangelicals*, ed. David F. Wells and John D. Woodbridge (Nashville: Abingdon, 1975), 27.

contested concept" (the phrase is W. B. Gallie's, who writes in the British analytical tradition).[7] Abraham believes there are alternate, competing specifications of those qualities central to the definition of evangelicalism. When a concept is "essentially contested," one finds various groups using it in different ways with no common standard. Even though the contestants recognize competing definitions, they continue to maintain the correctness of their own version, believing themselves to have convincing arguments. Abraham thinks the only hope is to seek an appreciation of the history of the contested concept. But will this work?

Abraham would have us understand the Wesleyan roots of American evangelicalism over against those who would emphasize its Reformed heritage. Abraham is rightly sensitive to the present dominance of Reformed practitioners of evangelical historiography (such as Noll, Marsden, Hatch, and Carpenter). Yet a focus on American evangelicalism's primary debt to pietist, rather than Puritan, traditions in America is similarly reductive, not simply a necessary part of the "contest." By the nineteenth century, almost all American Protestants were evangelical. This coalition reflected a "merger of Pietist and Reformed heritages."[8]

A Family Resemblance

D. Bloesch suggests that the term *evangelical* remains "fluid."[9] D. Hubbard admits that the term is presently "shrouded in controversy."[10] L. Sweet believes it "eludes definition."[11] T. Weber considers the definition of evangelicalism "one of the biggest problems in American religious historiography."[12] D. Dayton understands there to be no "univocal defi-

---

[6] William J. Abraham, "E Pluribus Unum: Towards a Definitive Definition of Evangelicalism," (unpublished paper), 4.

[7] William J. Abraham, *The Coming Great Revival: Recovering the Full Evangelical Tradition* (San Francisco: Harper & Row, 1984), 72.

[8] George M. Marsden, "Fundamentalism and American Evangelicalism, " in *The Variety of American Evangelicalism*, ed. Donald W. Dayton and Robert K. Johnston (Knoxville: University of Tennessee Press, 1991). Compare William G. McLoughlin, *Evangelicals, 1800-1900*, ed. William G. McLoughlin (New York: Harper & Row, 1968), 5; C. Norman Kraus, "Evangelicalism: The Great Coalition," in *Evangelicalism and Anabaptism*, ed. C. Norman Kraus (Scottdale, PA: Herald Press, 1979), 43-59; and Carpenter, "The Fundamentalist Leaven," 267.

[9] Donald G. Bloesch, *The Future of Evangelical Christianity: A Call for Unity and Diversity* (Garden City, NJ: Doubleday, 1983), 9.

[10] David Allan Hubbard, *What We Evangelicals Believe* (Pasadena, CA: Fuller Theological Seminary, 1979), 7.

[11] Leonard I. Sweet, "Nineteenth-Century Evangelicalism" in *Encyclopedia of the American Religious Experience*, ed. Charles Lippy and Peter Williams (New York: Charles Scribner's Sons, 1988), 2:875.

[12] Timothy P. Weber, "Premillennialism and the Branches of Evangelicalism," in *American Evangelicalism*.

nition of evangelicalism."[13] And C. N. Kraus believes "the movement defies a precise theological definition."[14]

Such a definitional impasse suggests the need of a new model for describing American evangelicalism. In the 1981 *Annual Review of Psychology*, Carolyn Mervis and Eleanor Rosch summarize contemporary research in the field of categorization. As they define it, a "category" exists whenever two or more items are made equivalent. Such categorization can be done poorly, but it is "one of the most basic functions of living creatures," allowing an organism to interact profitably with "the infinitely distinguishable objects and events it experiences." Traditionally, categories have consisted of "a specification of those qualities that a thing must have to be a member of the class" (intention—for example, a flat surface about waist high, space for one's legs to fit under the surface) and a listing of "things that have those qualities" (extension—for example, dining-room tables, card tables, kitchen tables, picnic tables). Categories are, thus, "seen as determinately established by necessary and sufficient criteria for membership," and "the role of rationality is to abstract out what is essential to a situation while ignoring what is inessential."[15] (For example, a surface waist high is essential; four legs are not, for a pedestal works fine.)

One might say that categories traditionally have been viewed as more or less *black or white*. While recognizing the tidiness of such a definitional approach, Mervis and Rosch, with their colleagues, have begun to understand the limitations of such "exactitude" as well. They have become increasingly aware that categorization deals only more or less with black and white.

For example, growing empirical evidence supports the conclusion that, within a category, all members need not be, nor are they, equally representative, as has often been assumed. Whether one is considering "colors," or "dogs," or "furniture," test subjects are able to agree on certain exemplars that are "more representative than others." Moreover, our language helps us code these gradients of representatives through the use of qualifying terms or "hedges." We might say, for example, that "a penguin is technically a bird," even though we would not say, "a sparrow is technically a bird." In the latter case, the word technically is redundant, while in the former it recognizes that not all birds are equally birdlike. Researchers recognize that "category members differ in the

---

[13] Donald W. Dayton, "The Limits of Evangelicalism: The Pentecostal Tradition."

[14] C. Norman Kraus, "Evangelicalism: A Mennonite Critique."

[15] Carolyn B. Mervis and Eleanor Rosch, "Categorization of Natural Objects," *Annual Review of Psychology* 32 (1981), 89, 94, 90, 95.

extent to which they share attributes with other category members. They call this variable family resemblance (after Wittgenstein 1953 [*Philosophical Investigations*]). Items which have the highest family resemblance scores are those with the most shared attributes."[16]

This notion of "family resemblance" helps explain a variety of phenomena. As in any family, category boundaries are not always well defined. The poorer members (that is, less representative) of categories often contain attributes from other categories which cause lines to be blurred and decisions to remain probalistic. (For example, is a daughter-in-law a member of the family, or not?) On the other hand, the most representative members of a family are recognized rapidly and easily, even if the family is not named. Again, although the recognition of family members can occur without the subject being told the rules of family membership, the human mind does tend to categorize and classify in ways that involve abstraction, that is, creatively sorting out "which elements of a situation are 'essential' and which irrelevant."[17]

This notion of family resemblance, as Mervis and Rosch describe the term, is a helpful one in coming to understand American evangelicalism. Rather than seek exclusive categories, it is useful to recognize the familial nature of American evangelicalism. Just as with other categorization, so with the term "evangelical," we must allow category boundaries a certain open-endedness. One observes this fluidity with regard to the term "evangelical," as we often and rightly use qualifying terms: "basically evangelical," "generally evangelical," "strict evangelical," "progressive evangelical," "conservative evangelical," "mainline evangelical," "establishment evangelical," and so on.[18]

Several examples are useful in helping one to understand the importance of evangelicalism's family resemblance. In his book *The Coming Great Revival*, William Abraham points out that the term *evangelical* has meant different things in different ages. One only needs to consider the distinctives of Luther, Calvin, and Wesley to sense profoundly different accounts of the Christian tradition. Yet Abraham admits:

> What holds the various expressions together as one tradition is not one agreed set of doctrines; rather unity resides in family resemblance. Despite differences of emphasis and expression, there is sufficient

---

[16] Ibid., 96, 99.

[17] Ibid., 103.

[18] Compare Kenneth S. Kantzer, "The Future of the Church and Evangelicalism," in *Evangelicals Face the Future*, ed. Donald E. Hoke (South Pasadena, CA.: William Carey Library, 1978), 132.

common appearance for both outsiders and insiders to identify a single evangelical tradition within the Christian tradition as a whole.[19]

Abraham opts methodologically not to follow through with the notion of family resemblance, choosing to develop the model of an "essentially contested concept" instead. Reacting against those within neofundamentalism who have attempted doctrinally to "suitably can" what he believes is in reality "a complex vision of the Christian tradition," Abraham chooses his own "suitable can," an alternate, Wesleyan model, one clear-cut and identifiable.

Abraham does not want Wesley to be "tamed by placing him in the categories of the fundamentalist paradigm,"[20] and he is right to resist. If, however, what is under consideration is not fundamentalism, one of evangelicalism's multiple expressions, but the broader familial category of evangelicalism itself, then such a fear is ungrounded. Although American evangelicalism historically has been influenced by fundamentalism, it is not synonymous with the movement. One need only observe, as George Marsden has, the irony of some who shun the use of the term *evangelical* because of its association with fundamentalism, while "with most who would call themselves fundamentalist in the 1980s, the designation evangelical is still anathema."[21]

If Abraham stumbles over the concept of evangelicalism when defined more out of the Princeton tradition than the Finney tradition, David Wells, one strongly identified with the Reformed tradition within evangelicalism, has no less serious a dilemma.[22] Wanting a theological definition of evangelicalism rooted in a "simple enumeration of doctrinal points to which evangelicals agree," Wells nonetheless recognizes that such an approach "only deals with part of the reality." Wells would understand evangelicals as essentially "a doctrinal people," something Abraham would dispute. Even Wells recognizes certain cultural and sociological factors within evangelicalism that must be taken into account doctrinally. He writes:

> It is true that a rough doctrinal agenda has been consistently maintained from the time of the Protestant Reformation to the present, but in every age that doctrine has been formulated in relation to, and sometimes as a

---

[19] Abraham, *The Coming Great Revival.*

[20] Ibid., 67.

[21] Marsden, "Fundamentalism and American Evangelicalism."

[22] Wells, a professor at Gordon-Conwell Theological Seminary; Mark Noll of Wheaton College, and Cornelius Plantinga, Jr., of Calvin Seminary, were recently awarded a $400,000 grant for a four-year project to strengthen evangelical theology from a Reformed perspective.

result of, a confusion with the expectations, norms, and events that shaped that age's cognitive horizon. For this reason, it is true to say that evangelicalism has meant something different in every age.[23]

Wells thus bemoans the diversity of the evangelical family, even while allowing for its necessity.

Samuel S. Hill, Jr., in his article, "The Shape and Shapes of Popular Southern Piety," offers more integrated understanding of evangelicalism's family resemblance than either Abraham or Wells. Hill outlines four particular versions of evangelicalism in the American South. Those who are "truth-oriented" he labels "fundamentalists." He calls those who are "conversion oriented," the "evangelistic"; those who are "spiritually-oriented," the "devotional"; and those evangelical Protestants who are "service-oriented," the "ethical." Hill finds many independent Baptist churches as well as the Churches of Christ (in their considerable variety) to be "truth-oriented." The Southern Baptists are largely "conversion-oriented," while the black churches and Southern Methodists are devotionally or "spiritually-oriented." Hill finds individuals such as Clarence Jordan and Will D. Campbell representatives of "service-oriented" Southern evangelical Protestantism. Despite the considerable differences these traditions represent, Hill believes they are nevertheless "four distinct versions of one family of Protestant Christianity." The emphases vary from what you "believe," to what you "get," to who you "are," to what you "do." Moreover, while these variant forms are identifiable, they are far from discreet. (One need only consider the current "truth-oriented" battle for the Bible going on in the "evangelistic" Southern Baptist Convention.) "Yet," writes Hill, "one [orientation] is likely to be dominant, standing as the animating principle, with the others recessive."[24] (Could we understand the current battle within the Southern Baptist churches as a fight over which of evangelicalism's possible "animating principles" will dominate?)

The notion of family resemblance can be tested by considering the case of Mennonite churches. Mennonites, as C. Norman Kraus recognizes, have always been within the evangelical tradition. They are part of the "family." Yet Anabaptists are more "prophetic" than "evangelistic," less apologetic and rationalistic with regard to Scripture than hermeneutical;

---

[23] David F. Wells, "'No Offense: I am an Evangelical': A Search for Self-Definition," in *A Time to Speak: The Evangelical-Jewish Encounter*, ed. A. James Rudin and Marvin R. Wilson (Grand Rapids: Eerdmans, 1987), 30, 32.

[24] Samuel S. Hill, Jr., "The Shape and Shapes of Popular Southern Piety," in *Varieties of Southern Evangelicalism*, ed. David Edwin Harrell, Jr. (Macon, GA.: Mercer University Press, 1981), 99-103.

and more concrete and communal with regard to the church than is typical of wider evangelicalism. Moreover, to the degree that evangelicalism is defined by the "Calvinist faction, especially in its dispensationalist guise," Mennonites have shunned too close an identification. In Kraus's words, "The traditional Mennonite understanding of what is primary and what is secondary in the gospel differs from the American evangelical consensus."

Yet, despite such tensions, most commentators on American evangelicalism would conclude that just as penguins are really birds, so Anabaptists are really evangelicals. An emphasis on personal religious experience, an insistence upon witness and mission, a loyalty to biblical authority, an understanding of salvation by grace through faith—such family resemblances within most of evangelicalism are identified by Kraus as true to Anabaptist-Mennonites and are enough to define Anabaptists within evangelicalism's orb.[25] This is true, even as differences regarding scriptural interpretation, church, and society cause the Mennonites to be viewed by Kraus as less representative examples of evangelicalism in America.

Definitions or Descriptions?

The present contest over the definition of American evangelicalism has caused frustration, hostility, and, increasingly, I am afraid, boredom. Incessant argument over what constitutes the pure "core" of doctrine has turned evangelicals inward and threatens to undermine their effective evangelism and mission. The latest evidence of this sad but oft-repeated phenomenon is the decade of controversy in the Southern Baptist Convention, which now appears to be slowing church growth.

Seeking to avoid such peril, some have attempted to posit evangelism as the *only* valid trademark of American evangelicalism. Is this our "family resemblance"? Such a perspective was strongly evident in the summer of 1989, for example, at the Lausanne II Consultation of Future Evangelical Concerns. Evangelist and Lausanne president Leighton Ford argued that evangelicals might become unified, if not by theological agreement, then by a commitment to a common mission. This, in turn, led Carl F. H. Henry to question in his rejoinder "How much pragmatism can evangelical Christianity accommodate without jeopardizing its own evangelical ingredient?" Henry's own creedal propensity caused him to be particularly sensitive to a coalition built simply on evangelistic utility. He cynically proposed a tagline which the evangelical movement one day might be forced to use: "Doctrinal views professed by those involved are not necessarily those of the New Testament."[26]

---

[25] Compare C. Norman Kraus, "Anabaptism and Evangelicalism," in Kraus, *Evangelicalism and Anabaptism*, 175, 177.

While Henry would opt for creedalism over pragmatism, neither will suffice as the key to an understanding of the family—American evangelicalism. Timothy Weber is correct in warning against the temptation to define evangelicalism in either theological or existential/spiritual terms. Some want to force on evangelicalism a kind of theological uniformity that historically it never had, while others want to speak almost exclusively of an evangelical spirit without specifying any theological boundaries. "As is often the case," reasons Weber, "the truth lies somewhere in between these two extremes. From my perspective, evangelicalism is both a set of theological convictions and an ethos."[27] In short, common understandings both of faith and of mission knit this otherwise disparate group of Christian subcultures together—these provide a family resemblance. Put most simply, for all of their variety and particularity, contemporary American evangelicals have a commonality centered on a threefold commitment: a dedication to the gospel that is expressed in a personal faith in Christ as Lord, an understanding of the gospel as defined authoritatively by Scripture, and a desire to communicate the gospel both in evangelism and social reform. Evangelicals are those who believe the gospel is to be experienced personally, defined biblically, and communicated passionately.

For some years now, historian Timothy Smith and his students at Johns Hopkins University have been at work on an analysis of twelve North American evangelical "movements." Smith's work is to be published in a forthcoming book, *The American Evangelical Mosaic*. In an essay already published, Smith delineates the descriptive parameters of his project. He sees four historical evangelical movements in America— Methodist Arminianism, Puritan Calvinism, pietism, and the "peace churches." All four had a "thoroughgoing commitment to the authority of the Old and New Testaments." All were:

> permeated with the promise of a personal experience of salvation from sin, received in a moment of living faith, which Jesus called being "born again" . . . Finally, all four of these inwardly diverse movements found that both the Scriptures and this inward experience of love for God and one's neighbor impelled them to missionary evangelism.[28]

---

[26] Carl F. H. Henry, "Response to Conference Findings," in *Evangelicals Face the Future*, ed. D. Hoke, 164.

[27] Weber, "Premillennialism and the Branches of Evangelicalism."

[28] Timothy Smith, "Evangelical Christianity and American Culture," in Rudin and Wilson, *A Time to Speak*, 60.

Smith summarizes his preliminary findings: "These three characteristics—commitment to Scriptural authority, the experience of regeneration or 'new life in Christ,' and the passion for evangelism—have marked evangelicals ever since."

Gabriel Fackre, in his entry on "Evangelicalism" in *The Westminster Dictionary of Christian Theology*, argues similarly, although his referent is the classical evangelicalism of the Reformation. He notes that the term came into use during the Reformation to identify Protestants as they held "to the belief in justification by grace through faith and the supreme authority of Scripture (often considered the material and formal principles of Reformational teaching)." Fackre then observes a subsequent "interiorization and intensification" of the meaning, as evangelicalism came to refer to those who emphasized "personal conversion and a rigorous moral life," who concentrated "attention on the Bible as a guide to conviction and behavior," and who sought to disseminate the Christian faith so conceived with a special zeal. Here, again, are the same three descriptors.[29]

"Word" or "Spirit"

If evangelicals as a family are those who emphasize: (1) that the Bible is authoritative and reliable; (2) that salvation comes through personal trust in Christ and in His atoning work; and (3) that a spiritually transformed life is marked by a commitment to social outreach and evangelism, then how are we to understand evangelicalism's familial differences? Gabriel Fackre provides a beginning point by focusing his description of evangelicalism on the two formative principles of Reformation teaching: justification and scriptural authority. Fackre understands the controversy that often surfaces among evangelicals relating to their focus on one or the other of these emphases.

Lutherans, for example, "prioritize the transforming power of the gospel over Scripture and theories of biblical authority." They sense that the evangelical coalition in its "Presbyterian" expression does not affirm "the centrality of justification by grace through faith apart from works of the Law with the kind of vigor Lutherans desire. Evangelical priorities seem to be elsewhere, with holiness or the character of the Christian life."[30] Perhaps this is the reason why even the more theologically conservative Lutheran denominations, such as The Lutheran Church—Missouri Synod, have avoided formal identification with the National Association of Evangelicals. It might also explain why Robert Preuss,

---

[29] Gabriel Fackre, "Evangelicalism," *Westminster Dictionary of Christian Theology*, ed. Alan Richardson and John Bowden (Philadelphia: Westminster, 1983), 191.

[30] Mark Ellingsen, "Lutheranism," in *American Evangelicalism*.

former president of Concordia Seminary in Fort Wayne, Indiana, was the only Lutheran involved in the leadership of the International Conference on Biblical Inerrancy.

Such a differentiation—distinguishing those who stress the Reformation's material principle (justification) from those who stress its formal principle (Scripture)—speaks only to a partial listing of the evangelical family. Evangelical priorities are often elsewhere, on holiness and the character of the Christian life (that is, on the third prong of the evangelical description). Rather than stress the differences between those who speak of the gospel of Scripture and those who focus on the Scripture of the gospel, it is better to differentiate that both of these groups are subsets of a *theology of the Word* and that those other expressions of American evangelicalism which have emphasized a personal experience with Christ through His Spirit are oriented toward a *theology of the Spirit*. While one branch of the evangelical family has understood its informing center to be the Christ of Scripture, the other branch has stressed new life in Christ. To use Samuel Hill's language, what we have in contemporary evangelicalism is differing "animating principles."

Examples are easily multiplied. In his short personal statement of Who's Who in America, Carl F.H. Henry comments: "The Bible remains the world's most indispensable reading, and a personal walk with God remains man's unsurpassable privilege."[31] It is not accidental that Henry chose to begin with knowledge of God through Scripture and then turned to the experiential dimensions of the faith. Although the importance of both Word and Spirit are recognized, and although the two are in fact conjoined, a clear priority is evident here, as in other of Henry's writings.[32]

In one of his contemporary Christian songs, Michael Card sings, "Jesus loves me, this I know; *it's not just the Bible that tells me so*. I can feel it within my soul; Jesus loves me, this I know."[33] Card goes on in the several stanzas to talk of Jesus' death for us, of Card's desire to "shout the news" to the world, of the wonder of the atonement, and of the glory of the Christian life. His theology is classical, biblical evangelical Christianity. Yet it also is distinct in emphasis from what many evangelicals learned from the cradle on: "Jesus loves me! This I know, for the Bible tells me so."

---

[31] Carl F. H. Henry, quoted by Carl F. H. Henry and Kenneth S. Kantzer in their letter of July 1988 for the executive committee of Evangelical Affirmations, a conference held at Trinity Evangelical Divinity School, May 14-17, 1989.

[32] Compare Carl F.H. Henry, "Who Are the Evangelicals?," *Christianity Today*, (February 4, 1972), 23-24.

[33] Michael Card, "Jesus Loves Me (This I Know)," *The Best of Michael Card*, Milk and Honey Records (Grand Rapids: Zondervan, Singspiration Music, 1985).

Varieties of American Evangelicalism

Donald Dayton, Richard Hughes, and others have labeled this basic dichotomy in evangelicals emphasis the "Presbyterian" versus the "Pentecostal" paradigms.[34] Anabaptists, Holiness churches, Pentecostals, black churches, pietists, and Baptists are all oriented toward a theology of experience, one explicitly or implicitly grounded in the Spirit. Turning to the other central branch of evangelicalism's family tree, that grew from a theology of the Word, we note the orthodox Lutherans, the self-consciously Reformed, fundamentalism, and premillennialism. It is perhaps best to include restorationism and Adventism, too, though they have their own dynamics.

Two classic approaches to theology exist in American evangelicalism.[35] One begins with God's action in regard to humankind. The other focuses on *humankind's* experience of God in His creation and redemption. I have labeled the former a "theology of the Word." It tends toward creedal definition and is prone at its worst to literalism in biblical interpretation and legalism in regard to experience. The latter I have called a "theology of the Spirit." It tends toward the intuitive and interpersonal and is prone at its worst to mysticism or psychologism. One focuses on formal doctrine; the other, on Christian experience. Yet both belong to the family of American evangelicalism, for one can move from Spirit to Word or Word to Spirit without friction or reduction. Ultimately, within evangelicalism, as Calvin recognized long ago, Word and Spirit must be conjoined. The Word cannot take the place of the Spirit, but neither can it be ignored. Hans Küng is correct in recognizing that we "demonstrate to the world the good news of the gospel both with authority and love."[36]

---

[34] Compare Donald W. Dayton, "Whither Evangelicalism?" in *Sanctification and Liberation*, ed. Theodore Runyon (Nashville: Abingdon, 1981), 162-163: "The purpose of this chapter has been to demonstrate the debt of contemporary evangelicalism to the holiness movements of the last century, and to point to the impoverishment that has occurred as evangelicals have lost contact with that Arminian heritage and have been co-opted by fundamentalism, premillenialism, and biblical literalism. The creative alternative to reactionary versions of Calvinism is to be found, I believe, in those Wesleyan sources. And the challenge to Methodist theologians of an evangelical persuasion today is to make the evangelical world aware of that alternative."

[35] Compare Robert K. Johnston, "Of Tidy Doctrine and Truncated Experience," *Christianity Today*, (February 18, 1977), 10-14.

[36] Hans Küng, *The Church* (New York: Sheed and Ward, 1967), 149.

3

Baptist and Evangelical: One Northern
———————— Baptist's ————————
Perspective

Stanley J. Grenz

Are Southern Baptists evangelicals? The question had, until recently, never crossed my mind. I had never entertained the thought that Southern Baptists could be anything but evangelicals. Of course, I had noted the Mercer University Press book of 1983, *Are Southern Baptists"Evangelicals"?* Still, the whole matter appeared on the surface to be a purely academic question.

How else could one classify Southern Baptists? I asked myself. The options—if one is limited to the theological categories generally employed to characterize persons and groups—are quite restricted. These categories tend to allow for only three alternatives: fundamentalist, liberal, or evangelical.

Are Southern Baptists to be characterized by the first designation? Are they fundamentalists? Of course, I was aware of fundamentalists within the SBC; but the denomination that gave the nation Jimmy Carter could hardly be fundamentalist in its entirety, it seemed.

The second option, liberalism, loomed even more unlikely. In a denomination numbering over fourteen million one would naturally expect to find a few members with liberal leanings. How else could conservatives rally the troops and raise the battle flag?

Despite the presence of both fundamentalists and liberals within the SBC, however, it seemed to me that neither of these standard labels could serve as the appropriate characterization of the Convention on the whole. This meant that for the purposes of delineating the rank and file within the SBC there remained only one designation—evangelical.

The time during which I naively assumed that Southern Baptists were simply evangelical folk with a Dixie drawl has now come to an end, however. Reminiscent of Immanuel Kant I have been "awakened from my dogmatic slumber," or to borrow the phrase of Kierkegaardian existentialism, I have fallen from my previous state of "dreaming innocence." I now realize that it may, indeed, be the case that my sisters and brothers in the SBC, these with whom I share a kindred spirit as "Baptists," do not share with me the self-designation *evangelical*.

My blissful ignorance destroyed and my curiosity aroused, I must raise anew the question, "What is an evangelical?" I cannot simply engage in the cool endeavor of objective analysis. Rather, I am forced to enter again into the painful business of self-analysis as well, seeking to discover what it means for me to view myself as a Baptist and as evangelical.

The Evangelicals: Who Are They?

From childhood I have always thought of myself as an evangelical. I looked upon the evangelical organizations (which I only later learned were "parachurch") and the evangelical leaders (whom I only later discovered are not all Baptist, although most are in some sense baptistic, if Martin Marty's thesis concerning the baptistification of America is correct) as my organizations and my leaders.

As I progressed into adolescence, I graduated from Child Evangelism Fellowship into Youth for Christ. While a university student, I participated at one time or another in Campus Crusade for Christ, InterVarsity, and the Navigators, with the Baptist Student Union thrown in for good measure because I was also a Baptist. (In the context of the 1960s on the campus of the University of Colorado all these groups, with the notable exception of the BSU, I now insightfully note, joined forces under the banner of the World Christian Liberation Front.)

The great contemporary evangelical heroes were household words during my younger years. I looked uncritically to Hal Lindsay (*The Late Great Planet Earth*), Josh McDowell (*Evidence that Demands a Verdict*), and Billy Graham as possessing the ultimate answers for young, inquisitive minds. As I began to try my own intellectual wings and explore the rationality of the faith, the ranks of my heroes were augmented by Francis Schaeffer (*Escape from Reason*), Paul Little (*Know What You Believe*), C. S. Lewis (*Mere Christianity*), and the theologians publishing in *Christianity Today*. Only later did the awareness fully dawn that these affinities had taken me beyond my denominational label and placed me in the middle of the then-mushrooming evangelical movement.

My entire life, I have seen myself as a Baptist and as an evangelical. The evangelical-Southern Baptist dialogue, in contrast, moves from a different orientation: not the Baptist and evangelical, which characterizes my outlook, but Baptist (and by that is meant *Southern* Baptist) or evangelical. As you can see, posing such an alternative is as foreign to my frame of reference as grits, crawfish, "y'all," and Lottie Moon offerings. For me, the matter need not be—cannot be—an either/or. If anything, it must be a both/and.

For this reason, even the analysis of George Marsden, perhaps the dean of "evangelical watchers," fails to place the situation within my purview. He speaks of "card-carrying evangelicals," referring to those who identify themselves as evangelicals first and members of a denomination second. My perspective, however, moves from yet a different option. It is as a member of my denomination that I am an evangelical, and this because I participate in an evangelical denomination, namely, the family of Baptists, and more specifically, the North American Baptist Conference.

Perhaps the best service I can perform, then, is to voice this option for reflection and scrutiny. My task may be that of encouraging Southern Baptists to ascertain to what extent being a Southern Baptist also means they too are "ex officio" (by virtue of their presence in the Baptist family, more specifically, by virtue of their involvement in the Southern Baptist expression of that family) in some sense of the term evangelical. The task at that point will be to consider the ramifications and practical implications that might arise out of such a discovery.

But now to the question, what is an evangelical?

Marsden's Categories: Two Senses of the Term

Perhaps more so than any scholar, Duke University historian George Marsden has set out to observe and describe the evangelical movement. He offers two basic understandings of the term.

First, *evangelical* may be used in a broad sense, as a Christian who subscribes to certain viewpoints. The most significant of these are the authority of Scripture, God's historical saving work in Christ, salvation solely through faith in Christ's work, the importance of evangelism and missions, and an emphasis on a transformed life.

In addition to this broad sense, *evangelical* may be used more narrowly as the designation for those whom Marsden calls "card-carrying evangelicals." These persons are Christians who see themselves as part of a transdenominational movement from which they gain their primary religious identity.

This latter part of the description is crucial for Marsden. The key question, he maintains, is that of the source of a person's primary self-understanding. Evangelicals, in his analysis, look to the movement, and not to their particular denomination, for this identity. They are evangelicals first, and only then adherents of a denominational tradition. This orientation, in turn, explains in part the relatively great degree of denominational fluidity characteristic of evangelicals, in contrast to Southern Baptists.

Personal View

While I appreciate Marsden's analysis and am convinced of its general validity, I would offer a slightly different perspective. *Evangelical*, I would maintain, refers primarily to a specific vision of what it means to be a Christian. This vision is less easily described as "felt." What is "evangelical"? I cannot offer an objective, scientific description of it, but I know it when I see it. Or better, I sense it, when I find myself in an evangelical atmosphere.

This evangelical vision of what it means to be a Christian includes various aspects. Basically, it entails a shared way of being Christian, a certain piety. This piety is present despite, or in the midst of, differences and diversity. It may be expressed through diverse worship forms. It transcends differences in racial, ethnic, or sociological and social backgrounds. It may be found in church buildings of differing types and styles. It even crosses political and language barriers. (Evangelicalism is present in a small group of Christians from different countries who meet in a hamlet in Bulgaria and sing "How Great Thou Art" simultaneously in three languages.)

Despite differences among the people it encompasses, evangelicalism means that all share a sense of belonging. They sense that "these are My people." Evangelicalism entails shared hymns, a shared desire to make the Bible live in personal and community life, a shared understanding of the church as a fellowship of believers, and a shared way of praying. (Mainline churches "say prayers"; evangelicals join in "a word of prayer.")

Evangelicalism involves a shared sense that personal faith is to be vibrant and central to life. Above all, evangelicalism means shared stories. Evangelicals offer testimonies or narratives of their life experiences. Although the details of the stories differ, the same basic format provides their structure, and the same basic motifs are woven throughout the various accounts.

I must add, however, that all evangelicals do not agree on this perspective on the genius of evangelicalism. Holding to it marks me in some circles. It means that, at best, I am an evangelical of a different sort in their eyes, focusing too much on piety and too little on doctrine. Some evangelicals would even exclude me from their number. Nevertheless, I would argue that this vision of the faith lies at the heart of what the evangelical party within the church throughout its history has sought to maintain.

A Historical Perspective: The Rise of the Evangelical Movement in America

What is the source of this shared vision of what it means to be a Christian? Where did the evangelical movement arise?

Before moving to a historical perspective on the movement, a word of preface must be offered. Evangelicalism in both the broader and the narrower sense of the term obviously transcends the boundaries of the United States. It is found in Europe, for example, in the Evangelical Alliance. The evangelical wing of the Anglican Church boasts a venerable history. At the same time, something distinctly American marks the movement. Evangelicalism is bound up with the ethos of America in a way unparalled anywhere else in the world. This country has been especially successful in exporting the evangelical vision through its missionary endeavors. Therefore, it is proper to look at the specifically American dimension of this wider phenomenon.

Evangelical Beginnings in the Reformation

Although evangelically oriented reform movements existed within and beside the dominant church during the Middle Ages, the initial beginnings of evangelicalism are best located in the Reformation call to a return to biblical doctrine and in its emphasis on personal salvation. These beginnings have been reflected even into the present in church nomenclature in Germany, where "evangelical" (*evangelish*) refers to the Protestant, or specifically Lutheran Church, in contrast to the Roman Catholic Church. For this reason, a new word had to be coined for the Anglo-American evangelical movement as it moved into Germany, namely, *evangelikal*.

Beyond the Reformation itself, evangelicalism is indebted to certain subsequent developments within European Protestantism. Two such developments are most significant. Pietism on the Continent (and later

Methodism in England) fostered a quest for vibrant personal religion coupled with a social consciousness in the midst of the dead orthodoxy of the state churches. Puritanism in England bequeathed the quest for certainty of personal election and the vision of the building as a truly Christian nation.

Evangelicals in Early America

The beginnings of evangelicalism in North America date to the Great Awakening of the colonial era, a revival of such significance that it has been called the American "national conversion." This even left a lasting legacy on American religious life in the form of an emphasis on "experiential religion," that is, a vision of being Christian that emphasizes that religious affiliation must be experienced in life.

Instructive illustrations of the ethos of American evangelicalism at this point in history as well as its close connection with the fortunes of the Baptists may be found in the Awakening in New England and, more specifically, in the experience of the Baptist, Isaac Backus. The event that changed the ecclesiastical face of the region was the arrival of the British evangelist, George Whitefield, in the early 1740s. The revival he precipitated was not enthusiastically greeted everywhere. Rather, it produced a deep division within the established Congregational churches of Connecticut and Massachusetts.

At first the "New Lights"—those who had been touched by revival or who supported the revivalists—were content to remain within the established churches, seeking to be catalysts for the new life the revival had produced in them and for the ecclesiastical reform it demanded. Inevitably, however, conflicts arose as their efforts were met with antagonism and opposition, especially among the clergy, and as the revival party, in turn, began questioning the spiritual integrity of an ecclesiastical system that opposed itinerant preaching and failed to emphasize what had become a hallmark of the revival—the necessity of personal conversion. These fundamental disagreements led finally to schism as many New Lights began holding worship services apart from the established churches, earning for themselves the name "Separates."

The Separates' program included a renewed emphasis on the authority of the New Testament in all ecclesiastical matters. This "back to the Bible" movement introduced a new and explosive controversy among the schismatic congregation: the issue of baptism. The ensuing debate eventually resulted in the demise of the Separate movements, as many adherents came to adopt an immersionist position and to form close-communion churches. These "Separate-Baptist" congregations soon joined fellowship with the older Baptists of New England. In so doing, they brought new life to the immersionist cause and redefined what it meant to be a Baptist American.

One man's ecclesiastical pilgrimage was typical of many Separate-Baptists. Isaac Backus became the leading figure in raising the Baptist banner and in redefining the nature of the Baptist movement in eighteenth-century New England. His importance for Baptists in America lies in at least four dimensions. First, he was instrumental in bringing together the older Baptist churches and the newly forming antipedobaptistic Separate churches into one denomination. Second, he became the bearer of the theological thought which came to characterize the denomination as a whole at this crucial stage in its establishment. The evangelical Calvinism which he inherited from the Separates replaced the Arminianism which had become prevalent in the older Baptist churches. Third, Backus played an instrumental role in winning for the denomination a place in the Reformation tradition. He located this outcast group within the Protestant world of Reformation and then helped to win for it a place of equality among the leading denominations of America. Finally, Backus articulated anew the traditional Baptist call for some sort of broad religious liberty and struggled with the ramifications of that call for New England society.[1]

The role Backus played during the formative years of his denomination was so crucial that historian Mary Hewitt Mitchell, in her book *The Great Awakening and Other Revivals,*[2] has termed him "the father of American Baptists." Similarly, Backus' efforts on behalf of separation of church and state led William Henry Allison, writing in the *Dictionary of American Biography*, to say concerning him, "no individual in America since Roger Williams stands out so preeminently as the champion of religious liberty."[3]

Isaac Backus was born on a Connecticut farm in 1724. Prior to the Awakening, his parents were nominal Congregationalists. The fervent preaching of the itinerants that was sweeping the area in 1731 resulted in revival in the life of young Isaac's recently widowed, severely depressed mother. Isaac was deeply impressed with what he saw happening in his home congregation in the neighboring community of

---

[1] For a more detailed analysis, see Stanley J. Grenz, "Isaac Backus" in *Baptist Theologians,* ed. Timothy George and David S. Dockery (Nashville: Broadman, 1990), 102-20.

[2] See Mary Hewitt Mitchell, *The Great Awakening and Other Revivals* (New Haven: Yale, 1924).

[3] See William Henry Allison, "Isaac Backus," in *Dictionary of American Biography,* ed. Allen Johnson (New York: Scribner's, 1928).

Norwich and desired the conversion so many others were experiencing. Not knowing how one received such an experience, he went to his minister, who, in keeping with the outlook of New England rationalist theology (if the sinner leads an upright life, God will in due time grant him salvation), advised his inquirer, "Be not discouraged, but see if God does not appear for your help." Backus found this advice totally unacceptable and continued his search for salvation until he finally concluded that personal striving was totally useless. Only then was his quest rewarded. On August 24, 1741, while alone in a field, he experienced conversion. Soon after his experience of "divine light," Backus received the "inner witness" which assured him that he was indeed a true saint predestined for salvation.

Five years later (September 1746) he received a second divine encounter, "an internal call to preach the gospel." In the meantime the Backus family had become part of the Separate congregation that had formed in the community. Immediately after receiving his call, Isaac "tested his gift" by preaching the Sunday sermon at the New Light church. He spent the next year on the itinerant circuit, and then at the age of twenty-four, lacking any formal theological education, he was called to the pastorate of a similar group in Titicut Parish, Massachusetts.

It is important to note that these events transpired while young Backus was still a New Light Congregationalist. Only subsequently did he join the ranks of the Baptists. When he did, he not only brought this New Light outlook with him, he was also instrumental in its spread throughout the New England Baptist denomination. The ethos Isaac Backus exemplified, therefore, was not primarily Baptist. It was typically evangelical. This typically evangelical vision of what it means to be a Christian, in turn, became to a large extent the ethos of the Baptists.

Nineteenth-Century Evangelicals

Although the eighteenth century witnessed the formation of the ethos of American evangelicalism, the actual heyday of the movement came in the next century, for this was, indeed, the era of the evangelical movement. Three features came to dominate and characterize the nineteenth-century American religious experience. The first was revivalism. The Great Awakening that occurred during the beginnings of national life was repeated on a smaller scale again and again throughout the next hundred years. Revival methodology, which first came under scrutiny with the research of Jonathan Edwards during the Great Awakening, was transformed into a masterful art with Charles Finney, before attaining the precision of a science through that skilled practitioner, Billy Sunday.

Second, the nineteenth century was the era of the evangelical establishment. At this time evangelicalism was *the* American religious experience. As the dominant religious force in the nation, Protestants set out to fulfill the dream of the Puritan colonists and make the United States into the city on a hill it was intended to become. In this task evangelical clergy entered into a working relationship with civic leaders and politicians, as together they set out to fulfill the nation's manifest destiny. In this century the United States was quite Protestant, and American Protestantism was evangelical.

Third, the nineteenth century was an era of the denominational model of the church. At the birth of the nation no single church group could claim dominance over the religious life of the whole. The Anglican Church, which was strong in the South, had been wounded by the earlier organizational link with England. In New England the Congregationalists had formed the establishment, but their privileged status unraveled under the challenge of the Baptists and other dissenters. Throughout the land the Methodists and Baptists were on the rise. This hitherto unheard of religious situation—in which no church had gained national ascendancy, no one body could claim the allegiance of the people as a whole, no one tradition enjoyed national preference, patronage, and prestige—called for a new ecclesiology.

The American churches responded with an ingenious innovation—denominationalism. This position postulated that the one body of Christ is denominated in the various ecclesiastical bodies and traditions reflected in the land. That is, the various churches were viewed as denominations of the one church that lies beyond the separate church organizations.

Nineteenth-century denominationalism had two important results. On the one hand, it required that some sort of cooperation replace competition among the various traditions. In keeping with the spirit of cooperation, church bodies entered into arrangements for the "winning of the West." On the other hand, it led to the growth of voluntary societies as agencies for the advancement of the various aspects of the church's mandate. Christians who belonged to separate church traditions could by means of their involvement in these societies join together in causes on behalf of the kingdom.

A first crucial factor was immigration. From the beginning the United States had been founded by migrations from Europe. After the Civil War a new wave of immigration brought a new breed to this land, non-Protestant people (specifically Catholics and later Jews), in greater numbers than before. Many Protestants perceived the new arrivals as an alien threat. To some extent this perception was accurate. The nineteenth century drew to a close in the midst of sociological disruption. With the balance shifting away from the Protestants, room would need to be made for other religious traditions. The nation would never be the same again.

A second crucial factor was introduced by the European scientific community. The most significant challenge was Darwinism, which constituted a watershed for the religious self-understanding of Western society. As a result of the impact of the evolutionary theories credited to Darwin, the nineteenth century ended in the midst of intellectual disruption. Despite the efforts of religious conservatives, the older perceptions of the genesis of humankind began to give way under the barrage of new ideas. The nation would never be the same again.

Finally, and in part as an outworking of the revolution in science, the evangelical establishment was battered by the rise of theological modernism. New voices sounding forth from Germany and elsewhere sought to reconcile the new science with the old faith. These efforts met with resistance, and the impact of this struggle led to theological disruption within evangelicalism.

Under the impact of these changes, the nineteenth-century evangelical establishment was divided by a theological dispute now termed the modernist-fundamentalist controversy. The division focused on the acceptance or rejection of German liberalism, the central issue being framed as fidelity to the fundamental doctrines of the Christian church. The conflict also took an ethical turn. Nineteenth-century evangelicalism had been characterized by a vision for the social order of the American nation, a vision that had led some evangelicals into social activism in various areas, including abolitionism. As the fundamentalist-modernist controversy flared, so did a controversy concerning social activism. In the face of the dislocation and injustice brought by increasing industrialization, some evangelicals moved into the area of radical economic reform, even calling for a Christian socialism. Others rejected this move and turned instead toward the eradication of personal vices such as alcohol consumption as the cure for the nation's ills. The disagreement between these two positions brought about the crisis over the so-called social gospel.

When these controversies subsided, the heirs of the nineteenth-century evangelical movement found themselves no longer in control of most major Protestant denominations. Instead, these church bodies had "defected" to form a new modernist establishment. In response, the fragments of the old-line evangelical establishment regrouped under the fundamentalist banner.

The Evangelical Movement

Since the Second World War, the American religious community has witnessed the emergence of a new, albeit minority coalition, formerly called the new evangelicalism, but now generally designed simply as "the evangelical movement." An early impetus toward this new coalition came with the publication of Carl F. H. Henry's book, *The Uneasy Conscience of Modern Fundamentalism.* Henry chastised his fellow fundamentalists for their separation from society and their lack of a social vision. About the same time several fundamentalist church bodies laid the groundwork for an ecumenical organization to rival the National Council of Churches called the National Association of Evangelicals.

The newer coalition that formed the new evangelicalism and participated in the NAE consisted of at least three strands of religious groups representing three quite diverse backgrounds and interests. The first strand included many of the older fundamentalists, those who were party to the earlier modernist-fundamentalist controversy in the mainline denominations. Some had in the meantime severed their former denominational connections and formed splinter bodies (for example, the Presbyterian heirs of the Princeton theology who left the national church and formed several new synods and schools). Other individuals, however, had remained within the older bodies, but nevertheless offered leadership to the new movement.

A second strand in the new coalition was formed by dispensationalists. Dispensationlism was imported to North America from England in the nineteenth century and gained widespread reception in part through the Bible prophecy conference movement. As a result, in the years before and after the turn of the century, dispensationlists were able to develop a network of schools, including Dallas Theological Seminary, as an alternative to denominational institutions.

Finally, the new evangelical movement included various holiness and Pentecostal groups. In the nineteenth and early twentieth centuries, they had largely remained on the fringe of American religious life, but in recent decades many of these groups have ranked among the fastest-growing bodies in the United States and elsewhere.

These, then, became the "card-carrying" evangelicals of Marsden's narrower definition.

The Relationship of the SBC to This Historical Development

The Southern Baptist Convention has an interesting and perhaps unique relationship to the ebb and flow of the evangelical movement in America. This relationship may be characterized by a dialectic of participation and aloofness.

Early Baptist Evangelicalism in the South

Prior to the formation of the SBC in the 1840s, Baptists in the South participated *as Baptists* in the development of the evangelical establishment in the United States. During the colonial and revolutionary eras little of substance distinguished Baptists in the South from their counterparts in the North.

Baptists everywhere went through similar experiences. They all participated in the struggle of the seventeenth and early eighteenth centuries to move toward respectability as a minority group within the wider culture dominated by other Christian traditions. Baptists everywhere experienced immense growth during the Awakenings and in the frontier. In each region Baptists were hampered by the rift (which was subsequently healed) between the older Regular Baptists and the newer Separate Baptists.

The experience of Isaac Backus was typical of the group of persons—whether in the North or in the South—who swelled the ranks of that once-despised sect and made the Baptist denomination a central player in the shaping of the American religious ethos. As a result, Baptists in the South, like their Northern counterparts, fit within the broad evangelical party that dominated American religious life in the early decades of the nineteenth century.

The Split with the North

The nineteenth century also introduced factors that would lead the Baptists in the South to part ways with their colleagues in the North. The slavery issue was not what actually led the South to remain on an independent road. Other denominations experienced schism over this issue, only to be reunited in the postwar era.

Two other differences among the Baptists were more important than slavery in leading the South to go its way alone. The first was the Baptist success in the region. The expansion of the Baptist denomination in Dixie made for a great affinity between those of the Southern experience as such and the ethos of being Baptist in the South. As a result, Southern Baptist life became closely tied with Southern culture, a reality evidenced even today, in that to enter an SBC church often is to experience a taste of Dixie, regardless of geographic location. This forms an immense contrast to the North, where no one denomination was as successful in displacing the others and therefore no one denomination came to be linked with the ethos of the region.

The second factor was the difference in denominational polity that came to characterize Baptists in the two regions. Baptists in the North followed the society model, with its emphasis on voluntary involvement and a multiplicity of loyalties. In the South, however, a different model— a centralized convention, rather than voluntary, cooperating societies— took firm root. This model was able to direct the focus of Baptists in the South toward one central organization, in contrast to the diffusion of attention and loyalty among the various societies characteristic of the Northern approach.

It must be added, however, that the society model fit well in the more pluralistic North, for it allowed coalitions to form around issues. The North was more diverse, and societies allowed diverse people to come together as participants in single causes they held in common. In the South, the success of the Baptists, the smaller number of denominations that divided up the religious pie, and the consolidation of Baptist strength in specific locales made for a greater homogeneity of religious life. This homogeneity precluded the need for the society model and fostered the success of the centralized approach. As a result the SBC was able to engender a denominational loyalty far beyond that enjoyed by its Northern counterpart, which actually formed no unified body but was splintered into a number of associated societies.

The SBC on Its Own

The SBC was prepared by its experience in the nineteenth century to be independent. The immediate reason the Convention did not join the evangelical coalition that emerged in the twentieth century lies elsewhere. The SBC did not participate in the modernist-fundamentalist controversy.

This is not to suggest that Baptists in the South have always been exempt from theological controversy. A quick look at the nineteenth century dispels this misconception. Nevertheless, the major disputes that arose in Southern Baptist life—as the Convention found itself dealing with groups that developed within its ranks such as the Campbellites, the anti-mission movement, and the Landmarkists—were controversies of a largely Baptist, rather than of a transdenominational, nature. As a result, Southern Baptists did not view their feudings as skirmishes that were components of a larger, transdenominational war. Nor were the antagonists in these various disputes generally prone to appeal to compatriots in other denominations.

The assertion that the SBC did not participate in the modernist-fundamentalist controversy must, however, be qualified slightly. The Convention was touched by theological strife in the twentieth century. The dispute in the SBC differed from that experienced in other denominations in several ways. Those who carried the fundamentalist label in the SBC (for example, J. Frank Norris) were quite different from the fundamentalists of the North, lacking, for example, the intellectual erudition of leaders such as J. G. Machen or James Orr. Second, the SBC was not fertile soil for modernist thinking, and, therefore, in contrast to other denominations, it did not develop a sizable liberal faction. Finally, the outcome of the controversy was different. No major schism ensued. Although certain elements left the Convention, SBC life was not seriously disrupted.

Why the SBC Stayed Apart

At this point we can offer some conclusions as to why the SBC did not become a part of the evangelical coalition that began to emerge in the 1940s. It appears that the charting of an independent course was not because Southern Baptists sensed no affinities with the evangelicals. On the contrary, by and large SBC churches and people share the same piety, if not the theology, that characterizes those who identify with the evangelical movement. Rather than the lack of felt affinities, then, a different overarching reason should be noted. Southern Baptists did not join the new evangelical coalition simply because they sensed no necessity to do so. This lack of a sense of compulsion may be viewed in three areas.

First, as noted above, there was no historical necessity to drive the SBC into the coalition. By the turn of the century denominations in the North had already developed a relatively long tradition of cooperation, a tradition lacking in the more single denominational orientation that characterized religious life in the South. Further, the Northern denominations, including the Northern Baptists, had all moved through the theological and ethical controversies of the turn of the century, which gave birth to splinter groups and a cadre of evangelical exponents who remained in their churches despite the modernist victories.

Second, the practical necessity was absent. By the 1940s the SBC had grown so large, both numerically and financially, that it could remain an entity to itself. Its self-sufficiency meant that in contrast to the smaller bodies who formed the new coalition, the SBC did not sense that cooperation was necessary for the completion of the mandate of the church. This attitude, which dies a difficult death, remains widespread in SBC circles today.

As a result of these two factors, a third arose. The SBC sensed no theological necessity to join the coalition. Because their history has been characterized by phenomenal growth and by self-sufficiency, Southern Baptists have difficulty thinking in ecumenical terms. They often sense no need to join with Christians from other traditions to become more completely the essence of the church of Jesus Christ or to give expression to the oneness of the body of Christ.

Already in the nineteenth century Northern Baptists had moved to denominationalism as an ecclesiology. Because of the pluralism of their context and their relatively smaller size vis-a-vis the Christian community as a whole and vis-a-vis the surrounding society, they were more open to working with other groups and to seeing themselves as part of a larger whole. Thus, they more readily came to view the one body of Christ as expressed in the various denominations of Christians, all of which enjoy a common denominator, namely, fellowship in the one, universal church.

Southern Baptists, however, retained a more sectarian outlook. Whereas Northern Baptists embraced other denominations as Christian churches, their counterparts in the South debated the question concerning the status of non-Baptist traditions. As the strength of the Landmark movement and its persistence even after its failure to take over the Convention organization show, Southern Baptists in the nineteenth century tended to see other Christian groups either as constituting no true church whatsoever or, at best, as inferior expressions of the church. Even late in the twentieth century Landmarkism remains a potent force in some SBC churches. (As a university student I interviewed for a position as youth director in an SBC church in Colorado. The pastor indicated that my immersion at the hand of my North American Baptist father would perhaps not be acceptable.)

Not unlike the pre-Vatican II Roman Catholic Church, the SBC tended to see itself *as* the body of Christ. This ecclesiology eliminated the theological necessity for inter-denominational cooperation. As a result, when viewed in terms of E. Troeltsch's categories, the SBC in the South posed an interesting contradiction. As Baptists, the Convention was sectarian, but within the context of life in the South the SBC fulfilled many of the functions of church-type bodies.

The SBC never became a part of the new evangelical coalition. This situation is understandable, given the differing historical development of denominational life in the North and in the South. Yet, I perceived that as a whole Southern Baptists and evangelicals are kindred spirits, especially in terms of piety.

The factors which led the SBC to go it alone are beginning to change. The Convention avoided the earlier modernist-fundamentalist controversy, only to be embroiled now in an internal battle that overshadows whatever squabbling is occurring in other denominations, one which could potentially produce a great loss of churches and people, if not wholesale schism. At the same time, the impressive growth and financial stability that characterized the past decades has slowed, forcing funding cut-backs and worry over declining baptism figures. Some signs indicate that these developments and the expansion of the SBC into the North, which has transpired in this century, are leading to theological reassessment in several areas, including questions of ecclesiology.

In short, Southern Baptists are now at a crossroads in their history. The glue that bound the Convention together may be growing a bit stiff and brittle. Perhaps this is God's doing, for He may be challenging this great body of the people of God to rethink who they are in relation to the greater reality of the body of Christ.

4

Baptist or Evangelical: One Southern
———— Baptist's ————
Perspective

H. Leon McBeth

My response to the relationship between Southern Baptists and American evangelicals will be more personal perhaps than is the custom for such papers. I will use Dr. Marsden's paper as a beginning point to reflect on personal experiences. Thus my paper will involve less literature analysis and footnotes, and more candid reflection upon my own personal response to the general movement of evangelicalism.

First, I would like to express my deep appreciation to George Marsden not only for the chapter in this book but for his other writings, particularly for his book *Fundamentalism in American Culture: The Shaping of Twentieth Century Evangelicalism, 1870-1925.*[1] My students welcomed it because it gave them something to balance Ernest Sandeen's *The Roots of Fundamentalism.*[2]

More recently all of us have benefited from Marsden's history of Fuller Theological Seminary. The title is quite revealing: *Reforming Fundamentalism: Fuller Seminary and the New Evangelicalism.*[3] This book gives us not only a fascinating history of an important institution in America but also provides, I think, a role model for what effective historical writing and interpretation should be.

---

[1] George Marsden, *Fundamentalism in American Culture: The Shaping of Twentieth Century Evangelism, 1870-1925* (New York: Oxford University Press, 1980).

[2] Ernest Sandeen, *The Roots of Fundamentalism* (Chicago: University of Chicago Press, 1970).

[3] George Marsden, *Reforming Fundamentalism: Fuller Seminary and the New Evangelicalism* (Grand Rapids: William B. Eerdmans, 1987).

Although it is probably unnecessary, I feel the need to emphasize that in this chapter I speak only for myself, for one Southern Baptist. I cannot speak for University Baptist Church, where I am a member, nor for any local congregation. I cannot speak for Southwestern Baptist Theological Seminary, where I teach, nor for any seminary. I cannot speak for Southern Baptists, with whose Convention I am affiliated. I speak for myself, and the misgivings expressed here are mine.

Areas of Agreement

I find Marsden's thesis quite instructive, informative, and interesting. Anything that includes up to fifty million Americans will in some way influence all of us. Quite rightly Marsden points out the difficulty of defining evangelicalism. His introductory definitions gave me a chuckle; I have *known* people who fit those definitions, who wanted to fight about religion.

We may not know exactly what evangelicalism is, but we know that it is important. A few years ago the Religion Writers of America designated 1976 as "the year of the evangelical." As the so-called mainline denominations—and that is another troublesome term hard to define—continue to recede on the horizon of America's religious landscape, the so-called evangelical groups loom larger in the American consciousness.

We do not know exactly who the evangelicals are, but we see them everywhere. They crowd the television screen with preachers and programs, with bouncy talk shows, with sawdust-trail revivalism, with psychological self-help, with various cathedrals crystal and otherwise, all with prosperous, beautiful people. We see evangelicals in the newspapers, on the cover of *Time* and *Newsweek*, in PAC and lobby groups in Washington. To paraphrase King David in the Psalm, whither shall we flee to escape the pervasive presence of the evangelicals?

A Personal Pilgrimage

My own background provided very little exposure to this group I now know as evangelicals. I grew up in Sunday School and church; daily Bible reading and prayer formed a part of my home and family circle in my childhood. I never encountered the term evangelical until college. Not one of my family, friends, Sunday School teachers, or pastors ever mentioned the word, much less claimed to be one. I realize it is possible to encounter the essence without the verbiage, but I think all of us would have been astonished, and perhaps offended, to have been called an evangelical.

Like most Anglo-American, Protestant Christians, I have struggled with labels. As a child I was a "missionary Baptist," a term my mother used all her life to identify herself. She grew up in Arkansas, where it was necessary for Baptists to distinguish themselves from the predestinarianism of the Primitive or "Hardshell" Baptist tradition; and from the Arminianism of the Freewill Baptist tradition. I was perfectly happy to be a Missionary Baptist.

Somewhere along the way in the youth organization we called "Training Union," I learned that I was, in fact, a Southern Baptist. Our church was affiliated with something called the Southern Baptist Convention, which had various boards for home and foreign missions. We helped fund these missionary endeavors through the Cooperative Program, a Southern Baptist version of the United Way. I was perfectly happy to be a Southern Baptist.

When I was in high school, we had a Baptist heritage study course in my church, with a teacher from a nearby Baptist college. I had grown up in the Landmark Baptist tradition, though I did not know it then and had never heard the term. We believed that the Baptist church was a true church because it had been founded by Jesus and John the Baptist. After all, one does not read in the Bible about John the Methodist. In the Landmark tradition, we made a big deal of the idea that Baptists are not Protestants; we go all the way back to Jesus and the Apostles and thus antedate the Reformation. I learned in that study course how Baptists as a denomination really came into existence, and that we really are Protestants. That was no problem for me; I was perfectly happy to be a Protestant.

Then in seminary, I came across the works of Winthrup Hudson, an outstanding Baptist historian and churchman. In one of his works, Hudson said Baptists are a part of English Puritanism; that as a separate denomination we emerged in the early-seventeenth century from the intense desire for biblical reform as found in the English Puritan protest movement. He said that Baptists today represent the conservative wing of Puritanism. That was no problem for me; I was perfectly content to be a Puritan or the descendant of Puritans.

Thus my personal pilgrimage continued. As I continued to learn about myself and my world, my identity grew and expanded. Different people assigned me labels, and I accepted them.

Now in these latter years, people are lining up to assign me a new set of labels. Some people, looking at what is happening in the Southern Baptist Convention, tell me that I am now a fundamentalist. Others tell me that I am now an evangelical. I do not want to be either an evangelical or a fundamentalist, at least not as I understand the terms. I am weary of other people defining who I am. I want to decide for myself who I am.

I recall the words of the Separate Baptists of old Virginia in the 1770s when they were discussing a merger with the so-called Regular Baptists of the Charleston tradition. "Excuse us in love," the Separate Baptists said, "for we are acquainted with our own order but not so well with yours; and if there is a difference we might ignorantly jump into that which might make us rue it." I commend that word of caution to Southern Baptists today who are alternately urged to define themselves as evangelicals, fundamentalists, ecumenists, liberals, inerrantists, premillennialists, dispensationalists, or whatever.

Earlier Understanding of Evangelicalism

The effort to define evangelical and set boundaries for those who wear that label is not new in America. Many will recall that Robert Baird in 1843 wrote *Religion in America*, the first comprehensive history of American Christianity. Baird was a Presbyterian missionary to Europe and wrote to help Europeans make sense of the mosaic of American denominations. The first panoramic view of American Christianity was also an effort to export the American system of voluntarism to other countries.

Baird divided American denominations into two main groups: the "evangelical denominations," and what he called the "unevangelical denominations." In the evangelical section, Baird deals with Episcopalians, Presbyterians, Methodists, Lutherans, Congregational, Reformed, Baptists, and many others. He says that all of the evangelical churches stem in some fashion from the Protestant Reformation. He groups all of them into three sub-sections on the basis of church government: episcopal, presbyterian, and congregational. In basic theology, however, Baird portrayed all of these denominations as one group. He said:

> But when viewed in relation to the great doctrines which are universally conceded by Protestants to be fundamental and necessary to salvation, then they all form but one body, recognizing Christ as their common Head. They resemble the different parts of a great temple, all constituting one whole; or the various corps of an army, which though ranged in various divisions, each having an organization perfect in itself, yet compose but one great host, and under the command of one Chief.[4]

---

[4] Robert Baird, *Religion in America*, abridged by Henry Warner Bowden (New York: Harper Torchbook, 1970), 210.

In essence, this makes almost everyone in America evangelicals except Roman Catholics and Mormons, and Baird was hard-pressed to say any good word about either of them.

As to the "unevangelical" groups, Baird gave them short shrift. He said, "We come now to speak of those that are considered by Orthodox Protestants as unevangelical; and under this head we shall . . . range all those sects that either renounce, or fail faithfully to exhibit the fundamental and saving truths of the Gospel."[5] In this category Baird treated Roman Catholics, Unitarians, Universalists, Jews, Rappites, Shakers, Mormons, Atheists, Deists, and Socialists. This calls to mind Sydney E. Ahlstrom's classic work, *A Religious History of the American People*, where he includes a section on "countervailing religion" and treats some of the same groups.

All of our efforts to define and classify the species and sub-species of evangelicalism may look as quaint in the twenty-first century as Baird's nineteenth-century list looks to us.

Evangelicalism in America

In his paper Marsden struggles, as we all do, with the problem of defining evangelicalism. I find considerable help in his distinction between a *broad* and *narrow* use of the term. *The New International Dictionary of the Christian Church* says the term *evangelical* means "pertaining to the Gospel," or "conforming to the basic doctrines of the Gospel."[6] This dictionary goes on to define an evangelical as someone who believes in the grace of God as revealed in Jesus Christ who died for our sins. I believe we can put that down as an example of a broad definition. By that definition surely we are all evangelicals. Each of us values the Bible as the Word of God, accepts the atoning death and resurrection of Jesus Christ the Son of God, values the church as the people of God, and feels the tug of missions and evangelism as a part of the work of God's people.

If we could leave it at that, we might all relax and adjourn for coffee and conversation. However, we cannot, for that broad definition is not the only one we have to face. There is also the narrow view or narrow definition.

It is the "card-carrying evangelicals," if I may adapt Marsden's distinction, that troubles Southern Baptists the most. I think he is right on

---

[5] Baird, *Religion in America*, 257.

[6] J. D. Douglas, ed., *The New International Dictionary of the Christian Church* (Grand Rapids: Zondervan, 1974), 358.

target when he says Southern Baptists are not sure whether they are evangelicals or not. Many of us react strongly against identification with the more narrowly defined evangelicals. I recall the story of the nineteenth-century Missouri storekeeper whose last name was James. To avoid misunderstanding and to relate to his customers, he put a sign in his window, "No relation to Jesse." When Southern Baptists are identified with some of the prominent evangelicals who crowd the television screen and popular magazine and book stands today, we want to say, "No relation to Jerry, or Pat, or Chuck, or Francis."

Allow me to respond at this point to one of Marsden's statements. After naming off various groups of fundamentalists, evangelicals, black Pentecostals, and charismatics, Marsden says, "And then, of course, there are Southern Baptists who do not associate much with any of the above." My first reaction is that Marsden knows us very well; surely he has been reading our mail. In fact, it appears to me that Marsden has understood the complexities and ambiguities of Southern Baptist relations to evangelicals better perhaps than most writers, whether from within or without the denomination.

If the statement is valid, and I think it is, let us ask, "Why have Southern Baptists not associated closely with the groups named?" No doubt many reasons could be named, but some version of the following should be included.

Regional Isolation

For much of their history Southern Baptists have been just that, Southern. That regional isolation has begun to break down in the twentieth century with expansion of SBC churches to the North, the far West, and the Northeast. Even within my ministry, the terms "Our Baptist Southland" and "all across the South" were standard vocabulary. While "broad evangelicalism" or adherence to the gospel was common in the South, "organized evangelicalism" or "narrow evangelicalism" was more common in the North. It was found in places like Chicago and its suburbs, in Detroit, and especially in Grand Rapids, communities where Southern Baptists did not generally reside.

Programmatic

Quite early the Southern Baptist Convention developed a tightly organized and highly promoted program of local, regional, and international ministries. Through the Foreign Mission Board in Richmond we sought to address the challenge of world evangelism. Through the Home Mission Board in Atlanta we marshalled our resources to win converts and plant churches throughout the Southland (and, in time, throughout the nation). Through the Baptist Sunday School Board in Nashville we sought to develop a publication and educational ministry that would train laypersons in Bible study, Baptist doctrines, and denominational distinctives.

Our local churches formed not only Sunday Schools for all ages, but also Training Union, Woman's Missionary Union, Men's Brotherhood, Girls' Auxiliary, and Royal Ambassadors, to say nothing of graded choir programs, the summer camp programs, and, in later years, the ubiquitous youth choir tours and winter ski trips. We have not associated much with others partly because we have not had time. A few years ago I saw a cartoon of a Baptist teenager who had achieved perfect attendance in all the church organizations in which he was enrolled; he said, "I have not been home in six weeks."

Ecclesiastical

Churchly reasons also explain Southern Baptist standoffishness. Our doctrine of the church, our concept of believer's baptism by immersion, and our view of the Lord's Supper as a church ordinance have made us less comfortable with persons who may not share one or more of these views. Admittedly, we have sometimes elevated secondary issues to primary importance.

I recall an experience a summer or two ago on the isle of Iona, just off the west coast of Scotland. My wife and I made what I suppose you could call a pilgrimage to that historic place; and, of course, we were properly impressed with the remoteness, the wild beauty, and the historic significance of the place. On the backside of that tiny island we watched for a few minutes as a farmer dipped his sheep. He had prepared a huge vat with foaming green liquid. A narrow passageway or chute led from one holding pen to the vat. The farmer would pick up the sheep, drop them into the vat, and they would literally disappear under that foaming green liquid. Then, thoroughly drenched, the sheep would swim out into a small holding pen. One sheep struggled violently. When the farmer tried to throw him in, the sheep hit the side of the vat. The result was that this sheep went only about halfway under. He swam out and joined his fully immersed fellows in the holding pen. The farmer sent his small son to cut this half-dipped sheep out of the group and drive him back to the first pen to have another go at it. As we watched that fascinating spectacle, I said to Ada, "Here on the island of Saint Columbia, we have just seen a dramatic reenactment of Baptist history."

Though we may be a bit less doctrinaire than we used to be, Baptists still care deeply about baptism and its ancient form of total immersion. We still feel uncomfortable with God's other sheep who have had only a partial dipping.

Theological

Traditionally, Baptists have believed passionately in religious liberty for all. No part of our witness for four centuries has been more insistent and consistent than this: that the response of the individual soul to God must be free and uncoerced. We believe that no civil or ecclesiastical powers should pressure or force an individual to say yes or no to the claims of the gospel. The great leaders in our heritage took a courageous stand for complete religious liberty. In our ranks, the names of John Smyth, Thomas Helwys, Roger Williams, Isaac Backus, John Leland, and a host of others remind us of our commitment to spiritual liberty for all. We also believe that the best way to guarantee that liberty is to keep church and state separate. We recognize that such separatism is not complete and never was, and never can be. Yet, we believe that civil and spiritual powers operate in separate realms. We believe that separation of church and state gives us our best and most dependable assurance of preserving the liberty that is priceless to us.

Many of the new evangelicals in America, it seems to me, do not really understand religious liberty; and even fewer understand separation of church and state. When they are made to understand, it turns out that many do not really share our convictions. Many of the evangelicals come from different historical roots; their ancestors were in power when ours were in prison. Perhaps that is why we look at religious liberty differently today.

I will say with the Separate Baptists of old, "Excuse me in love," but I do not want to buddy up with the evangelicals. I am uncomfortable with the term, and more uncomfortable with the people who flaunt it.

I am uncomfortable with the political agenda of some of the narrowly-defined evangelicals. The easy identification of Republican conservatism with the will of God makes me want to give them assigned readings in the prophets, the gospels, and church history. They seem to assume that the church is the Republican Party at prayer, that the GOP is the Christian party of Christian America. They uncritically endorse the weirdest nominees and most extreme agendas of that political group as if the political agenda were handed down from Mount Sinai. Those who seek to baptize any political system seem to have missed the first and most basic lesson of church history: namely, that political power corrupts the church.

I am uncomfortable with that narrow evangelical concept of social morality which goes little beyond zeal against abortion; their concern for the unborn does not always extend to the born. The efforts of some zealots to mandate the teaching of "creation science" and to impose government-sponsored prayers upon public school students strike me as misguided.

Sometimes card-carrying evangelicals communicate spiritual pride or even arrogance in that label. "We are evangelicals," they say. Where does that leave the rest of us? With Baird's "unevangelical"? The strict Calvinists today use the phrase "the doctrines of grace" as a synonym for Calvinisn; a Calvinist is one who holds the doctrines of grace. I am not a Calvinist, but I too lay hold of the doctrines of grace as resolutely as Joab laid hold of the horns of the altar (1 Kings 2:28f). I am not an evangelical, but I hold firmly to the basic biblical gospel. The narrow evangelicals have no monopoly on the *euangellion*, the good news in Jesus Christ.

Many of us Baptists also fear that the new evangelical is really the old fundamentalist in a new blazer. In his chapter on "The New Evangelicalism" in his history of Fuller Seminary, Marsden speaks of "the struggle to free the fundamentalist heritage from its peculiarities."[7] He speaks of "refurbishing fundamentalism" and he quotes a popular fundamentalist monthly that "in short, fundamentalism has become evangelicalism."[8]

That is precisely what I fear. To a Baptist, fundamentalism does not mean the gentle-spirited Machen or even the scholarly Warfield. To us the word recalls the likes of J. Frank Norris, W. B. Riley, and T. T. Shields. Surely no compassionate person will blame us for cringing at the thought that such people might come among us again wearing a different label.

If you are an evangelical in the broad sense of that term, I give you my hand for I am your brother in Christ. If you are a narrow, "card-carrying," militant, antidenominational, antiecclesiastical, organized evangelical, then leave me alone. Make no mistake: I am not one of you. My hopes are not your hopes; my hurts are not your hurts; my values are not your values; my views are not your views; and my intentions are not your intentions.

---

[7] Marsden, *Reforming Fundamentalism*, 153.
[8] Ibid., 162.

PART II

In
———————— Dialogue ————————

5

Is "Evangelical" a Yankee Word? Relations Between Northern Evangelicals

&

the Southern Baptist Convention in the Twentieth Century

Joel A. Carpenter

Over a decade ago *Newsweek* published a cover story on evangelical Christianity in America. One of the more striking and memorable quotes in that article came from Foy Valentine, who was then the head of the Christian Life Commission of the Southern Baptist Convention. Valentine was asked whether Southern Baptists were evangelicals. He answered most emphatically, with scarcely concealed irritation,

> Southern Baptists are not evangelicals. That's a Yankee word. They want to claim us because we are big and successful and growing every year. But we have our own traditions, our own hymns, and more students in our seminaries than they have in all theirs put together. We don't share politics or their fussy fundamentalism, and we don't want to get involved in their theological witch-hunts.[1]

These remarks point to some important features of the relationship that contemporary Northern evangelicals and their ancestors have experienced with Southern Baptists over the past century. In particular they

---

[1] Quoted in Kenneth L. Woodward, et. al., "The Evangelicals," *Newsweek*, October 25, 1976, 76. Apparently Valentine had changed his mind about being called an evangelical. In 1973 he was a featured speaker at the Thanksgiving Workshop on Evangelicals and Social Concern, which marked the beginning of Evangelicals for Social Action, a progressive evangelical organization devoted to issues of social witness. In his address, which was subsequently published as "Engagement—The Christian's Agenda," in *The Chicago Declaration*, ed. Ronald J. Sider (Carol Stream, Ill: Creation House, 1974), 57-77, Valentine repeatedly identified with the evangelicals.

highlight several areas of long-standing tension and thus provide the perfect starting point for this essay. Its purpose is to attempt to clarify, from an historical vantage point, the ongoing relationship between Southern Baptists and so-called evangelicals.

One learns very quickly in an American context to speak of evangelicals or evangelicalism advisedly, for such a discussion cannot proceed very far before it runs headlong into the problem of definition. What, or who, is an evangelical? Are Southern Baptists evangelicals? Are fundamentalists evangelicals? How about Pentecostals? Charismatic Roman Catholics? Mennonites? Lutherans? It is important to recognize that there is a problem of definition. Evangelical is an illusive concept, and it has rarely been used with any precision.

Fortunately, George Marsden has taken pains to explain his understanding of how to define evangelical. There are, he argues, three important senses of what is meant by the term. First is the broad, five-or-six point conceptual profile of evangelicals' characteristic beliefs and emphases. Next is the American evangelical mosaic of varied movements and traditions that have expressed these traits. Most historians of American religion would have no trouble whatsoever seeing that the Southern Baptists and other Baptists in the South belong here, as a "classic" evangelical tradition.[2]

This essay, however, will work with Marsden's third definition of evangelical as the self-ascribed label for the diverse transdenominational movement or coalition that has arisen since World War II. Marsden calls the people in this movement "card-carrying evangelicals." Evangelicalism in this sense was envisioned and organized by a reforming party within Northern fundamentalism. The shape of this movement is complex, network-like, and embodied mostly in parachurch agencies such as InterVarsity Christian Fellowship, *Christianity Today* magazine, World

---

[2] I realize that the use of "evangelical" to describe Southern Baptists has been the subject of an ongoing debate, as illustrated in *Are Southern Baptists "Evangelicals"?*, ed. James Leo Garrett, Jr., E. Glenn Hinson, and James E. Tull (Macon, GA: Mercer, 1983). As will became apparent below, I think that both Garrett and Hinson, who take what appear to be opposing views, have a point. It all depends upon how one defines evangelical, who defines it, and in what sense the term is used. The best discussions of how to define "evangelical" are George Marsden, "Introduction: The Evangelical Denomination," in *Evangelicalism and Modern America*, ed. Marsden (Grand Rapids: Eerdmans, 1984), vii-xvi, on which my definition depends most heavily; also see Marsden's chapter in this volume; Timothy L. Smith, "The Evangelical Kaleidoscope and the Call to Christian Unity," *Christian Scholar's Review* 15 (1986): 125-140; and Cullen Murphy, "Protestantism and the Evangelicals," *Wilson Quarterly* 5 (Autumn 1981): 105-116, which was written in consultation with Timothy Smith.

Vision, Campus Crusade for Christ, Moody Bible Institute, Seattle Pacific University, Trinity Evangelical Divinity School, and the Billy Graham Evangelistic Association. As Marsden describes it, evangelicalism was dominated early on by post-fundamentalist theologians and ministry leaders, but it also includes some people from all of the other movements and traditions that have embodied evangelical beliefs and emphases. Perhaps the key test for membership in this evangelical coalition is to find out whether someone identifies more with his or her home denomination or with this parachurch network. Thus the family ministries leader James Dobson is more an evangelical than a Nazarene; the social theologian Ron Sider is more an evangelical than a member of the Brethren in Christ; and Billy Graham is more an evangelical than a Southern Baptist.[3]

This book, according to the above definition, is focused on the relationship between Southern Baptists—who are the heirs of one of the "classic" American evangelical traditions—and the "card-carrying" denizens of this "new evangelical" coalition, which is about fifty years old. The relationships between these two traditions go back further in time than the 1940s, however, so fundamentalism, the tradition that was dominant in forming and leading the new evangelicalism, will be the reference point for earlier comparisons.

When Foy Valentine insisted that Southern Baptists were not evangelicals, he obviously had the "card-carrying evangelicals"—and their fundamentalist ancestors—in mind. His statement pointed to at least three major areas of perceived differences and sometimes outright antagonism.

First, the word *Yankee* points to the cultural distance between the two groups. Until recent decades, when Pentecostal, charismatic, and neofundamentalist groups and leaders from the Sunbelt have become integrated into the evangelical coalition, the movement was dominated by Northern leaders and institutions. Historic cultural differences, tensions, and isolation between the North and South in American religion have strongly colored the relationships between "new evangelicals" and Southern Baptists.[4]

A second area of tension that surfaces in the Valentine quote has to do with organizational differences. Southern religion has been more denominational than its Northern counterpart, and Valentine's litany of

---

[3] Marsden, "The Evangelical Denomination," vii-xvi.

[4] The best work on this fundamental division in American religion and its rootedness in diverging cultures is Samuel S. Hill, Jr., *The South and the North in American Religion* (Athens, GA: University of Georgia Press, 1980).

Southern Baptists' uniqueness points to their intensely denominational character. By contrast, the new evangelical coalition has been transdenominational and dependent upon parachurch agencies.[5] As a result, the evangelicals have generally thought of the Southern Baptists as parochial and uncooperative, while the Southern Baptists have seen evangelicals' work as a threat to the Convention's great treasure and reason for existence—the Cooperative Program.

The third area of stress has to do with historic theological differences. Valentine's denial of any Southern Baptist interest in Northern evangelicals' "fussy fundamentalism" is obviously the cry of a progressive who resented the growing influence of fundamentalism within the Convention and saw it as a Yankee imposition. The story is not that simple, as we shall see. Southern Baptists have both been attracted to and put off by fundamentalism for as long as the fundamentalist movement has existed. Today it is mostly the Convention liberals and moderate conservatives who object to fundamentalism, but in years past some of the most adamantly conservative Southern Baptist leaders attacked fundamentalism for, of all things, being too liberal. Genuine differences in theological perspective have made for strained relations.

These areas of tension are still strong and doubtless will remain for years to come. Nevertheless, each is breaking down. Parachurch evangelicalism and the Southern Baptist Convention are coming into increasing contact and interpenetration, and they are growing more like each other. The question before them is whether they can be good neighbors, friends, and partners in the years to come. It is outside the scope of this brief study to provide any answers, but perhaps this paper can contribute to mutual understanding.

Yankee Versus Southern: The Cultural Tension

Several times in recent decades, the Southern Baptist Convention has entertained proposals to change its name. After all, Southern Baptists have planted congregations in every state of the United States, quite a few in Mexican and Canadian provinces, and thousands in nations around the world. Nevertheless, each time such motions arise, they are soundly defeated. Obviously, great significance has been invested in the name Southern; it carries a heavy burden. In the wake of the Civil War when the South's attempt to become its own nation was smashed by the

---

[5] Marsden, "The Evangelical Denomination," xi-xvi; Richard G. Hutcheson, *Mainline Churches and the Evangelicals: A Challenging Crisis?* (Atlanta: John Knox, 1981), 62-79; Joel Carpenter, "Parachurch: Impatient to Do God's Work," *Christianity Today,* (October 17, 1986), 27.

Northern armies, Southern churches remained perhaps the most important independent institutions that the South had. As a result the churches became major expressions of Southern nationalism. Evangelical, revivalistic, conservative Protestant religion, historian Kenneth K. Bailey pointed out, became one of the foremost means of expressing the South's "mental independence."[6] Since then, the Southern Baptist Convention has grown to become the dominant church of the South, enjoying at least as much stature as the Roman Catholic Church has in the Northern urban centers.

Religious dominance has meant cultural dominance as well. Evangelical Christianity pervades Southern culture, and the Southern Baptist Convention has became part of the Southern establishment. Once largely the religious choice of the region's plain and poor, today the Southern Baptist Convention has prestigious downtown congregations and large suburban churches in every Southern city. These congregations are prominent on the civic landscape as well as the religious terrain. Mayors, governors, members of congress, and even presidents have called them their church homes, alongside legions of corporate executives and urban professionals. Southern Baptists have insisted on the formal separation of church and state, but their leaders, lay and pastoral, have been immersed up to their Sunday School and Rotary pins in the main currents of Southern civic life.

Yankee fundamentalists and their kin, on the other hand, have struggled in a pluralistic world where religion's public place has been progressively constricted. From the 1920s until very recently, evangelical Protestants ranked far behind mainline Protestantism, Roman Catholicism, and the small but influential Jewish community in public influence. Now even these more influential faiths have gradually lost ground in the public arena. Evangelicals thus have a deeply ingrained minority mentality which gives their triumphal talk of restoring "Christian America" a wistful sound; it is in fact their "Lost Cause." Their ranks have included tiny immigrant denominations, holiness and Pentecostal groups, and the fundamentalists. These are the Rodney Dangerfields of American religion; their sense of marginality stems from their lack of public respect.[7]

---

[6] Kenneth K. Bailey, "Southern White Protestantism at the Turn of the Century," *American Historical Review* 68 (April 1963), 618-635. See also Bailey's longer work, which takes this story closer to the present, *Southern White Protestantism in the Twentieth Century* (New York: Harper & Row, 1964).

[7] R. Laurence Moore, *Religious Outsiders and the Making of Americans* (New York: Oxford, 1986), in which chapters 5 and 6 provide an illuminating discussion of evangelicals' complex sense of marginality.

Until the 1940s when the Youth for Christ revivals and the formation of the National Association of Evangelicals brought them a bit more unity, prominence, and evangelistic momentum, Yankee evangelicals were scattered "faithful remnants" of a once-dominant religious tradition.

These major differences—ascendancy versus marginalizaton, cultural custodianship versus cultural alienation—have contributed, along with other Yankee-Southern differences, to a divergence in cultural styles. This cultural contrast has been an important source of mutual distaste and standoffishness. Northern fundamentalists, for their part, tried to set the tone for Yankee evangelicalism by cultivating a persona of prim rectitude and emotional restraint. They stressed rationalistic doctrinal precision and enforced severe behavioral structures against even the appearance of worldliness. Novelist Shirley Nelson wrote the following about the fundamentalists in the 1940s: they "simply spurned the world's frenetic search for empty pleasure. They did not smoke nor drink nor dance nor attend the theater nor concern themselves unduly with fashions and fads." One of Nelson's characters thought she could always spot a fundamentalist girl on the street, "her face cool and relaxed . . . among the strained and painted, and . . . she could tell the boys, too, by a certain clearness in their eyes."[8]

On the other hand, Southern Baptists often seemed to Yankees to behave like the Junior Chamber of Commerce at prayer. They came off as flashy, self-aggrandizing, emotionally cloying, theologically sloppy, and somewhat worldly in personal behavior. The Irish fundamentalist evangelist J. Edwin Orr, who visited the South during his American tour in 1935, complained that "quite a majority of believers" in the South went to 'the movies' once a week, as well as other questionable amusements," and that "the unpainted face was more an exception than the rule." The "converted Christians," Orr complained, behaved "almost exactly as the non-Christians do—there is no separation."[9] When the Southern Baptist and Yankee fundamentalist encountered each other, the cultural clash could be palpable. One famous instance was Billy Graham's arrival at Wheaton College in the fall of 1940 as a freshly ordained Southern Baptist preacher. In his colorful and imaginative biography of Graham, Marshall Frady wrote that "in his implausibly gorgeous pinstripe suits and flowered neckties of lime and chartreuse and mauve,"

---

[8] Shirley Nelson, *The Last Year of the War* (New York: Harper & Row, 1978), 5.
[9] J. Edwin Orr, *This Is the Victory* (London: Marshall, Morgan, and Scott, 1936), 91-92.

Billy felt "abysmally misplaced" on Wheaton's staid campus of prince-nez sanctitude."[10]

Nevertheless, the opportunities for Yankee fundamentalist evangelicals and Southern Baptists to encounter each other have grown throughout the twentieth century. Even during the 1920s, 1930s, and early 1940s, when the mutual isolation was still great, contacts became fairly frequent. Four prominent leaders of the fundamentalist crusade of the 1920s—John Roach Straton of New York, J. S. Massee of Brooklyn and Boston, A. C. Dixon of Chicago and Baltimore, and William Bell Riley of Minneapolis—were Southerners who started their pastoral ministries in the Southern Baptist Convention before heading north.[11] On the other side, the Atlanta Baptist Tabernacle, pastored by Dr. Len Broughton and then in the 1920s by a Yankee named Will Houghton, was one of the few prominent fundamentalist centers at that time in the South.[12]

Another important source of contacts were the fundamentalist institutions that grew up in the South beginning in the 1920s, notably Dallas Theological Seminary, founded in 1924, and the Columbia Bible College, established in 1926 in Columbia, South Carolina. Bob Jones, a Southern Methodist evangelist who became a fundamentalist crusader, established his college in Florida in the mid-1920s and then moved it to Cleveland, Tennessee, in the early 1930s.[13] Other important bridges between Yankee fundamentalists and Southern Baptists during the 1930s and 1940s included the South's most famous preachers, Baptists George Truett of Dallas and Robert G. Lee of Memphis, who became

---

[10] Marshal Frady, *Billy Graham: A Parable of American Righteousness* (Boston: Little, Brown, 1979), 134.

[11] C. Allyn Russell, *Voices of American Fundamentalism: Seven Biographical Studies* (Philadelphia: Westminster, 1976), 50 (Straton), 82 (Riley), 111 (Massee); Helen C. A. Dixon, *A. C. Dixon: A Romance of Preaching* (New York: G. P. Putnam's Sons, 1931).

[12] Wilbur M. Smith, *A Watchman on the Wall: The Life Story of Will H. Houghton* (Grand Rapids: Eerdmans, 1951), 69-80; William R. Glass, "The Ministry of Leonard G. Broughton at Temple Baptist Church, 1898-1912: A Source of Southern Fundamentalism," *American Baptist Quarterly* 4 (March 1985), 35-60. Houghton later became the pastor of Calvary Baptist Church in New York City and then the president of the Moody Bible Institute.

[13] These nondenominational schools seemed to attract few Southerners in general or Southern Baptists in particular until after World War II. Firm evidence of this pattern is readily available at Dallas Theological Seminary. See Robert E. Wenger, "Social Thought in American Fundamentalism, 1918-1933" (Ph.D. diss., University of Nebraska, 1973), 64-65, and Rudolf A. Renfer, "A History of Dallas Theological Seminary" (Ph.D. diss., University of Texas, 1959), 183, 189, 249, 264-267.

widely known and greatly admired on the Northern fundamentalist Bible conference circuit. Perhaps the most popular Southern Baptist on this circuit was the folksy preacher from North Carolina, Vance Havner. Yankee fundamentalists and Southern Baptists may have had their disagreements in these years, but they were beginning to get better acquainted.

Since the Second World War the cultural factors prompting Northern-Southern difference and dissonance have been dissolving. The interstate highway system, new corporate and commercial development, network radio and television, and the growth of university education prompted the South of the 1950s and 1960s to experience rapid cultural change and, ultimately, to lose much of its cultural distinctiveness. When the maelstrom of 1960s public affairs—the civil-rights revolution, the Vietnam War, and the so-called youth movement—put the white, middle class-dominated vision of the American Dream under siege, none were more profoundly shocked and threatened than Southern white Protestants. Furthermore, the migration of economic and political power to the Sunbelt during the 1970s and 1980s continued to open the South to the kind of cultural pluralism and secularity that operated in the rest of the nation.[14] The Southern Baptist Convention was rocked by controversy throughout these years, experiencing intense debates over social responsibility and religious authority.[15]

Analysts of cultural change in the South often overlook the other side of this shift, however. Since World War II the South has experienced great cultural dynamism. It has exported its culture, both high and popular, to the nation and the world. The South has been a veritable factory of American poets and prophets, ranging from Martin Luther King, Jr. to Oral Roberts, from Flannery O'Connor to B. B. King, and from Clarence Jordan to Michael Jordan, not to mention Billy Graham, Elvis Presley, and the Williams boys—Hank and Tennessee. Much of this renaissance has been religious. We have witnessed, for example, the rapid growth of Pentecostal and independent fundamentalist churches. Once merely the sectarian sprouts on the margins of the Southern religious seedbeds, now these groups' largest denominations, such as the Assemblies of God (2 million) and the Baptist Bible Fellowship (1.5 million), are among the nation's largest Protestant bodies. So what consti-

---

[14] Bill J. Leonard, "Southern Baptists and Southern Culture," *American Baptist Quarterly* 4 (June 1985), 200-212; Walter B. Shurden, "The Problem of Authority in the Southern Baptist Convention," *Review and Expositor* 75 (Spring 1978), 219-233.

[15] For suggestive and valuable commentaries on these changes, see Claude L. Howe, Jr., "Factors Affecting Cooperation Since 1945," *Baptist History and Heritage* 24 (January 1989), 30-40.

tutes the American religious mainline these days? The nation's religious configuration is shifting, and Southern-based religious dynamism is a major force.[16]

Nevertheless, the most powerful vehicle of Southern religious expansion is the Southern Baptist Convention. On the eve of World War II, the Convention had nearly five million members in nineteen states. By the late 1950s the Southern Baptists were in forty-three states and had grown to nearly nine million members. In 1963, they surpassed the Methodist Church to become the nation's largest Protestant denomination at 10.2 million. Southern Baptist home missionaries were planting churches in Wisconsin and Ontario, and Baptist Student Unions sprouted in such unlikely places as the University of Connecticut and at Wheaton College, the new evangelicals' flagship college, in suburban Chicago.

Alongside expansion, however, has come assimilation. While Southern Baptists are still a special people, and their denominational ethos is still distinctive, they are becoming more like the rest of American Christians, if only for the simple reason that there are increasing numbers of "strangers" in their ranks.[17] Economic growth has brought increasing numbers of Yankee evangelicals into Southern Baptist territory and, hence, into their congregations. One Canadian Plymouth Brethren family joining the First Baptist Church of a West Texas oil town or one construction executive from Detroit who is a Moody Bible Institute graduate leading North Carolina Baptists' lay evangelism efforts may not bring any great transformation. With such cases multiplying and with addition of new congregations from the home missions frontiers, it has not taken long for Southern Baptists to begin looking a little more like Yankee evangelicals. Penetrating both regional religious cultures are the Pentecostals, charismatics, and resurgent fundamentalists. Southern Baptists' denominational distinctiveness and regional hegemony are not what they were a few years ago.

---

[16] David Edwin Harrell, Jr. is particularly insightful on Southern cultural and religious dynamism. See Harrell, *Oral Roberts: An American Life* (Bloomington: Indiana University Press, 1985); *Pat Robertson: A Personal, Religious and Political Portrait* (San Francisco: Harper & Row, 1987); "The South: Seedbed of Sectarianism," in *Varieties of Southern Evangelicalism*, ed. Harrell (Macon, GA: Mercer University Press, 1981), 45-57; and "American Revivalism from Graham to Robertson," paper presented at a conference, "Modern Christian Revivalism: A Comparative Perspective," 1 April 1989, Wheaton College, Wheaton, Illinois, in which Harrell provided a recent sharpening and elaboration of this theme.

[17] Leonard, "Southern Baptists and Southern Culture," 209.

The scattered "little flocks" of Northern evangelicalism have experienced a parallel resurgence. An early sign was the formation of the National Association of Evangelicals in 1942-43.[18] The new evangelical coalition which the NAE pioneered proved to be well-equipped to take advantage of the postwar trends in American culture. This new brand of "old-time religion," rather than being inherently anti-modern and dysfunctional, proved to be very adaptive. Its ready use of mass communications is a case in point. By the 1940s, Charles E. Fuller, a fundamentalist from Southern California, was attracting the nation's largest Sunday evening audience with his "Old-Fashioned Revival Hour." With the Second World War and the subsequent "Cold War" tensions prompting Americans to reaffirm traditional values, fundamentalists and other evangelicals felt more welcome than they had in decades to work for a revival in America. The creative restyling of their message resulted in the "Youth for Christ" movement in the mid-to-late 1940s. Emerging from this new evangelistic thrust came Billy Graham, who became revivalist to the nation and the leading symbol of a rising evangelical coalition.[19]

Graham was also an important emblem and catalyst of the growing interaction of Northern evangelicals and Southern Baptists. While Youth for Christ pioneered the way with its broadly cooperative rallies, the Graham crusades have marked the zenith of ecumenical cooperation, far transcending both the NAE and the National Council of Churches. Despite their traditional reluctance at becoming involved in "union meetings," Southern Baptists cooperated in the Youth for Christ and Graham crusades, and by their sheer size and enthusiasm became key players in the new urban revivalism. The magazine that Graham helped to found, *Christianity Today*, returned the favor by eagerly reporting the Southern Baptists' triumphal march as they set records for growth, scope of activity, and ebullient optimism.

Yankee evangelicals, who have pursued their own imperial "world visions" of Christian advance and of "remaking the modern mind," have wanted to claim that their ranks include the Southern Baptists because, as Foy Valentine put it, the SBC is "big and successful and growing every

---

[18] For a fuller discussion of the formation of the NAE and its significance, see my essay, "The Fundamentalist Leaven and the Rise of an Evangelical United Front," in *The Evangelical Tradition in America*, ed. Leonard I. Sweet (Macon, GA: Mercer, 1984), 257-288.

[19] My essay, "Youth for Christ and the New Evangelicals' Place in the Life of the Nation," in *Religion and the Life of the Nation: American Recoveries*, ed. Rowland A. Sherrill (Urbana and Chicago: University of Illinois Press, 1990), 128-151, documents and assesses these developments.

year."[20] Yearning to recover their respect and influence, the evangelicals have taken vicarious pride in the SBC's accomplishments and clout and have hoped that some of the glory would rub off on them. Nevertheless, the Southern Baptist Convention has continued to resist fellowship and cooperation with other evangelicals. A major reason for this reluctance has been a fundamental incompatibility in organizational structures and values.

"We Have Our Own": Organizational Trustees

A second major difference between the Southern Baptist Convention and the evangelical coalition has to do with how each tradition is organized. "Evangelicalism" is a transdenominational network dominated by parachurch agencies, while the Southern Baptist Convention has been the most self-sufficient and fiercely loyal of the major Protestant denominations. Valentine's remark, "We have our own," followed by the boast that "our own" is "more . . .than they have" says it very well.

A key feature of the history of the Southern Baptist Convention has been its commitment to denominational solidarity and collective denominational enterprises. Cultural historians suggest that this cooperation has been aided by the relative homogeneity of Southern culture. With the major exception of the twenty percent of its population that has been African-American, the South has been overwhelmingly Celtic and Anglo-Saxon.[21] Although it has produced a welter of sects, Southern religion reflects this relative uniformity. As late as the 1960s, nearly eighty percent of all church members in six Southern states belonged to Baptist and Methodist denominations.[22]

Regional homogeneity cannot be the entire explanation, however, because the South is an internally diverse region. Moreover, the Southern Baptist Convention overarches a variety of Baptist subtraditions, persuasions, and styles. Southern denominationalism, as Kenneth K. Bailey showed, has been a vehicle for Southern nationalism; it carries

---

[20] Carl F. H. Henry, *Remaking the Modern Mind* (Grand Rapids: Eerdmans, 1946) is an early example of the neo-evangelicals' hopes and ambitions on the intellectual front. The best available discussion of neo-evangelicalism and its agenda is George M. Marsden, *Reforming Fundamentalism: Fuller Seminary and the New Evangelicalism* (Grand Rapids: Eerdmans, 1987), especially chapter 3, "Rebuilding Western Civilization," and Chapter 4, "Redefining the Fundamentalist Mission."

[21] Hill, *The South and the North in American Religion*, 76-79.

[22] Wayne Flynt, "One in the Spirit, Many in the Flesh: Southern Evangelicals," in *Varieties of Southern Evangelicalism*, 23. This statistic should be qualified, for it masks some diversity. The Baptists and Methodists are both internally fragmented into several denominations which reflect differences in race, class, and doctrine.

both religious and regional aspirations and loyalties. Therefore, a Southern Baptist may not enter into religious fellowship and enterprises outside of Southern Baptist channels without becoming, in the eyes of many, something of a traitor.

This explanation has helped me, as an outsider, to understand one of the mysteries of the Southern Baptist faith: how a local congregation that so proudly proclaims its sovereign independence can feel so utterly constrained to support only Southern Baptist ministries. I confronted this mystery while in graduate school when the pastor of my adopted church home, the University Baptist Church of Baltimore, recruited me to lead the college-career Sunday School class. As a Yankee evangelical used to a free-market religious economy, I naively suggested that I would like to consider some Bible study materials published by InterVarsity Press. My pastor was very surprised by my request, but he quickly recovered his composure. Very kindly he explained that University Baptist was a cooperating Baptist church and that others in the Baltimore Association would wonder about our loyalty if we used non-Baptist materials. Besides, he assured me, the Sunday School Board's Advance Adult Bible study series was really the finest to be had anywhere. Well, we ordered them, and I was genuinely impressed by the material's high quality; but I was still mystified by what I considered to be a large measure of unfreedom in a locally sovereign Baptist church.

That was an important lesson, however, in measuring Southern Baptist denominational solidarity and loyalty. Using denominational materials and gathering in those Lottie Moon missionary offerings help even the smallest congregations participate in the Southern Baptist Convention's march from victory until victory. Southern Baptists have built the nations's largest Protestant denomination on such solidarity; they have outgrown the Northern Baptists on Yankee turf; and they have sent out the largest Protestant foreign missionary force. These are the results of millions of ordinary people's hopes and dreams for a New Jerusalem—and a New South.

By contrast, Yankee Protestantism has always allowed and even encouraged the development of non-denominational voluntary associations. In the South, popular aspirations have often been channeled into collective denominational enterprises; in the North, the democratic spirit fostered grassroots initiatives. Hundreds of ad hoc, special-purpose voluntary societies have sprung up in recurrent waves over the past two centuries. The North's ethnic and religious pluralism also seems to have encouraged the voluntary approach, which even the past century's trend toward corporate consolidation and bureaucratization has not dampened. In fact, as the managerial revolution has permeated American religion, it seems to have provoked several waves of populist religious entrepreneurship.[23]

The theological controversies that have racked the Northern denominations over the past century have also been powerful stimulants for independent religious initiative. Beginning with the Methodist fight over the holiness movement in the 1880s and 1890s, continuing through the fundamentalist-modernist wars of the 1920s and 1930s, and ever since, millions of Protestants, particularly in the North, have lost confidence in the character and programs of the mainline denominations. Not only have new sects proliferated, but even those who never left the major denominations have turned to non-denominational agencies for fellowship and ministry.

Thus when progressive fundamentalists and other evangelicals began to work for more fellowship and cooperation in the 1940s, they did it by networking, not by forming an evangelical super-denomination. The National Association of Evangelicals was more a symbol than a structure, in that sense. Beneath and even outside and around its rubric, the real action took place, as evangelicals developed informal relationships between their small denominations, the myriad independent agencies, and leading preachers. The result was a new movement, a quasi-denomination without firm organizational boundaries, connected more by like-mindedness and mutual recognition than centralized organization. So while the Southern Baptist Convention is something like a corporation that services a network of regional offices and an international franchise system, the evangelicals are like a bunch of small public-action groups that, despite their independence and bewildering variety, somehow have built cooperative networks.

These fundamentally different ways of putting their faith to work have made for tensions and misunderstandings between Southern Baptists and the parachurch evangelicals. Evangelicals typically find it hard to believe that people would restrict their Christian witness to denominational channels. In their experience bureaucratic denominations inevitably become corrupt and stifle spirituality and initiative. Lurking behind their suspicion is their inherited belief in the inevitable, progressive apostasy of the organized church. Many Southern Baptists find it hard to believe that parachurch evangelicalism amounts to much when its efforts are so fragmented and diversified. Faithful Christians who care about the

---

[23] Ben Primer, *Protestants and American Business Methods* (Ann Arbor: UMI Research Press, 1979).

distinctive beliefs and calling of their home denominations will not support just any group that comes asking for help. In their experience, independent religious activity tends to be the work of demagogues and schismatics.

Therefore, while the parachurch evangelicals have yearned to add Southern Baptists' scope and influence to their own, they have failed to achieve much integration. Both groups have their own imperial plan of winning America and the world, and neither has felt the need to share leadership with the other. So far, Southern Baptists have said, "we have our own," and have added, it seems, "we're self-sufficient so we don't need your piecemeal outfits, which we're big enough to buy and sell; and everything we do is better, anyway." Evangelical leaders continue to believe that Southern Baptists should join them in a grand imperial alliance. Evangelicals assume their own vision is the nobler one, because it transcends denominational lines. Many evangelicals do not realize that Southern Baptists feel threatened by the parachurch mode of operation and see no reason to subsume their work under evangelicals' parallel and competing structures.

These organizational differences will persist, no doubt, but once again, historical trends are levelling out the differences. In this case the changes are occurring most rapidly on the Southern Baptist side. Put briefly, Southern Baptist solidarity is waning. Theological pluralism has been growing in the denomination. The Southern Baptists have a small but influential contingent influenced by the old-line Protestant theological centers. Meanwhile, due to the influence of dispensational theology and the one-man, jumbo-church independent Baptist movement, a fundamentalist right wing has flourished. Aided by the naturally conservative Southern Baptist climate and the recent flare-up over biblical inerrancy among parachurch evangelicals, these militants have mounted a seemingly invincible coalition. As a result, the vast conservative middle of the SBC constituency seems hopelessly polarized. The resulting "Holy Wars" thus mark a rite of passage from the Southern Baptist Convention. It has finally encountered the crisis of religious authority that every other major Christian denomination, including the Roman Catholic Church, has had to face.[24]

Because of its growing pluralism, both cultural and religious, the Southern Baptist Convention might well become more like the American

---

[24] E. Glenn Hinson, "Baptists and Evangelicals: What is the Difference?" *Baptist History and Heritage* 16 (April 1981), 20-32; Nancy T. Ammerman, "The New South and the New Baptists," *Christian Century*, (May 14, 1986), 486-488.

Baptist Convention and the Presbyterian Church (USA), with some large cooperative programs and a pluralistic holding company for special-purpose agencies. If the denomination does not make internal accommodations, Southern Baptists will probably create more parachurch agencies to represent more closely the interests of its diversifying constituencies. This may be sad news, for there is much to be admired about the solidarity that the SBC has enjoyed and much to be regretted about Northern Protestantism's fragmentation. Nevertheless, one cannot substitute regret for analysis, and I am afraid that pluralism and voluntarism have caught up with the Convention.[25]

"Fussy Fundamentalism": Theological Tensions

The cultural and organizational differences that have stood between the evangelicals and the Southern Baptists are important, but what has been most troubling for the moderates and the progressives in the Convention has been what Valentine called Yankee "fussy fundamentalism." As George Marsden's recent history of Fuller Theological Seminary and the "new evangelicalism" has shown, a fundamentalist legacy has indeed set much of the agenda for Northern evangelicals.

The "theological witch-hunts" Valentine referred to no doubt included the controversy then raging around Harold Lindsell's book, *The Battle for the Bible*. Lindsell was by no means the inventor of this controversy, but his leading role in it and his particular interest in Southern Baptists are instructive. Ever since he participated in a controversy over biblical inerrancy at Fuller Theological Seminary in 1962 and 1963, Lindsell has been a champion of the inerrantist position. The editor of *Christianity Today* from 1968 to 1978, Lindsell emerged as one of the most influential leaders of evangelicalism's conservative wing and a tenacious opponent of the more progressive or "open" evangelicalism for which Fuller Seminary had become the leading institution.

A New Yorker who had been ordained a Southern Baptist during a brief sojourn in South Carolina, Lindsell took a special interest in the Southern Baptist Convention's several controversies over inerrancy and

---

[25] There has, of course, been much discussion of late regarding a formal secession of moderates from the Convention. If prior splits among American Protestants are any indication, however, only a small minority of the most alienated will leave, and the rest will still seek less formal ways to meet their diverse needs within a denomination that has lost its working consensus on many fronts. Robert Wuthnow, *The Restructuring of American Religion: Society and Faith since World War II* (Princeton: Princeton University Press, 1988), 71-240, argues that the denominational way of organizing American religious life is rapidly waning and that the ascendant patter is the proliferation of special-purpose groups.

higher criticism that flared up sporadically in the 1950s, 1960s, and 1970s. Lindsell's manifesto, *The Battle for the Bible* (1976), includes a chapter-length exposition on Southern Baptist progressives, and its 1979 sequel, *The Bible in the Balance*, argues the Southern Baptist case further. These works came just in time, it appears, to provide ammunition for the militant conservatives then mobilizing in the Convention. So at the same time that Valentine was insisting that Southern Baptists did not want any part of Yankee evangelicals' "fussy fundamentalism," a sizeable contingent of Southern Baptists, notably the Baptist Faith and Message Fellowship (founded in 1973), were in fact mounting a fundamentalist crusade. It certainly did not help relations between Northern evangelicals and the moderates and progressives in the Convention to have some of the most influential of the former cheering on the Convention fundamentalists from the editorial and news sections of one of the nation's most widely read Protestant magazines.[26]

Tensions over fundamentalism are nothing new for Southern Baptists, since there have been at least a few Southern outposts of this movement since its inception. Interestingly enough, it has not always been the more progressive leaders in the Convention who have been uneasy about fundamentalism. In earlier years, conservatives were often the Southern Baptists' most outspoken opponents of fundamentalism. This might seem odd, given the stereotype of fundamentalism—that it was rural, Southern, and mostly Baptist. Fundamentalism, as a distinct, coherent movement, differs markedly from the other varieties of conservative or evangelical Protestantism. As Valentine put it, Southern Baptists have their own traditions. Although they took a conservative stand during the nationwide controversies of the 1920s, Southern Baptist leaders have usually been very hesitant, if not hostile, when it came to relating to real fundamentalists. In their estimation this was an alien competing movement.

The fundamentalist movement is rooted in the popular revivalism of the 1880s and 1890s, as eminent urban pastors, evangelists, and Bible teachers who tended to be associated with Dwight L. Moody formed a premillennialist movement. Contrary to the stereotype, this interdenominational network was largely Northern and urban in its centers of strength. By the early twentieth century, Southern hubs, such as the annual Bible conference at the Atlanta Baptist Tabernacle, appeared.

---

[26] For an illuminating account of the inerrancy controversies among Northern evangelicals, see Marsden, *Reforming Fundamentalism*, chapters 11, 12, 13, and the sequel.

For the most part this proto-fundamentalist movement did not make much of an impact on the Southern Baptist Convention.[27]

At the same time Southern Baptists were preoccupied with another movement, Landmarkism. Many Landmarkers, following the example of James R. Graves, were premillennialists. Premillennialism did not become a major issue in the Landmark controversies, however, because eschatology was not a matter of dogmatic importance in Southern Baptist theological circles. The *Abstract of Principles*, a theological standard written for The Southern Baptist Theological Seminary, did not even mention the millennium. By the 1920s, the Scofield Reference Bible, Bible and missionary training institutes, and itinerant premillennialist teachers and their periodicals began to prompt some interest in Southern Baptist ranks. Southern Baptist theological leaders such as B. H. Carroll, the founder of Southwestern Seminary; E. Y. Mullins, the president of Southern Seminary; and Southwestern professor W. T. Conner responded with vigorous critiques of premillennialism. After all, the Convention was not fully finished with the Landmark challenge, and premillennialism may have seemed to pose a related threat.[28]

A more likely cause for Convention leaders' concern, however, was that the Bible-school millenarian movement was perceived as a trespasser. It challenged the authority of Southern Baptist theological guardians and encroached on the domain of Southern Baptist programs. One of the ironies of Southern Baptist history is that the very ideas that propelled the Landmark schism—Baptist apostolic succession and exclusivity—also served to strengthen the Convention and put it on guard against "foreign" ideas and movements.[29] Dispensational premillennialism was alien, and so were its advocates, for this movement included both "alien immersionists" and paedobaptists. According to Landmark doctrine, the "Bible schoolers" were seriously in error because they practiced open communion and engaged in interdenominational activities.

---

[27] Ernest R. Sandeen, *The Roots of Fundamentalism: British and American Millenarianism, 1800-1930* (Chicago: University of Chicago Press, 1970), remains the best history of this movement; but see also Timothy P. Weber, *Living in the Shadow of the Second Coming: American Premillennialism, 1875-1982*, rev. ed. (Chicago: University of Chicago Press, 1987).

[28] Emmett H. Cantwell, "Millennial Teachings among Major Southern Baptist Theologians from 1845 to 1945: (M.Th. thesis, Southwestern Baptist Theological Seminary, 1960), 49-50, 65-67, 77-79; and James M. Morton, "The Millenarian Movement in America and Its Effect upon the Faith and Fellowship of the Southern Baptist Convention: (M.Th. thesis, Golden Gate Baptist Theological Seminary, 1962), 47, 53-56, 104-105; provide the substance for the two preceding paragraphs.

[29] James Leo Garrett, Jr., "Are Southern Baptists 'Evangelicals'?", 94-96.

Southern Baptist cooperative programs, which had just withstood the Landmarkers' challenge, now seemed threatened by the Yankee-dominated fundamentalist movement's nondenominational missionary societies, publications, schools, evangelistic crusades, and Bible conferences.[30]

It did not help matters that most Southern fundamentalists since the 1920s have been notably irascible and disruptive. The relatively more irenic types of fundamentalists who staffed Columbia Bible College and Dallas Theological Seminary were much in the minority until very recently. Fundamentalism among Southern Baptists often took an extreme turn toward populist anti-institutionalism and anti-intellectualism. Since there was not much modernism to fight in the South, fundamentalism was used instead to build personal empires and bombard the denominational headquarters. The most notorious case was J. Frank Norris, the Baptist renegade from Fort Worth, who waged guerilla war against the Convention for thirty years and was responsible for the defection of scores of congregations. If this was fundamentalism, Southern Baptist leaders wanted nothing of it.[31]

Norris-type independent Baptist agitators thus fed a stereotype that made it difficult for less combative fundamentalists, who were similar to mainstream Southern Baptists in many respects, to get a fair-minded hearing. When the *Moody Monthly* published an issue in 1941 entirely devoted to premillennial prophecy, Southern Baptist Seminary's missions professor William Owen Carver overreacted. Interpreting it as "a campaign . . . to promote a new wave of millennialism among Southern Baptist churches," he published an article attacking dispensational theology in the Sunday School Board's periodical, *Pastor's Periscope*. Carver may have had a right to be touchy, since he had been slashed at

---

[30] For classic Southern Baptist critiques of interdenominational fundamentalism, see "Southern Baptists Concerned about Fundamentalist Invasion: Dr. L. R. Scarborough, President of the Southwestern Theological Seminary, Discusses the Movement," *The Baptist*, (October 7, 1991), 1111; and the editorial, "Essentials and Non-Essentials," *Baptist and Reflector* (May 9, 1940), 2. A helpful summary of fundamentalist-Southern Baptist relations in the 1920s is in James J. Thompson, Jr., *Tried as by Fire: Southern Baptists and the Religious Controversies of the 1920s* (Macon, GA : Mercer, 1982), 137-165.

[31] On Norris and the Convention, see Patsy S. Ledbetter, "Crusade for the Faith: The Protestant Fundamentalist Movement in Texas" (Ph.D. dissertation, North Texas State University, 1975), 70-91, 200-209, 228-236, 257-260; and C. Allyn Russell, "J. Frank Norris, Violent Fundamentalist," in Russell, *Voices of American Fundamentalism*, 20-46. See also Kenneth C. Hubbard's excellent study, "Anti-Conventionism in the Southern Baptist Convention, 1940-1960" (Th.D. dissertation, Southwestern Baptist Theological Seminary, 1968).

in print some time earlier by one of fundamentalism's most influential power brokers, Charles G. Trumbull of the *Sunday School Times*.[32] Indeed, "anti-Convention" sentiment within SBC territory seemed to go hand-in-hand with premillennial, fundamentalist teaching and evangelism. By the 1940s the menace came not only from Norris but from a number of itinerant evangelists, most notably John R. Rice, editor of the widely-disseminated newspaper, the *Sword of the Lord*.[33]

Given these continuing threats, more formal lines of fellowship between Southern Baptists and other evangelicals still seemed out of the question. In 1942 Robert G. Lee, O. W. Taylor of the *Tennessee Baptist and Reflector*, Russell Bradley Jones of Georgia, and two or three other Southern Baptist notables attended the first meeting of the National Association of Evangelicals in St. Louis. Afterward, Taylor voiced what seemed to be the party line: "There were brethren in the meeting who manifested a fine spirit and said some really good things," Taylor admitted; he did not question the "motives and sincerity of the sponsors" of the NAE. Still he concluded that "our people already have" the values expressed in the NAE and "need not further organizational set-up to possess them."[34] At a time when the Convention was facing a growing interest in premillennialism among its people, suffering from free-lance evangelists like John R. Rice who were sowing discontent among Convention churches, and still fending off Norris's attacks, the last thing Southern Baptist leaders thought they needed was some entangling alliance with Yankee fundamentalists, holiness come-outers, immigrants, and tongue-speakers.

Nevertheless, contacts between fundamentalist evangelicals and Southern Baptists continued. At the 1944 Founder's Week Conference at the Moody Bible Institute, for example, four prominent Southern Baptist pastors were featured speakers: Harold L. Fickett of Galveston, Vance Havner of North Carolina, Robert G. Lee of Memphis, and William R. White of the Sunday School Board.[35] After World War II such contacts increased. Premillennialist fellowships grew in (and sometimes

---

[32] Cited in William Owen Carver, *Out of His Treasure* (Nashville: Broadman Press, 1956), 76-81, 96-97.

[33] Hubbard, "Anti-Conventionism," 86, 89, 96, 98, 101; Morton, "The Millenarian Movement," 47, 62-66, 87-89; Robert A. Baker, "Premillennial Baptist Groups," in *Encyclopedia of Southern Baptist*, 2 vols., (Nashville: Broadman, 1958), 1:111.

[34] Editorial, "Meeting of Evangelicals in St. Louis," *Baptist and Reflector* (May 7, 1942), 3.

[35] Founder's Week Conference program bulletin, January 31—February 6, 1944, Moodyana Room, Moody Bible Institute, Chicago.

out of) the Convention, and Vance Havner, who was lionized in Yankee evangelical circles and perhaps for that reason shunned by his own denomination, eventually earned a welcome to Southern Baptist Conference grounds. Billy Graham provided the most influential bridge of all.

While Convention officials and theologians remained critical of the "fussy fundamentalism" to be found in parachurch evangelical circles, its views and religious products—especially its books and tapes—have continued to be absorbed into Southern Baptist life at the grassroots level. Dispensationalism, fundamentalism's most distinctive doctrine, has made major inroads in the Southern Baptist Convention, probably through its dissemination by graduates of the growing fundamentalist Bible colleges and seminaries in the South, via radio and television preachers, by Hal Lindsay's *The Late Great Planet Earth*—the best-seller of the 1970s— and by the ever-popular *Scofield Reference Bible*. By the mid-1980s, Southern Baptist pastors fell into three roughly equal groups of opinion concerning the end-times. One-third were amillennialists; one-third were traditional premillennialists, and one-third were dispensationalists.[36] So the "fussy fundamentalism" Foy Valentine rejected is no longer just a Yankee import. Indeed, it probably never was, for as our story shows, the interdenominational fundamentalist movement always had a hearing and some networks of support in the South. Now Southern Baptists clearly have their own brand, and today, it seems, this fundamentalist party controls the Convention's national agencies.

Conclusion

This brings us to the current end of a long and complex story, one which is, unfortunately, still only partially told. What does it tell us? First, it reveals that Southern Baptists' and parachurch evangelicals' encounters have not always been on the best of terms or conducted with a clear understanding of the other side's perspective. Furthermore, the history of these relations suggests that there is no guarantee that having known each other better would have made them better appreciate or like each other. Finally, this shared history shows that these traditions are obviously kin and obviously struggling along parallel and increasingly intersecting tracks over the questions of being faithful Christians in the modern world.

Such perspectives may seem mildly interesting to contemporary Southern Baptists, but how useful are they? The Southern Baptist Con-

---

[36] James Guth, "The Politics of Armageddon," paper presented April 12, 1988, at Wheaton College, Wheaton, Illinois.

vention is experiencing a civil war and reconstruction, it seems. Such nice distinctions as developed in this essay may seem somewhat irrelevant to the current crisis. Is not this exercise something like holding a seminar while your building is under siege? Perhaps. Quite possibly what Southern Baptists need most is to understand themselves. Since the Convention's historians and analysts of contemporary religion have reflected the denomination's tendency to be most adept at self-scrutiny and not nearly so well-versed in understanding the larger American religious scene, perhaps they should save the broader context for another time and play to their strengths in a time of urgent need. Nevertheless, Southern Baptists' "holy wars" have not taken place in a vacuum. A better understanding of Southern Baptists' relationships with other traditions and movements in American religion and society should be of some use.

Let me offer a few suggestions in closing. First, Yankee evangelicals arguably have been the most important "significant others" for Southern Baptists in the twentieth century. Both have, in different ways, represented conservative responses to secularizing trends in American culture and alternatives to mainline Protestantism's accommodations to those trends. Even though Southern Baptists' relationships with mainline Protestants and Roman Catholics have grown more cordial over the past few decades, there is probably more of direct relevance for SBC leaders to learn from their evangelical cousins. Since the Southern Baptist Convention is increasingly less Southern, and even the South's distinctiveness is eroding, the positive and negative examples that Yankee evangelicals can provide should prove instructive. They have been struggling for a century now to maintain a dynamic yet authentically Christian witness—what church historian Richard Lovelace calls "live orthodoxy"—in a pluralistic modern setting. Southern Baptists should feel free to study the Northern evangelicals' record as a means to avoid repeating their mistakes and to build on their successes.[37]

Perhaps the place to start, however, is to break down stereotypes and distorted impressions of each other. Certainly a great deal of misapprehension about who the parachurch evangelicals are and what they stand for exists in the Southern Baptist Convention. Actually, they comprise a vast and varied mosaic. Within it one can find rough counterparts for most Southern Baptist persuasions on matters of theology, worship, and personal and social ethics. Just as Northern evangelicals distort mat-

---

[37] See especially Lovelace's recent summation, "Evangelicalism: Recovering a Tradition of Spiritual Depth," *Reformed Journal* 40 (September 1990): 20-25.

ters by insisting on treating the Southern Baptist "holy wars" as a contest with clear lines drawn between conservative evangelicals and mainline Protestant-type liberals, so Southern Baptist intellectuals tend to see their Yankee evangelical neighbors through a glass darkly, with lenses provided by Jerry Falwell.

As we have seen, important historical reasons have led to such stereotyping on both sides. With a clearer understanding of our traditions' relations over time—and the cultural and religious factors that colored those associations—evangelicals and Southern Baptists can build more friendships and partnerships. Given the increasingly similar social world we inhabit, that would only make good sense. Given the ongoing tensions and outright conflicts each tradition experiences, an understanding and sympathetic bearing of each other's burdens could prove a comfort and a help to beleaguered parties. One would also hope that it would have a broadening, softening, influence on those who now have the upper hand. It might be irresponsibly sanguine to expect that these would be the result of closer fellowship (but church history can and should fuel hope in the Spirit's working) as well as a sober understanding of our shortcomings.

So a final word from one representative of Yankee evangelicalism: we would like to know you better, we care about your struggles, and we pray for God's shalom in the Southern Baptist Convention. Certainly we have much to learn about each other. Mutual isolation has brought distortions and stereotypes. Our cultural and religious outlooks and styles still clash. Wheaton, Fuller, and Gordon types still bear the stigma, at least in SBC moderates' perception, of doctrinal fussiness, for we insist that in this day and age such discrimination and discernment are necessary. Louisville and Fort Worth and Wake Forest types will probably always strike us as a bit too openly triumphal (we are proud, too, but we like to act humble) and too enamored with the latest fads of the Protestant theological establishment. The newly ascendant SBC conservatives will strike most Northern evangelicals as having retained too much that was wrong with fundamentalism, both in style and in doctrine. The more we know about what we have inherited from our respective pasts and the more we know about each other, the better equipped we will be to serve each other, our respective faith families, and the world in which we live.

6

American Evangelical Responses
—————— to ——————
Southern Baptists

David S. Dockery

Joel Carpenter has carefully advanced the discussion for us, moving beyond George Marsden's excellent and illuminating analysis of American evangelicalism to help us see some of the common beliefs and practices between American evangelicals and Southern Baptists. Also, he has enabled us to see some of the differences between us, as well as some of the possibilities for cooperation among Southern Baptists and American evangelicals.

Carpenter demonstrates an understanding of Southern Baptists uncommon among American evangelicals. His understanding of American evangelicalism, including the important differences that he identifies between evangelicalism and fundamentalism, is heartily appreciated.[1] In this chapter, I shall seek to clarify and expand the discussion, while following Carpenter's three major points: (1) culture, (2) organization, and (3) theology.

J. Leo Garrett, Jr., in *Are Southern Baptists "Evangelicals"?* concluded his discussion by answering this question "yes, but . . .". He meant by this that we are Southern Baptists first and then evangelicals. Perhaps because Garrett was my mentor, but hopefully more out of personal conviction, I, nevertheless, share his conclusion. My response reflects this conviction. Thus, if Southern Baptists are evangelicals, we

---

[1] I have attempted to make this important distinction with application to the SBC in "The Inerrancy and Authority of Scripture: Affirmations and Clarifications" *Theological Educator* 37 (1988), 15-20. For expanded discussions of this matter see Donald Bloesch, *The Future of Evangelical Christianity: A Call for Unity Amid Diversity* (Garden City, NY: Doubleday, 1983); Douglas W. Frank, *Less Than Conquerors* (Grand Rapids: Eerdmans, 1986); and Robert E. Webber, *Common Roots: A Call to Evangelical Maturity* (Grand Rapids: Zondervan, 1978).

are denominational evangelicals. It is important, though, to raise the question at the beginning if one can be a denominational evangelical in the "card-carrying sense" that George Marsden, Richard Mouw, and Joel Carpenter are. The early movers and shapers of the American evangelical movement were predominantly Baptists. These included Carl F. H. Henry, E. J. Carnell, Billy Graham, Harold Lindsell, Bernard Ramm, Vernon Grounds, George Ladd, and their commentator in *The New Evangelicals*, Millard Erickson.[2] Yet each of these was/is an evangelical first and a Baptist second. Carnell in *The Case for Orthodox Theology* made caustic statements about the cultic nature of Baptist life.[3] Henry and Graham have probably spoken in more churches outside the Baptist world than within. This raises the question for Southern Baptists concerning the possibility of being evangelicals. This is not primarily our focus here, except as it has bearing on the discussion of evangelical responses to Southern Baptists.

My contribution to this discussion focuses on evangelical responses to Southern Baptists. I shall try to avoid moving into John Newport's or Richard Melick's territory concerning Southern Baptists' responses to evangelicals. Some overlap, however, is unavoidable. I shall also try to make some suggestions for possible ways to bring about beneficial cooperation among us in days ahead, with the hope that it can also address some issues in our own denominational unrest.

Culture

Carpenter has correctly noted that evangelical Christianity (not of the Gordon-Wheaton-Fuller variety) pervades Southern culture. Yet it is also more important to note that Southern culture has dominated the SBC (one of the reasons that the Gordon-Wheaton-Fuller type evangelicalism is not fully accepted in the SBC). This cultural impact has produced an isolationist mentality. Evangelicals have viewed the SBC as grandiose, provincial, parochial, and isolationist. The convention is big enough and its ministry is significant enough that generally Southern Baptists can do ministry by and for themselves without dependence on or interaction with other Christian communities. This has been both a strength and a weakness. It has simultaneously given vibrancy, direction, and purpose to its endeavors, while producing a seeming insularity. As

---

[2] See Millard J. Erickson, *The New Evangelicals* (Old Tappan, NJ: Revell, 1968); though Erickson himself is probably better identified as Baptist first and then an evangelical.

[3] See E. J. Carnell, *The Case for Orthodox Theology* (Philadelphia: Westminster, 1959).

Wheaton historian Mark Noll has commented, "the SBC is solid, populist, centralized and decentralized in a way that does not make sense to northern evangelicals. It is big, filled with dedication and potential; and only now is it beginning to emerge from cultural isolation."[4]

While moving out of its cultural isolation, it has had to come to grips with the changes in a Southern culture that is now almost as pluralistic as the rest of the United States. As this has taken place, it has encouraged the expansion of the SBC mission in North America. Some Northern and Canadian evangelicals do not understand or appreciate this expansion. While some welcome the SBC mission advance in these areas, several more do not understand the SBC drive to establish churches, missions, and schools in regions outside the South.[5]

This cultural pluralism and desire to move outside of our isolationism is not unrelated to our Convention squabble. Some see the movement of northern evangelical theology in SBC life as the final takeover of the South and Southern life. While this is a questionable reading of the situation, the pluralism and differences in the SBC between the East Coast, the Deep South, and the Southwest are extremely significant. Some of the differences between evangelicals and Southern Baptists, as well as differences between persons in the SBC, are as much cultural and sociological as they are theological. Certainly the recent work by Princeton sociologist Robert Wuthnow, *The Restructuring of American Religion: Society and Faith Since World War II*, provides evidence for this.[6]

Part of our denominational controversy is fueled by the desire of some to return to a time, culture, church patterns, and way of life characteristic of the 1950s. Likewise, some evangelical leaders are still trumpeting similar messages and articulating the same goals and strategies that they did in the early days of the evangelical movement. We must recognize that we are living in the 1990s, nearing the twenty-first century. What worked for the "million more in '54" campaign may not be applicable today. Southern Baptists and evangelicals must come to grips with the pluralism of our culture and contextualize our message (preaching), methods (in education and evangelism), and theology, while remaining faithful to the biblical revelation.

It can be granted that Southern Baptists are the most adamantly self-sufficient and fiercely loyal denomination in twentieth-century America.

---

[4] Mark Noll, personal correspondence, March 18, 1989.

[5] Stan Grenz, personal correspondence, April 4, 1989.

[6] See Robert Wuthnow, *The Restructuring of American Religion: Society and Faith Since World War II* (Princeton: Princeton University Press, 1988).

Foy Valentine's statement, "we have our own" is a common feeling throughout the SBC. We have our own seminaries; thus we do not need Bethel, Trinity, Gordon, Dallas, Denver, or Fuller. We have our own publishing arms; thus we do not need Zondervan, IVP, Eerdmans, Baker, or David C. Cook. We have our own mission boards (foreign and home), Christian Life Commission, Radio and Television Commission, *and most importantly, our own Annuity Board*. If Southern Baptists do not have the proper program or machinery, we borrow it, re-package it, or re-create it. We did not have a discipleship program like the Navigators, or Inter-Varsity, so we created MasterLife. We did not have a tool like Evangelism Explosion for training in personal evangelism, so we designed Continuing Witness Training. If Southern Baptists attend other schools, participate with other parachurch ministries, or use non-SBC literature it is as Carpenter has said, "akin to being unpatriotic." This mentality and organizational loyalty is very confusing to most American evangelicals.

Yet, ironically, within this monolithic structure, local churches in the SBC represent various spectrums of the evangelical and larger Protestant world. SBC churches might reflect a worship style similar to liturgical Anglicans or Lutherans. A church in the same community might manifest a classroom style like Bible churches. On the other hand, most SBC churches employ revivalistic services like Holiness churches, though still others might have open and free praise meetings that are quasi-charismatic. Church polity might be congregational, dictatorial, committee-led, or elder ruled. In this sense, we sometimes appear to be heirs to the Free Church tradition; at other times, we are more like independent Baptists; sometimes like little corporate structures, and occasionally semi-Presbyterian. In this diversity, however, is an overriding dedication to the Cooperative Program and related denominational structures such as the programs of the Baptist Sunday School Board, Lottie Moon, Woman's Missionary Union, and others. To fail to be committed to the denomination in this manner, as hinted at by Carpenter, would be considered schismatic. For evangelicals who think of agreement and unity in terms of thought worlds consistent with their cerebral Christianity, this organizational loyalty is incomparable.

Parachurch groups and other evangelical communities have longed to add Southern Baptists' influence and resources to their own but have failed to achieve much integration. As evangelical missiologist J. R. McQuilkin has noted, "because Southern Baptists are so intensely loyal, any mutually beneficial cooperation will have to be initiated by the SBC, not the other way around."[7] This will require Southern Baptists to over-

---

[7] J. Robertson McQuilkin, personal correspondence, April 11, 1989.

come their self-sufficiency. The SBC must move away from its triumphalist mentality. "Southern Baptists sometimes give other Christians the impression that if the SBC isn't doing it, it isn't being done."[8]

American evangelicals and Southern Baptists have competing agendas and a major mismatch of equipment and modes of operation. Perhaps we can still make progress in this area. Initial steps in recent days have seen an interest in developing common commitments, strategies, and cooperation in missions, as well as a sharing of resources, to carry out Bold Mission Thrust to reach the world for Christ. This is a healthy sign. How this can be worked out and the denominational/Convention loyalty can continue to exist as we know it remains a question.[9]

Another positive sign is the participation of several Southern Baptist scholars in the Institute for Biblical Research (IBR). While only six or eight faculty members from The Southern Baptist Theological Seminary participate in this progressive evangelical body, numerous representatives from Southwestern Baptist Theological Seminary and other SBC schools can be found in IBR, which makes possible a forum for dialogue and cooperating publishing ventures.

Perhaps by working together in missions, education, and social witness, we can learn from one another and not overly duplicate programs and literature. Educationally, by developing cooperating strategies through the Association of Theological Schools and co-participation in American Academy of Religion sessions such as the "Evangelical Theology Group," progress can be forged. In addition to IBR, we can seek to work together through the American College of Biblical Theologians. In missions we can join hands through the Evangelical Foreign Missions Association and in social witness through JustLife. This involves both American Evangelicals and Southern Baptists recognizing that they share: (1) a common experience (conversion, understood as a personal commitment to Jesus Christ as Savior and Lord); (2) a common authority (submission to the rule of God in His kingdom and commitment to the full authority of Scripture); and (3) a common mission (a commitment to the worldwide mission of the church, evangelism, and social witness).[10]

---

[8] Grenz, correspondence.

[9] For further insights on this movement see the chapter in this book by David F. D'Amico.

[10] For these insights I am indebted to Garth Roselle and Rob Johnston, personal correspondence, March 21, 1989.

Theology

Evangelical theology is quite diverse, as is Southern Baptist theology. Yet, the distinctives of evangelical theology, as different from fundamentalism, are not widely recognized by some portions of SBC life. The SBC, under the leadership of E. Y. Mullins and others, took a conservative position during the 1920s when it came to relating to fundamentalists or modernists. Because Mullins preferred a more centrist position, both because of temperament and ecclesiology, not to mention his more experiential theology contrasted with the Princetonians and dispensationlists, it was an uneasy alignment.[11] An identification by SBC leaders with American evangelicals is equally, if not more, uneasy today, primarily because in the early part of this century, the major questions for Southern Baptists were ecclesiological (matters of church identity and the Landmark issues) and not epistemological. Today, the ecclesiological question remains primary, but the epistemological, which is primary for the evangelical community, can no longer be bracketed by Southern Baptists.

Epistemic and systemic issues loom large for evangelical theology. Generally, the concern over such matters has produced an emphasis on precision in evangelical theology.[12] Generally, SBC progressives do not appreciate or understand the careful distinction evidenced in theological statements like the Chicago Statement on Biblical Inerrancy. Evangelicals need to recognize this and seek to do theological construction in more creative ways. This has been done by progressive evangelicals like Donald Bloesch, Millard Erickson, Klaus Bockmuehl, and Stan Grenz,[13] as well as by post-moderns like Thomas Oden[14] and advocates of the New Yale theology.

On the other hand, evangelicals generally see Southern Baptist theology falling into two categories: (1) one overly sympathetic and

---

[11] See William E. Ellis, *A Man of Books and a Man of the People: E. Y. Mullins and the Crisis of Moderate Southern Baptist Leadership* (Macon: Mercer University Press, 1985).

[12] See Carl F. H. Henry, *God, Revelation, and Authority*, 6 vols. (Waco: Word, 1983).

[13] See Donald Bloesch, *Essentials of Evangelical Theology*, 2 vols. (San Francisco: Harper and Row, 1978-79; Klaus Bockmuehl, "The Task of Systematic Theology," *Perspectives on Evangelical Theology*, ed. K. S. Kantzer and S. N. Gundry (Grand Rapids: Baker, 1979); Millard J. Erickson, *Christian Theology*, 3 vols. (Grand Rapids: Baker, 1986); and Stanley J. Grenz, *Revisioning Evangelical Theology* (Downers Grove: InterVarsity, 1993).

[14] Thomas Oden, *The Living God: Systematic Theology I* (San Francisco: Harper and Row, 1987).

enamored with the progressive wing of theology; and (2) the other doing theology in a fuzzy, somewhat pietistic sense (and even here, where the theological task is taking place, it is somewhat outdated). For instance, evangelical theologians would find the doctrine of the cross in Frank Stagg's theology to be incomplete and one-sided.[15] Likewise, evangelical theologians would be troubled by the rather naive articulation of the doctrine of the Trinity in the commentary on the *Baptist Faith and Message* (pp. 37-38). It would be perceived as having greater similarities with monarchianism than to classical formulations of the Trinity.

This sort of naive and problematic theologizing often occurs at the popular level. This populist theology occasionally articulates theological themes that sometimes reflect a modalistic understanding of the Trinity, a docetic Christology, a thorough-going subjective view of the atonement, or other views that are uninformed at best, while claiming to be conservative and orthodox.

Please, let no one understand that these examples represent the best of Southern Baptist theology. The list of good, careful, informed theology in SBC life could be multiplied, but unfortunately, because many of these theologians have not been very productive, they are not so well known in evangelical circles as we might wish. Broadman Press has produced a multi-volume lay-oriented series of theological works that exemplifies some of the more constructive theology taking place in the SBC. Several fine examples could be mentioned including John Newport's work on theological method, Bill Hendricks' volume on Christology, Wayne Ward on the Holy Spirit, and Bert Dominy on salvation. James Leo Garrett's *Systematic Theology* is the best Southern Baptist theology to date.[16]

SBC conservatives, who claim to have much in common with American evangelicals, have not provided SBC moderates and progressives with informed positions of evangelical alternatives. This has especially been the case with "red-flag, fussy-fundamentalist" issues raised by Carpenter, such as inerrancy and dispensational premillennialism. Evangelicals since Charles Hodge, in 1857, have maintained that inerrancy was not to be understood in terms of excessive harmonizations or mechanical dictation theories of inspiration. In his important essay on "Inspiration," he maintains:

---

[15] See Frank Stagg, *New Testament Theology* (Nashville: Broadman, 1962), 122-148.

[16] See James Leo Garrett, Jr., *Systematic Theology* (Grand Rapids: Eerdmans, 1990).

> From the beginning to the end of the Bible there is constant evidence of the calm self-control of the sacred writers. They all wrote and spoke as men in their age and circumstances might be expected to speak and write. It is, therefore, a perversion of the common doctrine to represent it as reducing the inspired penmen into mere machines, as though they were guided by an influence which destroyed or superseded their own activity.

He continues:

> Verbal inspiration, therefore, or that influence of the Spirit which controlled the sacred writers in the selection of their words, allowed them perfect freedom within the limits of truth. They were kept from error and guided to the use of words which expressed the mind of Christ, but within these limits they were free to use such language and to narrate such circumstances as suited their own taste or purpose.

Then he comments:

> The most serious difficulties which the advocate of the doctrine of inspiration has to encounter arise from the real or apparent inconsistencies, contradictions, and inaccuracies of the sacred volume. (With regard to this class of objections, we would repeat a remark already made, viz., that the cases of contradiction or inconsistencies are considering the age and character of the different books constituting the Bible, wonderfully few and trivial. Secondly, these inconsistencies do not concern matters of doctrine or duty, but numbers, dates, and historical details. Thirdly, in many cases the contradictions are merely apparent and readily admit of being fairly reconciled. Fourthly, with regard to those which cannot be satisfactorily explained, it is rational to confess our ignorance, but irrational to assume that what we cannot explain is inexplicable.)

He concludes that:

> A person's faith in the divinity of the Bible must be small indeed if it can be shaken because he [or she] cannot harmonize the conflicting dates and numbers in Kings and Chronicles. We are perfectly willing to let these difficulties remain and to allow the objectors to make the most of them.[17]

Yet contemporary Baptists like Harold Lindsell and John R. Rice have, I think, been more influential for the SBC right wing than have the Princetonians or James Orr, not to mention the creative work by the faculties of Gordon-Conwell, Trinity, Wheaton, Fuller, and others.

---

[17] See Mark Noll, *The Princeton Theology* (Grand Rapids: Baker, 1983), 135-141.

Similarly, the dispensationalism of the SBC right wing is, for the most part, out of touch with contemporary articulations of dispensational theology represented by Craig Blaising, Robert Saucy, and others. No longer does one find a strict disjunction between the Church and Israel. It is more common to find statements referring to two aspects of the one people of God, rather than two peoples of God, though there is still some type of a future for the nation of Israel. No longer are there distinctions between the kingdom of God and the kingdom of heaven; no longer are the ethical teachings of the Sermon on the Mount relegated to the millennium; no longer are the final judgments of God divided into dozens of separate judgments. These represent a few of the ongoing developments and modifications in dispensational thought.[18] It would be wrong, however, to conclude that dispensationalism dominates evangelical thought. Amillennialists, historic premillennnialists, and post millenialists are also present, but historic premillennialism tends to dominate the academic world because of George Ladd's influence.

I mention these matters only because our topic focuses on evangelical responses to Southern Baptists. Because of the ongoing examples of this type that could be mentioned, evangelicals have generally formed impressions that Southern Baptists' preoccupation with evangelism and the denominational machinery has seemingly produced a rather "a-theological" theology. Again, it goes both ways. Evangelicals' apparent unbalanced concerns with the doctrines of revelation and eschatology have given Southern Baptists cause to believe that evangelicals care little about Baptists' emphases on soteriology and ecclesiology. Both are no doubt overstated stereotypes, but unfortunately, we all tend to function more on the basis of appearance and perception rather than reality.

What Can We Learn from One Another?

What then can we do to overcome these shortcomings? We can recognize what we share in common. We can talk to and read each other with the hope of learning from each other. We can recognize the complementary strengths that we can share and, simultaneously, recognize the shortcomings in our fuzzy and incomplete thinking among the radical progressives, the rigid rationalists, as well as the fussy fundamentalists.

---

[18] See Craig Blaising and Darrell Bock, eds., *Dispensationalism, Israel and the Church* (Grand Rapids: Zondervan, 1992); C. Blaising, "Doctrinal Development in Orthodoxy," *Bib Sac* 145 (1988), 133-140; idem., "Development of Dispensationalism by Contemporary Dispensationalists," *Bib Sac* 145 (1988), 245-280; Robert Saucy, *The Case for Progressive Dispensationalism* (Grand Rapids: Zondervan, 1992).

Southern Baptists can recognize that the evangelical world represented by Joel Carpenter, George Marsden, and Stanley Grenz is quite different from the fundamentalism of John R. Rice and J. Frank Norris. Both groups must invite each other into their conversations, avoiding parochialism and isolationist tendencies. Where can we find a meeting ground that can bring together the concerns of the various groups that we have identified in this response (the SBC right, the evangelical community, and the SBC moderates)? It is perhaps naive and overly optimistic to think such common ground exists. Assuming the possibility of such, we must seek honest dialogue with one another like that represented between David L. Edwards and John R. W. Stott in *Evangelical Essentials: A Liberal-Evangelical Dialogue*.[19] While there is much to discuss, we should follow the proposal of Mark Ellingsen in *The Evangelical Movement*, who focuses on matters of Scripture, hermeneutics, and theological method.[20]

Ellingsen is an ecumenical Lutheran seeking dialogue with evangelicals. I think moderate Southern Baptists would find much in common with Ellingsen's perspective. In his final chapter, he suggests areas such as literary criticism, hermeneutics, and narrative theology as fruitful avenues of mutual exploration. *Perhaps* these areas, especially hermeneutics, would be helpful for us as well. In William E. Ellis' biography of E. Y. Mullins, he calls for Southern Baptists to rediscover their centrist heritage. Perhaps, together with American evangelicals, the pursuit of such common spheres of interest could serve as initial steps in that direction.

Evangelicals must recognize that the SBC has significant opportunity, with its denominational machinery in place, to reach the world for Christ. Also, they should understand that SBC seminaries are primarily concerned with equipping ministers to serve Baptist churches. They are not anti-academic, nor anti-intellectual, but they see themselves as servants to the churches. In his article in *Christianity Today* on the 1989 AAR/SBL meetings in Chicago, Rodney Clapp approvingly quotes Stanley Hauerwas, "Southern Baptists have this to say for them: their theologians still think their work should influence the church, and the church still cares what its theologians say."[21]

Perhaps our worlds are too different. Perhaps evangelicals are so overly concerned with epistemology, revelation, and theological preci-

---

[19] David L. Edwards and John R. W. Stott, *Evangelical Essentials: A Liberal-Evangelical Dialogue* (Downers Grove: InterVarsity, 1988).

[20] Mark Ellingsen, *The Evangelical Movement* (Minneapolis: Augsburg, 1988).

[21] Rodney Clapp, "The Ivory Tower Comes to the Windy City" *Christianity Today* (April 7, 1989), 16-21.

sion that they will always be "dressed-up, well-educated, fussy fundamentalists." Perhaps the SBC is overly concerned with ministry, piety, and experience, asking "How can we be saved, follow faithfully, and form believing communities?" while evangelicals concentrate on "What is truth?" If so, we must go our separate ways. If we are willing to put aside our own agendas and see the kingdom of God as bigger than the "card-carrying" evangelical world or the SBC, we can mutually benefit from and learn from one another so that we can work together. We must translate our discussion from academic concerns to common and fruitful avenues of ministry, evangelism, social witness, and missions. If we take Carpenter's challenge seriously, then together we reaffirm our commitment to biblical authority and become convinced afresh of its complete inspiration and truthfulness and its matchless ability to propel and guide people of faith. Thus, we can at least share a common starting place. Certainly we have much to learn from each other.

7

Southern Baptist Responses
——— to ———
American Evangelicals

John P. Newport

Definition of Southern Baptist

Before we can suggest Southern Baptist responses to non-Baptist evangelicals, we must give some definition or description of the basic groups in Southern Baptist life. I would like to define Southern Baptist life in terms of three strands.

Strand A is related to the thoughts of E. Y. Mullins and W. T. Conner. Mullins became a spokesman for what was called a consensus faction, rejecting modernism on the left with its disavowal of supernaturalism and rejecting fundamentalism on the right with its scholastic reliance on reason.[1] This strand is conservative and yet attempts to relate to and perhaps learn from the changing currents of theological and biblical studies. In this group we could place T. B. Maston who broke with the segregation situation in the South, and W. W. Barnes who denied the Landmark successionist theories. On the fringe of this group would be the Poteat types of North Carolina and scholars such as Glenn Hinson and Stewart Newman.

Strand A would claim to represent historic Baptist emphases on soul competency and religious freedom. For this group, the statement in the 1963 Southern Baptist Confession of Faith, "truth, without mixture or error, for its matter" would mean that the Bible contains all truth—"without mixture or error"—regarding matters of faith and doctrine and is making no technical claims regarding other areas, such as science and history.

---

[1] William E. Ellis, *A Man of Books and a Man of the People* (Macon, GA: Mercer, 1985), x, 41.

111

Strand B is composed of a large group representing practical and revival emphases. It stands for what Pinnock describes as "simple biblicism" or spontaneous inerrancy."[2] It represents what Mark Noll calls the "Baptist way" in affirming a fully truthful Bible.[3] In many ways this is the approach of A. T. Robertson and his student Herschel Hobbs. It perhaps would be related to John R. Sampey, L. R. Scarborough, P. I. Lipsey, Ronald Q. Leavell, and Gaines S. Dobbins. Intelligent, genteel, positive, and warm, this strand brings up memories of an upwardly mobile and fellowship oriented denomination. It was what I experienced at the Ridgecrest Student Week, in youth revivals, and in the warm fellowship of the meetings of the Southern Baptist Conventions. Along with Strand A, this group has traditionally emphasized denominational cooperation for missionary and institutional advancement.

Strand C is concerned with the Southern Baptist life that has always had a strongly conservative group bordering on fundamentalism. In earlier years there was the Landmark movement. The impact of dispensationalism and *The Scofield Bible* was and continues to be strong on many pastors and laypersons. The more extreme segments of this strand left the denomination with Frank Norris in the 1950s to form the World Baptist Fellowship or left to form other smaller Baptist groups. This group's view of the Bible has been called an elaborate, strict, or blunt inerrancy. Paige Patterson, a prominent leader, compares the Bible to a textbook on delicate cardiac surgery in which even the slightest error could produce fatal results. To say that the Bible is inerrant is to say that its writers were preserved from historical, philosophical, scientific, and theological error.

In general, this approach believes that a separatist stance is needed to protect the purity of the gospel. Higher biblical criticism and the social gospel are seen as great dangers. In the 1960s this group expressed its view in the Genesis controversy involving Ralph Elliott and Volume 1 of the Broadman Bible Commentary.

In 1973 the Baptist Faith and Message Fellowship (BFMF) was formed to push for their emphases in SBC schools, programs, and literature. In addition to a nationally circulated journal and efforts to provide Sunday School literature, the BFMF also sought to promote rival theological schools, particularly Luther Rice Seminary in Florida and Mid-America Baptist Seminary now located in Memphis.[4] This was neces-

---

[2] Clark H. Pinnock, "What is Biblical Inerrancy?" *The Proceedings of the Conference on Biblical Inerrancy 1987* (Nashville: Broadman Press, 1981), 76-77.

[3] Noll, "A Brief History of Inerrancy," in *Proceedings*, 18-19.

[4] C. R. Daley, "The New Conservative Fellowship Raises Questions," *Western Recorder*, April 28, 1973, 4; Leon McBeth, "Fundamentalism in the Southern Baptist Convention in Recent Years," *Review and Expositor* 79 (Winter 1982): 95.

sary, according to Jerry Vines and David Allen, because of the departure of such theologians as Eric C. Rust, Clyde Fant, James Cox, and Clyde Francisco from a strict inerrancy doctrine.[5]

The Change of Leadership
in the Southern Baptist Convention

From 1920 until 1979, the leadership of the Southern Baptist Convention was largely in the hands of representatives of strands A and B, although leaders of strand C were also active in many areas of Southern Baptist life. Since 1979 representatives of strand C have controlled the leadership often by a narrow margin.

Reasons for the Change

As we will see, many Southern Baptists have been and are strongly influenced by fundamentalist and evangelical teachings that undercut loyalty to SBC seminaries, agencies, and ministries in terms of both ideology and methodology.[6] Furthermore, there is a worldwide move toward fundamentalism and a resentment of intellectuals and so-called elites. Radio and television programs have accustomed the people to an emphasis on clear choices with great simplicity.

Paige Patterson suggests that the change in leadership in Southern Baptist life came because of theological, historical, and ecclesiastical reasons. First, the introduction of the historical-critical method in theology into Southern Baptist life brought conclusions that did not reflect the opinions of most Baptists. Second, the history of denominations shows that liberal beginnings lead to tragic endings. Many fundamental-conservatives fear that Southern Baptists are repeating this situation. Third, the danger of denominational centralization and the gradual development of a powerful ecclesiastical bureaucracy, if not in theory, at least in practice, increasingly threatens the autonomy of local churches.[7]

Patterson suggests that the change came because a large percentage of the Southern Baptist constituency wants the integration of inerrantists into the faculties, administrations, and boards of all Southern Baptist institutions and agencies. In addition they want the literature

---

[5] David Allen and Jerry Vines, "Biblical Authority and Homiletics," in *Authority and Interpretation: A Baptist Perspective*, ed. Duane A. Garrett and Richard R. Melick, Jr. (Grand Rapids: Baker, 1987), 157-173.

[6] Rob James, et al., "The Takeover in the Southern Baptist Convention: A Report of the Denominational Affairs Committee, River Road Baptist Church, Richmond, Virginia" (February 1989), 22.

[7] Paige Patterson, "Stalemate," *The Theological Educator* 30 (Winter 1984), 4, 6, 8.

and books published by the Sunday School Board to achieve the same parity within a reasonable period of time. They call for the assurance that the denominational press on both state and national levels will fairly represent the positions of the inerrantists and provide equal space for the apologetics of such a group. They also want assurances that the harassment of students who are inerrantists in the Southern Baptist Convention and state Baptist institutions will cease and that their viewpoints will be acknowledged as a legitimate academic option. In addition, they want a financial plan devised by which all Southern Baptists may participate together in a cooperative way without the necessity of supporting that which is morally and theologically repugnant to them.[8]

The Battle for the Bible

Many agree that the intellectual catalyst for a change of Southern Baptist leadership was the book published in 1976 entitled *The Battle for the Bible*. It reached its sixth printing early the next year. The author Harold Lindsell was editor of the evangelical biweekly, *Christianity Today*, and had spent most of his professional life in nondemoninational circles. Later, he joined a Southern Baptist church. Lindsell followed up in 1979 with a sequel, *The Bible in the Balance*. The book was timed for release at the Houston SBC that year, by which time Lindsell had become president of the Baptist Faith and Message Fellowship. His more recent book with a similar emphasis is *The New Paganism* (1987). A leader of the Baptist Faith and Message Fellowship, William Powell, became a committee of one to push the sale of Lindsell's books at the 1979 Southern Baptist Convention. Leon McBeth shows that in the earlier Elliott and Broadman controversies the term "inerrancy" was rarely used, even by ultraconservatives. He believes Lindsell's immensely popular *The Battle for the Bible* catapulted "inerrancy" into common use among Southern Baptists.[9]

The strand-C leaders in the Convention appear to see the doctrinal issues more or less as Lindsell views them. This strand sees strict inerrancy as the main test of orthodoxy. This is why the six Southern Baptist seminary presidents realized that it was important to deal with this issue at the 1987 Ridgecrest Inerrancy Conference.

---

[8] Paige Patterson, "My Definition of a Theological Conservative" (speech given at Southern Baptist Leadership Conference, November 12, 1982, Irving, Texas), 8.

[9] James, et al., "The Takeover in the Southern Baptist Convention," 13.

Influences of Old Princeton School and Dispensationalism

Donald Dayton maintains that dispensationalism and the Old Princeton theology have subconsciously dominated the views of Southern Baptist leaders in the last decade. He sees this influence coming from the Old Princeton view of inerrancy. Even more crucial are the affirmations of dispensational views, opposition to the social gospel, emphasis on Bible colleges, the centrality of soul-saving or witnessing, apostasy, and the importance of Israel in the last days. These emphases are seen in the writings and preaching of strand-C leaders. Granted the diversity of Southern Baptist life as outlined, Southern Baptist responses to evangelicals will vary, as we still see.

Definitions of Evangelicals

Evangelicals, like Southern Baptists, consist of many stands. The term *evangelical* goes back to the Protestant Reformation and is still included in the name of a number of Protestant denominational bodies. The term is also used to refer to groups that have come out of the revival and holiness movements. In a broad sense *evangelical* refers to those who agree on salvation by faith in Jesus Christ in a conversion experience, the centrality and absolute authority of the divinely inspired Bible, and the centrality of evangelism and missions.

Neoevangelicalism

However, for our purposes, *evangelical* in a more narrow sense refers to the group, primarily in North America, that is joined together through a common network of theological seminaries (for example Gordon-Conwell near Boston, Trinity near Chicago, Asbury in Kentucky, Regent College in Vancouver, or Fuller in Pasadena), publications (like *Christianity Today*), and *ad hoc* evangelical and social agencies (like the Billy Graham Evangelistic Association or World Vision). Post-fundamentalists or those individuals who have moved beyond the confrontational style or revivalistic fundamentalism to more civil forms of theological conservatism are seen as the representatives of this more narrow definition of the term *evangelical*.[10]

Dispensationalism

Donald Dayton takes seriously the work of Ernest Sandeen in *The Roots of Fundamentalism* and agrees with Sandeen in seeing the con-

---

[10] Mark A. Noll and David F. Wells, eds., *Christian Faith and Practice in the Modern World* (Grand Rapids: Eerdmans, 1988), 4.

temporary evangelical or neoevangelical or post-fundamentalist movement as primarily the overcoming of the dispensationalist vision. For Dayton dispensationlism marks a distinct break from the dominant evangelical ethos of the nineteenth century and pushes fundamentalism in directions clearly *discontinuous* with what went before.[11] Dayton maintains that the dispensational scheme of thought helps to explain many of the developments of the last century and many current phenomena. For example, more than other paradigms, it explains why the "social gospel" has become such a matter of controversy.[12]

Cultural attitudes are also illumined by the influence of dispensationalism. It is worth noticing that postmillennial revivalists in the nineteenth century founded Christian liberal arts colleges while twentieth-century revivalists influenced by dispensationalists have founded Bible colleges that dropped the broader study of the humanities for the streamlined Bible curriculum. This limited curriculum would provide the minimum biblical knowledge for the Christian worker, who because of the shortness of the time left for witness needed to get out into the "field" to maximize conversions before the end of the age.[13]

Dayton sees the essential theological task of neoevangelicals as rejecting dispensationalism from which most other problem issues flow. The dispensational issue was the fundamental issue behind the early manifesto of Carl F. H. Henry in *The Uneasy Conscience of Modern Fundamentalism* (1947).[14] Everett Harrison moved from Dallas Seminary to Fuller Seminary in part over his alienation from the heavy-handed use of dispensational categories in the interpretation of Scripture. The refutation of dispensationalism was the life work of George Eldon Ladd, a task which in sense determined his life and thinking to the end.

In recent years Harold Lindsell has rejected the term "fundamentalist" and prefers to use "evangelical." However, he denies the designation "evangelical" even to such conservative scholars and theologians as Daniel Fuller, David Hubbard, G. C. Berkouwer, F. F. Bruce, Bernard Ramm, Carl F. H. Henry, and Clark Pinnock. They are not evangelicals,

---

[11] Donald Dayton, "Response to Marsden: *Reforming Fundamentalism,*" paper presented at the American Academy of Religion, (November 21, 1988), 15.

[12] Dayton, "Non-Theological Factors: A Holiness Perspective," (Wesleyan/Holiness Study Project, 1988), 19-20.

[13] Sydney E. Ahlstrom, "From Puritanism to Evangelicalism: A Critical Perspective," in *The Evangelical,* ed. Wells and Woodbridge (Nashville: Abingdon, 1975), 287.

[14] Donald W. Dayton, "An Analysis of the Self-Understanding of American Evangelicalism With a Critique of Its Correlated Historiography" (Wesleyan/Holiness Study Project, January 28-30, 1988), 14.

Lindsell believes, because most of them do not accept his strict view of inerrancy.[15]

The Old Princeton Theology

Dayton contends that the established Evangelical Movement centered around Wheaton and Trinity, after overcoming dispensationalism, has sought to transform evangelicalism into the tradition of "reformed orthodoxy." He calls this effort the "presbyterianization of evangelicalism." Dayton goes so far as to contend that the vitality of evangelicalism is being destroyed by this trajectory. The broader roots of evangelicalism call for more social concern, more openness to dialogue, a more experiential orientation, and a more practical and ethical style of theology. In effect, instead of enriching the whole of Christendom out of their own history, the neoevangelicals are selling their inheritance for a mess of pottage.[16]

Holiness and Pietistic Groups

Dayton maintains that evangelicalism also includes the holiness or pietistic emphasis that has blossomed out into Pentecostalism and the wider charismatic movement. Thus in the United States, for example, the NAE is roughly one-third holiness churches and one-third a cluster of primarily Baptists and Presbyterians and other groups comfortable with the label "evangelical."[17] This holiness division of evangelicalism emphasizes the "higher Christian life" expressed in "baptism of the Holy Spirit" or in the more moderate Keswick "infilling" of the Holy Spirit. It is committed to the "faith principle" expressed in divine healing or faith missions.[18]

There is one other influence in the complexity of fundamentalism and evangelicalism that has implications for Southern Baptists: the new religious right. The new religious right is a strange combination of post-millennialists, amillenialists, and dispensationalists. In theory, at least, this right-wing vision of America and dispensationlism are incompatible. For dispensationalists, America is part of the world system that is passing away. It is one of the Gentile powers that will be either destroyed at Armageddon or judged at Christ's coming. However, dispensationalists like Hal Lindsey and Jerry Falwell have become enthusiastic boosters of

---

[15] James Leo Garrett, Jr., E. Glenn Hinson, and James E. Tull, *Are Southern Baptist "Evangelicals"?* (Macon, GA: Mercer University, 1983), 25-26.

[16] Ibid., 21-23.

[17] Dayton, "Response to Marsden," 11.

[18] Ibid.

the American military and supporters of its interests around the world. Their decision to help preserve the nation forced them to set aside, or at least downplay, certain parts of their eschatology. They know that the world cannot be saved by their efforts, but they do their best to postpone its demise as long as possible so that, among other things, the Lord's work might prosper until the end.[19]

Summary

In summary, evangelicalism in a broader sense constitutes a union of groups which shows dispensational, Old Princeton, Moral Majority, and holiness and charismatic influences. It emphasizes crossing denominational lines. It has set up a new communication network. Power belongs to those who command the schools, television, and publications. Realignments are related to various issues such as abortion, the death penalty, women in ministry, inerrancy, eschatology, and formality in worship services instead of traditional denominational doctrines. There is usually a negative attitude toward liberal scholarship. For the sake of efficiency and church growth, the pastor and the pulpit ministry are dominant, and an elder system is often used. Political issues are often closely aligned with the churches. The charismatic division of evangelicalism often emphasizes long leader-oriented celebrative worship services with minimal Sunday Schools and small groups.

Southern Baptist Perceptions of Evangelicals

Since there are three strands of Southern Baptist life and diverse groups among evangelicals, perceptions will differ.

Strand-A Perceptions

Southern Baptist leaders were invited to the founding meeting of the NAE in 1942. Some attended, but they declined to become members of this umbrella organization. Since then, some in strand A have avoided contact with the new evangelical coalition. "We are not evangelicals; that's a Yankee word," stated Southern Baptist executive Foy Valentine in 1976. "We don't share their . . . fussy fundamentalism." By 1980 Glenn Hinson saw most evangelicals as denying unique Baptist concepts such as voluntarism, the importance of religious experience, and soul competency.[20]

---

[19] Timothy P. Weber, *Living in the Shadow of the Second Coming: American Premillennialism, 1875-1982* (Chicago: The University of Chicago Press, 1983, 1987), 237-238.

[20] Joel Carpenter, "The Fundamentalist Leaven and the Rise of an Evangelical United Front," *The Evangelical Tradition in America*, ed. Leonard I. Sweet (Macon, GA: Mercer University, 1984), 283-284.

One conservative Southern Baptist seminary professor who has had experience both in the North and South suggests that following World War II and prior to 1976, Southern Baptist academic and denominational leadership in the strand-A group tended not to take seriously what they evidently saw as the evangelical "fringe." Rather, Southern Baptists needed to identify with the mainline denominations versus the evangelicals (NAE). Fuller, Wheaton, Trinity Evangelical, and Gordon-Conwell were largely ignored. Barth, Tillich, and in some instances, even Bultmann, were the academic heavyweights. According to this conservative professor, the strand-A group appeared in some cases to have reservations regarding discussion of the theological parameters of the Christian faith. They repeatedly emphasized that Southern Baptists are essentially noncreedal in their approach to theological issues (Christ alone is the ultimate authority; the Bible alone is our test of faith; the priesthood of the believer means that each Baptist is free to interpret the Bible for himself or herself). The strand-A group maintains that fundamentalism and some segments of evangelicalism are more than certain beliefs. As McBeth explains, fundamentalism is "at least as much a spirit and attitude as a set of theological beliefs."[21]

Strand-A leaders point out that E. Y. Mullins wrote in *The Task of the Theologian Today* that higher criticism is a method that can be used by conservative as well as liberal scholars. Baptists' historic confessions normally attribute a functional infallibility to the Bible in its "role as the supreme rule of faith, conduct and worship."[22]

Strand-B Perceptions

Representing the strand-B group, the six Southern Baptist Convention seminary presidents perceive fellowship with the presidents of the evangelical seminaries as valuable, and so they have joined and attend the Association of Evangelical Presidents. They also saw evangelical leaders as important speakers for the two seminary-sponsored conferences on biblical inerrancy and interpretation. In October 1986, the six seminary presidents sought to reflect a broad evangelical view by issuing the "Glorieta Statement." In this statement the seminary presidents agreed to hire faculty and to invite lecturers who hold inerrantist views. Some of the Southern Baptist seminaries have used evangelical leaders for lecture series, thus affirming that these leaders are important for

---

[21] H. Leon McBeth, "Fundamentalism in the Southern Baptist Convention in Recent Years," 85, 86.

[22] James L. Garrett, Jr., "Biblical Authority According to Baptist Confessions of Faith," *Review and Expositor* 76 (Winter 1979): 47-48.

academic understanding. Strand-B leaders point out that at the 1987 Ridgecrest Conference on Biblical Inerrancy six eminent inerrantist scholars, all of them non-Southern Baptists, clearly thought of inerrancy as a rather "large umbrella."[23]

The Southern Baptist Foreign Mission Board leadership feels it is essential in our time to relate to other evangelical missions agencies in terms of strategy and planning. Recently they have initiated conferences involving these evangelical groups.

Strand-C representatives have had mixed perceptions of neoevangelicals and a positive appreciation of an older type of fundamentalistic evangelicalism. Some leaders, such as Adrian Rogers, Paige Patterson, Jerry Vines, and Russ Bush, have been active in the inerrancy movement and conferences. Richard Land chose Carl F. H. Henry to be the key speaker for the "Inauguration Banquet" at the Spring 1989 Christian Life Conference in Kansas City. Most of the leaders of this group appreciate Harold Lindsell's view on inerrancy. There are exceptions. Richard R. Melick, Jr. of Mid-America Seminary has developed a carefully balanced view of hermeneutics and a nuanced view of inerrancy and authority.[24] While still at Criswell College, David Dockery expressed his criticisms of Lindsell's strict harmonizations.[25]

Prominent Southern Baptist fundamental-conservatives (including at least two who spoke at the 1987 Ridgecrest conference) are convinced that the old Princeton view should be "foundational" in the denomination's seminary education and in its organized convention life.[26] In other words, inerrancy is a "small" umbrella. Appreciation is expressed for groups that hold the strict inerrancy view such as Campus Crusade, Fellowship of Christian Athletes, and the Navigators.

For strand C, biblical research is primarily useful as a way of protecting Scripture. It is necessary to carry on academic work because erroneous critical opinions must be rebutted and correct views of Scripture reinforced. This stance may be called "critical anticriticism." Critical anticritics make a commitment to scholarship; they sometimes achieve widespread recognition for linguistic or historical competence; and they are concerned about professional certification.[27]

---

[23] Robison B. James, "Is Inerrancy the Issue? The Lessons of Ridgecrest 1987," in *The Unfettered Word*, ed. R. B. James (Waco: Word, 1987), 177-178.

[24] Richard R. Melick, Jr., "Contemporary Hermeneutics and Biblical Authority," *Authority and Interpretation*, 40.

[25] David S. Dockery, "The Divine-Human Authorship of Inspired Scripture," *Authority and Interpretation*, 40.

[26] Edgar V. McKnight, "A. T. Robertson: The Evangelical Middle is Biblical High Ground," *The Unfettered Word*, 92.

[27] Mark Noll, *Between Faith and Criticism* (San Francisco: Harper, 1986), 156.

This conception of the relationship between research and biblical infallibility provides considerable motivation for scholarship. Research can both disperse apparent problems with the doctrine of inspiration and demonstrate that supposed errors in Scripture lack certain support from scholarly evidence. At the same time, this view clearly awards pride of place to the doctrine of infallibility. If research is not the servant of infallibility, it will become its destroyer.[28]

It appears obvious that most strand-C leaders are also indebted to those older types of evangelicals or fundamentalists who favor dispensationalism. Jerry Vines in his article in the Spring 1988 *Theological Educator* follows the views of Charles Ryrie and John Walvoord of Dallas Seminary. He points out that he is followed in this view by such strand-C leaders as R. G. Lee, W. O. Vaught, W. A. Criswell, Charles Stanley, Adrian Rogers, Billy Graham, Homer Lindsay, Jr., Nelson Price, John Bisagno, Ed Young, Herschel Ford, Vance Havner, Fred Wolfe, T. A. Patterson, Gray Allison, Paige Patterson, and others.[29]

In all fairness, it should be noted that historical premillennialist scholars such as George E. Ladd, Robert Gundry, and Robert Mounce have attracted some strand-C leaders. In fact, some people within this group are finding in post-tribulationism a way of retaining their basic premillennialist orientation while entering, at least to some degree, the world of modern biblical scholarship. It is noteworthy that the evangelical leader J. I. Packer, who affirms a doctrine of inerrancy, disavowed Creation Science and dispensationalism at the 1988 Ridgecrest Conference on Biblical Interpretation. Walter Kaiser of Trinity stated at the same conference that the Bible does not forbid women to be engaged in pastoral leadership in churches.

Strand-C Southern Baptist leaders who are dispensationalists probably have some misgivings over the fact that prominent evangelical schools such as Fuller, Trinity, Wheaton, and Gordon-Conwell do not contain dispensationalism in their articles of faith.

Relationships Between Southern Baptists and Evangelicals

Limited Relationship Until 1979

According to Mark Ellingsen, Southern Baptists constitute one of the most prominent mainline churches seen by the broader religious world as sympathetic with the evangelical movement. In spite of similari-

---

[28] Noll, 157.

[29] Jerry Vines, "Eschatology: Premillennial or Amillennial?", *Theological Educator* 37 (Spring 1988): 141.

ties, however, the SBC has never joined the NAE, and a number of its theologians, as well as some of its theologically conservative members, refuse to identify with the evangelical movement.

More Active Relationship Since 1979

Beginning in 1979 the strand-C group has assumed a more dominant leadership role in the SBC, at least in the control of the national over against the state institutions. These leaders would tend to be more in sympathy with evangelicals and fundamentalists.

Especially notable is the acceptance of and sympathy with evangelical and fundamentalist parachurch organizations by strand-C leaders and churches. These include six organizations that minister to young people in high school, in college, and in the military: Campus Crusade for Christ, InterVarsity Christian Fellowship, Young Life, Youth for Christ, Navigators, and the Fellowship of Christian Athletes. Bill Gothard's Basic Conflicts Institutes are also popular with strand-C leaders. There has been an acceptance by many of Jerry Falwell's Liberty Broadcasting Network programs. Many children of strand-C leaders attend Liberty Baptist University. Some leaders encourage young people to attend Dallas Seminary. Their libraries are often dominated by books by such authors as Francis Schaeffer, James Dobson, Charles Swindoll, Tim LaHaye, Hal Lindsey, and Charles Ryrie. Strand-C churches frequently use Sunday School and Vacation Bible School literature from Scripture Press, Gospel Light, and David C. Cook publishing companies. *Christianity Today* and the *Fundamentalist Journal* are widely read.

The Chicago Inerrancy Conferences projected by the evangelical power structure in the North have used strand-C leaders such as Adrian Rogers and Paige Patterson. Jerry Vines was on the executive committee of the May 1989 Evangelical Affirmations Conference at Trinity Evangelical Divinity School. Robert Sloan of Baylor was a speaker on the program. Southern Baptist seminaries have employed scholars with evangelical connections such as Clark Pinnock, Earle Ellis, and Craig Skinner. In an attempt to resolve the crisis over the nature of the Bible and its interpretation, the six southern Baptist seminary presidents enlisted at least ten evangelical leaders to be speakers at the 1987 and 1988 biblical inerrancy and interpretation conferences at Ridgecrest.

Ties with the Religious Right

In recent years strand-C leaders have established ties with the Religious Right. In late 1987 and early 1988, a Bill Moyers documentary about the Southern Baptist controversy was aired on public television.

On this program Paul Pressler confirmed that he was a member of the Council for National Policy, a network organization for top leaders of the New Right and Christian Right. Paige Patterson and Paul Pressler have been sympathetic with the Conservative Caucus. Strand-C leaders Judge Sam Curren, Joseph Knott, III, and William Delahoyde are related to North Carolina Senator Jesse Helms and the political and religious right. Various strand-A leaders pointed out that these connections are behind much of the attempt to defund the Baptist Joint Committee on Public Affairs in Washington and to establish an alternative Southern Baptist presence there.

Tendency by the Evangelicals
to Ignore Southern Baptists

The relationship between Southern Baptists and evangelicals has been largely initiated by Southern Baptist leaders. In evangelical projects such as the *New Dictionary of Theology*, which has James I. Packer as consulting editor, few Southern Baptist scholars are used.[30] The 1984 *Evangelical Dictionary of Theology*, edited by Walter A. Elwell of Wheaton, uses few Southern Baptist writers among the two hundred authors. Seldom is a Southern Baptist used on the programs of the evangelical section of the American Academy of Religion or on the Evangelical Theological Society (ETS) programs. One gets the feeling that the Wheaton-oriented establishment evangelicalism is not too eager to expand the boundaries of evangelicalism to include Southern Baptists. This is true despite the fact that some Southern Baptist leaders have sought to build bridges with non-Baptist evangelicals.

Similarities Between
Southern Baptists and Evangelicals

Obvious similarities exist between Southern Baptists and certain groups of evangelicals. In a faculty retreat at Southwestern Seminary in the summer of 1979, a discussion was held on inerrancy. In a presentation, I pointed out that the International Council on Biblical Inerrancy, which held its first meeting in Chicago in 1978, obviously has a very positive approach toward the Bible.

In the exposition section, however, the inerrancy conference leaders make qualifications. "We must note the Bible's claims and character as a human product. In inspiration God utilized the culture and convention of the writer's milieu." All of the above statements were made by a

---

[30] Sinclair B. Ferguson and David F. Wright, *New Dictionary of Theology* (Downers Grove, IL: InterVarsity Press, 1988).

group that is supposedly more conservative than most Southwestern Seminary professors in their positive view of the Bible. Yet for over twenty years in courses on religious authority and interpretation at Southwestern Seminary, we have taught material similar to the exposition above.

The Differences Between
Southern Baptists and Evangelicals

The history and denominational posture of Southern Baptists set them apart from non-denominational evangelicals and call for their identification as "denominational evangelicals" for whom believers' baptism, congregational polity, denominational cooperation, religious freedom, and church-state separation continue to be major concerns.[31] Since the Baptist movement began (at least in its modern phase) in seventeenth-century England around concerns about the nature and function of the church, most of its distinctives have been in the area of ecclesiology. Baptist life began when a small group of Christian separatists took their stand on the principle of a regenerate church membership with its corollary, the baptism of believers only. They stood unequivocally for religious freedom, with its corollary, the separation of church and state. They believed that they derived these convictions from the Scriptures, which they sought to follow consistently as an authority subordinate only to the authority of God in Christ.

The Baptist convictions stated above would be considered in the Baptist fellowship to be statements of non-negotiable principles. One can be evangelical in virtually an ecclesiastical setting—a state church, a hierarchical church government, infant baptism—and still be, apparently, an evangelical, not a Baptist. A real Baptist believer holds tenaciously, courageously, and charitably to Baptist convictions.[32]

Most Southern Baptists in the strand A and B groups would disagree with Harold Lindsell's view of evangelicalism mentioned earlier if he pressed his doctrine of biblical inerrancy. The doctrine of biblical inerrancy, which Lindsell demands, necessitates the exclusion from the ranks of evangelicals such theologians as E. Y. Mullins and W. T. Conner. Lindsell would constrict or confine the label *evangelical* to those Southern Baptists who accept the Turretin-Hodge-Warfield-Lindsell doctrine of biblical inerrancy in all historical, geographical, and scientific matters and deny the label to any other Southern Baptists.[33] Most strand A and B

---

[31] Garrett, *Are Southern Baptists "Evangelicals"?*, 18-19.
[32] Ibid., 29-30.
[33] Ibid., 123-125.

leaders would affirm the historic Baptist conviction on separation of church and state and religious freedom which is different from the writings of Francis and Franky Schaeffer.[34]

Only very large and powerful groups (like the Southern Baptists) have been able to chart an independent course between fundamentalism and the more liberal groups associated with the National Council of Churches. In fact, Southern Baptists should focus on coming to ecclesiastical and cultural maturity, shedding a more sectarian past, establishing their own critical theological traditions, and moving toward a more responsible engagement with the world. This would involve finding a balance between evangelism and holistic ministry, authority and biblical interpretation, and doctrinal uniformity and personal freedom.

The Implications of the Relationship of Southern Baptists with Evangelicals

Constructive evangelicals, especially the neoevangelicals, have helped strands A, B, and C of Southern Baptist life avoid the extremes of the left and the right. The work of ten outstanding evangelicals in the two Ridgecrest conferences was meaningful. The lectures of evangelical scholars in Southern Baptist seminaries have offered models of devout scholarship and believing criticism in many cases. The writings of evangelical scholars (such as Millard Erickson, Everett Harrison, and George Ladd) have been widely used in Southern Baptist schools and churches. Southern Baptists should be grateful for these and other contributions.

However, Southern Baptists, in the context of their history, have developed certain distinctives which should be magnified. The importance of our work was assessed by Kenneth Kantzer, distinguished former editor of *Christianity Today*. In 1987 he said to Southern Baptists, "You are the pace-setter for evangelical bodies in the United States and, perhaps, in the world." What Southern Baptists do "sets the direction in which millions of others will go."[35]

Identity and purpose provide a sense of security. We need to develop an appropriate view of inerrancy and reverent or believing biblical criticism. There is also the challenge of blending personal piety, evangelism, and social concern. Many see a need to form churches and schools to meet the different needs of a varied and constantly changing, and in many cases upwardly mobile, culture. Likewise, Southern Baptists need to revi-

---

[34] Ronald W. Ruegsegger, ed., *Reflections on Francis Schaeffer* (Grand Rapids: Zondervan, 1986), 266.

[35] Kenneth S. Kantzer, "Parameters of Biblical Inerrancy," *The Proceedings of the Conference on Biblical Inerrancy 1987*, 111.

talize their communication in networks in terms of distinctive doctrines. The schools should develop plans to reach the laity at all levels with a balanced, biblical understanding of controversial subjects such as science and religion, eschatology, social issues, and proper hermeneutical principles.

Unfortunately Southern Baptists have produced a limited amount of distinctive theology. Some have suggested that Baptists have produced little theology because they have been preoccupied with evangelism and have come from the lower cultural and educational levels of society. These may be partial explanations. Others note that Baptists have been preoccupied with theological controversies that have dominated their intellectual energies. Not being well-furnished with a theology adequate for its own vision, the Baptist approach has suffered. This lack has allowed the Baptist view to fall captive to alien modes of self-understanding from both the left and the right. Therefore, not only Baptists but the entire people of God have been impoverished.

Suggested Emphases for a Baptist Theology

As we have seen, Southern Baptists enjoy a rich heritage in the conviction that the Bible is an absolutely reliable authority. They also have a legitimate concern to protect that conviction in the twentieth century when the academic world gives it so little credence. Nonetheless, the seemingly unending round of efforts to defend and refine the concept of biblical inerrancy offers diminishing returns. One strategy adopted by some thoughtful Southern Baptists is to embrace wholeheartedly a carefully nuanced doctrine of inerrancy, but then to move beyond that starting point to the pressing question of biblical interpretation and application. We must move beyond the external examination of Scripture to an internal appropriation of its message.[36]

Believers' churches have historically kept the interplay between Word and Spirit alive in a way that Protestant orthodoxy generally has not. This emphasis on the Bible is in keeping with the Baptist teaching on the restitution or restoration of the teachings or model of the early church.

The emphasis on missions and evangelism in Baptist theology is understood not as an attempt to control history for the ends we believe to be good. Rather it affirms the responsibility to witness to Christ and accept the suffering that witness entails. A part of the concept of the priesthood of all believers is that each Christian must witness or deny his or her own priesthood. A part of the genius of Southern Baptists is the development of the Cooperative Program. This approach is more effi-

---

[36] Kantzer, 196-197.

cient and economical in using resources in national and international missionary outreach.

In his *Axioms of Religion* Mullins argued that all other Baptist themes can be seen to rise from soul freedom, understood as competency of the individual soul in religion. This is an overstatement but surely highlights an important Baptist teaching. In the Reformation era and later, believers' churches believed that Christian discipleship could not be practiced alone. For them the Church was not an external aid, as for Calvin. Rather, it was the essential context for the practice and transmission of Christianity.[37]

A way of stating the unifying Baptist vision is in terms of the "already-not yet" stream of redemptive history centered in Jesus Christ. In general, eschatology has suffered from two attitudes in the church: neglect and overemphasis. In the Bible, however, eschatology is not merely a set of beliefs that may be pushed aside when the events are thought to be near. Although the Bible does not specify exactly when the consummating events will occur, it insists that the last times are already here. The eschatological atmosphere of the "already-not yet" should pervade every action and thought.

In short, the eschatological expectation of the first Christians bestowed a unique vantage point from which to view every dimension of reality. It also gave them a unique impulsion to act in light of this hope. Their eschatology was not merely a set of beliefs concerning future events but also the attitude or atmosphere aroused by these events.

The eschatological is thus not one element of Christianity, but it is the medium of Christian faith as such. It is the key in which everything is set. It is the glow that suffuses everything here and now in the dawn of an unexpected new day. Therefore, the eschatological outlook should be characteristic of all Christian proclamation, of every Christian existence, and of the whole church. It should be the unifying or organizing vision for a Baptist theology.[38]

Southern Baptists are varied. Evangelicals and fundamentalists are varied. Southern Baptists have been both helped and hurt by these groups. Is it not the essence of wisdom to study, evaluate, and dialogue with these kindred Christians? However, at the same time we should maintain and share distinctives which have been developed by Baptists as they have sought to be faithful to the Bible and Jesus Christ in the crucible of history.

---

[37] James William. McClendon, Jr., *Ethics: Systematic Theology* (Nashville: Abingdon Press, 1986), 20-41.

[38] Thomas N. Finger, *Christian Theology: An Eschatological Approach* (Nashville: Thomas Nelson, 1985), 1:99-103.

8

Southern Baptist Responses
——————— to ———————
American Evangelicals:
An Alternative Perspective

Richard R. Melick, Jr.

My assigned task is to respond to John Newport's perceptive paper. Dr. Newport has defined the various constituencies within the Southern Baptist Convention and has defined evangelicalism for his purposes. He continues with Southern Baptist perceptions of evangelicals and with the relationship between Southern Baptists and evangelicals. He then discusses similarities and differences between Southern Baptists and evangelicals and concludes with the implications of these relationships.

The thesis of the paper is concealed in its parts. Simply stated, it seems to be that evangelicalism (narrowly defined) has made recent negative inroads into the SBC through the conservative leadership of the Convention and that Southern Baptists should develop a theology closer to historic Baptist positions. Newport does, however, state that "Southern Baptists have been both helped and hurt" by both evangelicals and fundamentalists. The chapter contains some ambiguity, however, which might affect the thesis statement. The descriptions of the various groups entail both fundamentalist and evangelical categories. Thus the thesis statement may need to be changed with the insertion of the word "fundamental" for "evangelical." I would contend that the theological tensions arose within the Southern Baptist Convention and that a greater dialogue with evangelicals would prove productive toward a satisfying resolution. I share his conclusion that it would be helpful for us to take advantage of the constructive evangelical elements and to construct theological statements that reflect our own heritage. Southern Baptists have a unique and significant opportunity to do so.

I have some concern for a more precise definition of both South-ern Baptists and evangelicals. Without faulting Newport for his profiles, I would venture some clarifications as I see them. Dr. Newport calls for a new understanding of the diverse elements of the SBC. He advocates a "nontheological" categorization designed by the term "strands." The profile incorporates various and unrelated ideas, including theology, atti-tude, and activist descriptions. Nevertheless, these are helpful enough to provide a working framework for discussion.

The classifications are confusing. Strand A includes both theologi-cal and social activists, and the description provided speaks of the Bible allowing scientific mistakes. Similarly, some in strand B, the "intelligent, genteel, positive, and warm" group, actually have identified with the theological perspective of strand A, others with strand C. Finally, some in strand C evidence a theological stance radically different from dispen-sationalism and actively pursue some of the same social concerns as strand A. Like most categories, these are not clear cut and perhaps need further revision.

I would also suggest some further clarification as to fundamentalist and evangelical groups. In popular discussions a fundamentalist is "someone more conservative than I." However, as movements, these have some rather clear-cut, distinguishing features. The paper seems to draw too close a tie between evangelicalism and fundamentalism *today*. Both groups come from a similar environment at the end of the last cen-tury. George Marsden states, "Fundamentalists were especially militant evangelicals who battled against the modernists' accommodations of the gospel message to modern intellectual and cultural trends."[1] In actuality, the primary identifying characteristic of fundamentalism was its separat-ism, though distinctive theological positions came to be identified with it as well.

At a later date some moved from fundamentalism and became the "post-fundamentalist" evangelicals. These are the focus of Newport's paper. They primarily rejected the separatists' attitudes of fundamental-ism and, in large segments, rejected the theology of dispensationalism held by most fundamentalists. It would be helpful to distinguish between the more fundamentalistic groups and the more evangelical. Too often, perhaps because of shortness of space, the distinctions are blurred.

The Southern Baptist Convention today has both fundamentalists and evangelicals. They sometimes rally to the same issues, but they are

---

[1] George Marsden, *Evangelicalism and Modern America* (Grand Rapids: Eerdmans, 1984), xii.

distinct groups. A minority came from the "disgruntled evangelicals" of post-fundamentalism, but others have come to an evangelical position quite apart from any fundamentalist involvements. They have identified more with evangelical ideas, consciously or unknowingly. They rejected the radical separationism of the fundamentalists they knew, such as John R. Rice and Bob Jones. A clarification of these groups both among Southern Baptists and non-Southern Baptists would be helpful. It would perhaps open a more direct communication with non-Southern Baptist evangelicals. Many non-Baptist evangelicals have faced the same issues in their recent past.

A second concern relates to the question of the change in the SBC. Newport suggests that prior to 1979 strands A and B provided the Convention leadership. As he acknowledges, some strand-C leaders emerged. In actuality there were leaders, some quite vocal, who advocated the same bibliology as the post-1979 strand-C leaders, but many were, as Clark Pinnock has noted, "simple biblicists."[2] When Pinnock coined the term for us, he meant simple inerrantists. His assumption was that most Southern Baptists accepted all of the Bible as true (therefore accurate), but they differed on how to explain that accuracy. It hardly fits his discussion that "simple biblicism" would claim that the Bible was incorrect even in matters of science and history.[3] Some SBC presidents prior to 1979, however, had developed rather encompassing statements of inspiration. For example, W. A. Criswell preferred the term "literal," but Herschel Hobbs freely used the term "inerrant."

"Simple biblicism" sufficed for the first half of the twentieth century in Southern Baptist life, but it was challenged both from within and outside the Convention. The academic challenges came from the now famous controversies involving Crawford H. Toy, evolution, Ralph Elliott, and *The Broadman Bible Commentary* volume on Genesis. Many university students faced challenges from their professors at the point of their "simple biblicism." The challenges came from the secular classroom as well as from Baptist institutions. The fact is that "simple biblicism" will not answer the charges brought by modern thinkers. Pinnock stated:

---

[2] This term is employed because of Newport's seeming preference for it. It was taken from Clark Pinnock ("What is Biblical Inerrancy?", *The Proceedings of the Conference on Biblical Inerrancy 1987* [Nashville: Broadman Press, 1987], 75-76) and is understood in this discussion in the same fashion as Pinnock and, I assume, Newport.

[3] See Pinnock's presentation in the article mentioned above, particularly pp. 75-80. His "two necessary conditions" should also be heeded. To this point there has been little interest in satisfying his petition.

But the doctrine of Scripture cannot remain at the simple level. In the face of alien doctrine and unbelief, leaders of the church historically have seen the need from time to time to tighten up the theory of the Bible and not leave so many loose ends which could be misused by the enemies of Christ. No evangelical should deny the pastoral necessity involved here, to act on behalf of the well-being of the church facing spiritual and doctrinal danger.[4]

Thus while my emotional sympathies lie with "simple biblicism," there is a need for more adequate biblicism.

The statements on Scripture affirmed by the plenary sessions of the Southern Baptist Convention contained strong conservative views of the Bible. Newport states that in 1925 the SBC "officially affirmed the inerrancy of Scripture," and Herschel Hobbs publicly claimed that *The Baptist Faith and Message* statement was an inerrancy statement as well.[5] These were not interjections from alien theologies, but came from within the Convention itself to meet the demands of the day.

Thus the era of "simple biblicism" was first challenged by those who held to a defined, broader view of Scripture. The challenge was met initially by an intuitive reaction by the majority of the Convention over the years, then by theological statements. Two points are noteworthy. First, when many in the Convention found other definitions of inerrancy, they embraced the term—the concept was already incipiently there—

---

[4] Pinnock, 76.

[5] Discussions regarding this issue are recorded in the minutes of the "Proceedings" of the Southern Baptist Conventions in 1979 (p. 31), 1981 (pp. 35, 45), and 1985 (pp. 73, 87). In 1981 Hobbs clearly stated his position and the intent of the 1963 statement that the Bible "has truth without any mixture of error for its matter." He stated, "The Greek New Testament reads, 'all'—without the definite article—and that means every single part of the whole is God-breathed. And a God of truth does not breathe error." (1981 "Proceedings," 450.) This conviction also characterized his presidential address in 1963, which was devoted to a discussion of science and Christian faith, and his personal theology. This latter point is supported by his own public preaching when he said: "The other thing to note is that it has 'truth, without any mixture of error, for its matter.' Thus it is the inerrant word of God. The Holy Spirit no more protects a copyist from error than He does a typesetter. So when we speak of the Bible as 'truth, without any mixture of error,' we are referring to the original manuscripts. The Holy Spirit guarded the original writers from error." (Herschel H. Hobbs, "The Bible, God's Inerrant Word," *Great Decisions of the Church: Sermons From "The Baptist Hour,"* produced and distributed by Southern Baptist Radio and Television Commission, Fort Worth, Texas, nc. [as best it can be determined, the date was 1973], 11.) "As the inerrant Word of God, certain other things may be said about the Bible. For one thing it is scientifically accurate. But no proven scientific error has been found in it. I am confident that the science—note, I said, 'science'—of archaeology will eventually solve these in favor of the Bible. You do not need to discard your intelligence in order to believe the Bible to be the inerrant Word of God." (Ibid., 13-14.)

because it "fit." It was the solution which grew out of Southern Baptist history. Second, the term itself was not sacrosanct. At times a motion was made to include "inerrancy" in *The Baptist Faith and Message* statement, but the conservative leadership and conventions rejected the term both because the existing statement already meant inerrancy and because the word was not a magic term to guarantee its implementation.[6]

Newport follows Leon McBeth in arguing that Harold Lindsell's famous book *Battle for the Bible* was the "intellectual catalyst" for a change of Southern Baptist leadership. This must be considered carefully. What McBeth suggests is that the *term* "inerrancy" was supplied by Lindsell and that it affected the outcome of future elections.[7] Other factors, however, must be considered as well. In addition to the groundswell of conservative thought already discussed, W. A. Criswell provided a book that rallied some conservatives to his position. The book *Why I Preach that the Bible Is Literally True* (title supplied by the publisher, Broadman, not by Dr. Criswell) sold 30,000 copies, the great majority to Southern Baptists. Lindsell's book sold 145,000 in five years and went out of print;[8] but, as Newport states, only a portion of the book dealt with the Southern Baptist situation. By the time of the Lindsell book, Southern Baptists had already been emotionally charged by the recent history of the Convention and Criswell's contribution. The new leadership, therefore, did not arise overnight. Tensions and frustration were expressed for almost twenty years.

Beyond the questions of the leadership, however, is the puzzling question of the constituency. Leaders do not emerge without followers, and presidents cannot simply declare themselves in office. This is, perhaps, the crucial question regarding the 1979 changes: if the new leaders are out of step with the constituency, why do they occupy the positions they hold? I would contend that substantial support for the basic issue arose much earlier than 1979, and therefore the change,

---

[6] This counters the charge that the word itself is the key to conservative interests. These conventions which were dominated by conservatives chose to reject including the term "inerrancy."

[7] The term was in use among Southern Baptists prior to 1976, however, as evidenced from the previous note from the sermons of Herschell Hobbs dated about 1973. No doubt his message also contributed to the popularity of the term since he put his approval upon it. Compare Hobbs, "The Bible, God's Inerrant Word," 9-14.

[8] These numbers were supplied by the publishers, Broadman Press for *Why I Preach that the Bible Is Literally True*, and Zondervan Publishing House for *Battle for the Bible*.

while significant, was not revolutionary, though its implications certainly were!

Regarding the popularity of non-Southern Baptist evangelical scholars, Newport's statement is perceptive: "Historically, the SBC's identification with the evangelical movement and the latter's spiritual forefather, fundamentalism, is at best ambiguous." There was little communication and recognition between the groups. For example, few persons even knew the identities of the ten evangelical leaders who spoke at the inerrancy and interpretation conferences though they were established scholars and, for the most part, excellent choices. Many wondered why the seminary presidents would go outside the Convention to bring in "unknowns." Their teachings were even less known, as one program respondent openly stated: "Dr. Kantzer, we are grateful for your splendid presentation of your clearly modified form of the theory of inerrancy."[9]

In the matter of appreciation for dispensationalism and its schools, the puzzle remains. While it is clear that many strand-C leaders are dispensational, not all are, and one must ask: how did they get that way? Obviously the question is difficult to answer. Most of the current SBC leaders are too young for J. Frank Norris's influence and they are too Baptistic for the Trinity/Wheaton influence, which is not dispensational anyway. They were taught differently in Southern Baptist seminaries, yet they adopted dispensational theology. Why? The answer probably lies in two possibilities. One, it could be that the teaching made sense to them, even with the tools given them by their Southern Baptist seminaries. Another is that the ministry of the dispensational Southern Baptist pastors had an inherent attraction. Probably W. A. Criswell and R. G. Lee had as much to do with this as any. Their modeling an attractive style of ministry, the books from independent presses, especially Zondervan and Moody Press, and the ministry of Billy Graham, demonstrating a successful evangelistic message and method, attracted young preachers to their theology. The theology provided a systematic perspective and framework with which to grasp biblical truth. Is it the failure of our seminaries to argue effectively against it and/or to provide a compelling alternative?

The appreciation of other seminaries is a minor factor. A poll of the major evangelical seminaries reveals that comparatively few Southern Baptist students are enrolled. Dallas Seminary had a 1988 enrollment of 1,675 and only 146 listed their denomination as Southern

---

[9] *The Proceedings of the Conference on Biblical Inerrancy* (Nashville: Broadman, 1987), 129.

Baptist. The official number of graduates serving within the SBC is 101, but they are updating and believe the number may be closer to 200.[10] Trinity Evangelical Divinity School listed 20 Southern Baptist students out of 1,268.[11] At Gordon-Conwell, there are 20 Southern Baptist students at the Boston (nondegree) campus, and 19 at the Hamilton campus (out of 588 degree-seeking students).[12] Columbia Biblical Seminary in Columbia, South Carolina, listed 421 students, of which 60 specifically indicated Southern Baptist on their forms.[13] Western Conservative Baptist Seminary has 15 Southern Baptists out of 433 students.[14] Fuller Theological Seminary, excluding clinical psychology majors, has 1,402 students, of which 29 declared themselves to be Southern Baptist.[15] No doubt some only specify Baptist rather than Southern Baptist, but this means that in the evangelical seminaries surveyed, only 4.8 percent are Southern Baptist students.

In a similar vein, many emphasize the growing support for Mid-America Baptist Theological Seminary, the only non-Convention financed, accredited, Southern Baptist seminary.[16] Dispensationalism is not required of its professors, and, for that matter, an amillenial position would not, of itself, preclude one from teaching there.[17] A straw poll of its theology and Bible departments reveals that approximately 60 percent of the professors are not dispensationalists. George Ladd's *Theology of the New Testament* is the required textbook in the New Testament Theology class, and even those who claim dispensationalism generally say they are "modified dispensationalists."

---

[10] Provided by Jim Thames, Registrar, 3/8/89.

[11] Provided by James Terry, Registrar, 4/18/89.

[12] Supplied by Delbert Brown, Statistician, 3/17/89.

[13] Supplied by Lynette Wayne, Graduate Admissions Office, 3/8/89.

[14] Supplied by Etta Schwab, Records Office, 3/8/89.

[15] Supplied by David Keefer, Registrar's Office, 3/20/89. They also have seven of 218 in the clinical psychology program and three of 421 in extension programs.

[16] Newport mentions a specific group, the Baptist Faith and Message Fellowship, formed partially to support non-Southern Baptist seminaries. A common misconception is that this group supported Mid-America and that Mid-America sought their support. Neither is correct. Gray Allison attended the first meeting of the BFMF at their request to present the new school. He presented it and left the meeting before their proceedings. The group has never supported the seminary (from correspondence between Gray Allison, President of Mid-America and C. R. Daley, editor, *Western Recorder*, 1974-78).

[17] From an interview with Gray Allison, 4/13/89. The basic requirements are (1) agreement with the doctrinal statement, (2) earned, accredited doctorate (in the theology school), (3) pastoral experience, and (4) an active membership in a cooperating Baptist church.

On the other hand, the Convention seminaries have had a commendable openness to other traditions. A recent survey of faculty preparation reveals that in the six Convention-sponsored seminaries, all schools included, 14 percent have studied in nonevangelical international institutions and 19 percent have studied in nonevangelical American schools (total 33 percent). The number is highest at Southern Seminary, where 25 percent have studied internationally and 23 percent have studied in nonevangelical American schools. Only six of the collective faculties and one of the Southern faculty have studied in one of the "evangelical" schools.[18]

I would suggest, therefore, that the tensions have grown from within the Convention. Our isolation has been a strength. We have remained conservative in a complex religious scene. Isolation has also been a weakness, since we have sometimes failed to learn from others. Presbyterians, Lutherans, Methodists, Christian Reformed, Northern Baptists, and now Southern Baptists have split or face that danger. Since these groups differ widely in their theological positions and since the nature of Scripture has been the flagship of the controversy, the issue of scriptural authority is the central concern for everyone. Evangelicals have produced sane theological responses, in contrast to many fundamentalists, and Southern Baptists have opportunity to do so here.

In Newport's recommendations for the future, he advocates new theological investigation that is thoroughly Baptistic. In these things I concur. I would suggest the following:

- The strands he identifies may need to be redefined, both those within and outside the convention.
- Evangelicalism outside the Convention is largely ignored, and we might be wise to acknowledge its presence and seek productive, cooperative efforts in common concerns.
- Any dialogue or cooperation should be done without the loss of Baptist tradition, heritage, distinctive theologies, and denominational loyalties.
- Any new theological consensus must take into account the "rank-and-file" Southern Baptists and particularly the issues that they hold dear.
- We have opportunity and occasion for theological reflection and in so doing we may "set the pace" for many other Christian groups.

---

[18] These figures are based on the data derived from the current seminary bulletins. They include all faculty members in theology, education, and music.

I would particularly like to recommend theological discussion in the areas of our strength as Southern Baptists. These would include the immediate concerns of:

- The tension between biblical authority and the priesthood of the believer. Authority would involve the relationships between the Spirit and the Word. The priesthood of the believer would involve relationships among the Word, the conscience, and our heritage.
- The tension between personal evangelism and social concerns.
- Ecclesiology, particularly the relationships between the local church and the denomination.
- Various models of defining the inspiration and authority of the Scriptures in light of the expectations of the plenary Convention.
- The relationships between Scripture, epistemology, and hermeneutics.

These are pressing concerns along with the items Newport mentioned in his chapter. I agree with Newport's conclusion: "We need an appropriate view of inerrancy and reverent or believing biblical criticism."

PART III

Beliefs
&
Practices

9

Theological and Ethical Dimensions
———— of ————
American Evangelicals

Richard Mouw

In 1976 I was asked to participate in a Bicentennial event sponsored by the State of Pennsylvania at one of the university campuses in that state. There were four of us, a Rabbi, a Roman Catholic priest, a representative of mainline Protestantism, and myself representing conservative evangelical Christianity. Each of us was asked to give a morning lecture presentation on the role that our religious communities had in the history of our nation. In the afternoon we were asked to talk about where we saw our communities going in the future as far as our involvement in the American experiment, and then in the evening we had questions from the audience. I talked quite a bit about past, present, and future involvements of evangelicals in the American community. When the question time came in the evening, the very first question was directed to me. The person stood up at a rather large gathering on the university campus and said, "Dr. Mouw, you have talked a lot about evangelicalism today; you have given several different ways of understanding who the evangelicals are; but I still need a little more help, and maybe you could help me by answering this question: What is it that you as an evangelical Christian believe that nobody else on the platform believes?"

My good friend George Marsden, my next door neighbor for fifteen years, says that whenever I get backed up against the wall, I quote a hymn. That is what I did on this occasion. The previous Sunday morning at my home church in Grand Rapids, Michigan, we had sung a hymn. The third verse of that hymn was still playing in my mind, and so I quoted it. It is the hymn, "It is Well with My Soul," and the verse goes like this, "My sin—oh, the bliss of this glorious tho't:" and now here is the glorious thought, "My sin not in part, but the whole is nailed to the

138

cross and I bear it no more, Praise the Lord, praise the Lord, O my soul!"[1] I said I consider that to be a profoundly and uniquely evangelical confession. I can say with full confidence here and now, that it is once for all settled that my sins have been washed away through the blood of the cross and it is forever more well with my soul. If we evangelicals are right about the dangerous tendencies of a lot of the modernizing, secularizing compromises that have been made in much of Protestant theology, many people in the mainline churches will not sing, at least with the fervor, that which evangelicals sing: "It is well with my soul."[2] Now it is a simple answer, yet it symbolizes something very important about evangelical Christianity.

As I understand evangelicalism, we are a community of people who have been shaped by four great controversies in the history of the Christian church. The first was the break with Judaism. The second was a significant reaffirmation of many of the central issues in the break with Catholicism at the time of the Reformation. The third was a reaffirmation of those same central issues during the pietistic revivals of the seventeenth, eighteenth, and nineteenth centuries. Many groups reacted against the high intellectualizing orthodoxy that could preach hour-and-a-half or two hour sermons on the equal ultimacy of election and reprobation, or get into lengthy discourses on the doctrine of the Trinity but did not offer a presentation of the gospel whereby people entered into the assurance that they were the elect people of God. Those pietistic movements affirmed the importance of knowing the work of the cross in a very personal way in one's own life. Finally, in the last century the conservative theological movements have reacted or responded to the secularizing, modernizing efforts in much of Christianity whereby compromises influenced by various sorts and degrees have been the suppositions of the enlightenment. The key assumption here is that enlightened reasoning or enlightened human consciousness is the highest authority in the universe, a perspective that when driven to its logical conclusions robs the gospel of its power.

That is what it means to be an evangelical Christian—someone who has been shaped by those controversies. Central to those controversies are a couple of different questions: What is our authority? By what authority do we live? Can evangelicals lift up the authority of the Scriptures, *Sola scriptura*? Perhaps, even in a more poignant sense, the

---

[1] Words: Horatio G. Spafford, 1828-1888. Music: Philip P. Bliss, 1838-1876, *The Baptist Hymnal* (Convention Press, 1991).

[2] Ibid.

question is, who is Jesus Christ? How are we to understand the person and work of Jesus Christ, and how are we to present the saving work of Jesus Christ to a lost and dying world? What happened on the cross? Our response is, "My sins were nailed to the cross, and each of us can know once and for all that our debts have been cancelled, the accounts have been settled, and that we can say it is forevermore well with our souls."

This is my account of evangelicalism. Evangelical Christians are the kind of people who are so concerned with preserving the saving work of Jesus Christ in a person's life that we have centered our focus on the *evangel*, the gospel, to the degree that we are even willing to run the risk of turning the *evangel* into an "ism" and call ourselves by the term *evangelicalism*.

Now I also have my criticisms of evangelicalism although I am a "card-carrying" part of it. I spoke at an ecumenical conference recently. I was asked to deal with issues of social justice from an evangelical perspective. I said a lot of things that most of the people at the conference would agree with.

Later that night in the coffee shop I sat with the leader of one of the mainline denominations. It was as if he said, "OK, nobody else is listening; let me ask you a very confidential question. How does a guy like you survive in the evangelical world?" My response was something like this; I find it very helpful that I am really an evangelical. I must say that I am one and am pleased to be one. The evangelical arguments, the evangelical emphases, the evangelical experiences, and the evangelical expressions in proclamation are near and dear to my heart. I am an evangelical; yet I am a critical evangelical.

Ernest Stoeffler, a strong defender of the pietist movement, talks about some of the bad tendencies in pietism that have created some of the most significant defects or shortcomings in American Protestantism. He mentions three of those pietist defects in American Protestantism: anti-intellectualism, other worldliness, and ecclesiastical separatism. Evangelical Christians are people who are constantly plagued by these same three characteristics.

These are issues that we have to struggle with. It is good to struggle with them because the antidote to anti-intellectualism is not a thoroughgoing prointellectualism. The antidote to other worldliness is not thoroughgoing this worldliness. The antidote to ecclesiastical separatism is not a thoroughgoing ecclesiastical promiscuity. They are very dangerous tendencies.

The neoevangelical movement of the post-World War II period was consciously attempting to reform evangelicalism with reference to those three characteristics. It wanted to produce a new kind of conservative theological scholarship that was not anti-intellectual but that set forth in an intelligent way a biblical world and life view and a theological perspective that was capable of critical interaction with the other intellectual trends of theology and of the larger human culture.

An important emphasis was on involvement in this world. Carl F. H. Henry in 1947 wrote a book called *The Uneasy Conscience of Modern Fundamentalism*. He argued that the fundamentalist movement had been much too otherworldly and had irresponsibly extracted itself from the struggle for social reform. He called the fundamentalist and evangelical Christians back to an involvement in the corporate structures of societies and the larger cultural dialogue. He called them to efforts to reform society. Billy Graham addressed the ecclesiastical separatism issue. Graham was an important person in dealing with this issue because he introduced cooperative evangelism (which was a new thing for the fundamentalists), insisting on cooperating with people in the mainline churches and more recently even with Roman Catholics.

The neoevangelical movement in the post-World War II period has been struggling with some of the basic defects, or some of the defective tendencies, of the evangelical movement. Indeed, the new right in more recent years has been struggling with those same issues. Jerry Falwell, Tim LaHaye, and others have, in effect, been reformers of fundamentalism. We might think of them as neofundamentalists who have been addressing the same issues with a desire to reform the fundamentalist movement. Consider the issue of anti-intellectualism: Jerry Falwell established a university and now talks about the need for a new kind of fundamentalist scholarship. Tim LaHaye wrote a book in the late 1970s called *The Battle for the Mind*. Fundamentalists for a long time did not engage in the "battle for the mind." Recently they have begun to recognize that secular humanism is a genuine threat in society and that evangelical Christians have to respond with a disciplined mind. Now there are problems with it all because it is still the old militaristic "wipe out the enemy" kind of approach to things. Nevertheless, we have to hear the new emphasis in all of this. The fundamentalist community is committed to a battle for the mind, to an intellectual struggle. The Moral Majority is nothing if it is not a rejection of the older otherworldliness of the fundamentalist movement.

There are new patterns of ecumenical cooperation within the new right, not the sort that they dream of at 475 Riverside Drive in New York (headquarters for the National Council of Churches), or at the World Council headquarters in Geneva. What we see in it is an amazing ecumenical development in recent years where at least two parties who have been very hostile to each other, Roman Catholics and fundamentalists, have begun to forge new coalitions. The right wing of fundamentalism and the right wing of Roman Catholicism have entered into cooperative efforts. Bob Jones and others have criticized Jerry Falwell for having Phyllis Schafley speak in his church, not primarily because she is a woman, although that is certainly one of the problems, but because she is a Roman Catholic. The new right movement has in many ways been a reforming effort with regard to those three endemic problems: anti-intellectualism, otherworldliness, and ecclesiastical separatism. There is much to celebrate in that reformed movement. So this is a time of ferment, a time of new explorations in the conservative evangelical community.

Observations

I want to make four observations about this ferment, about these recent changes, and about the dialogue that is going on today. The first two I am only going to touch on very quickly, and I am going to concentrate a little more on the other two.

Biblical Authority

Evangelicals are struggling with crucial issues about biblical authority. We all know about the battle for the Bible. I would just observe here that unfortunately these explorations do take on that kind of militaristic tone—the *battle* for the Bible, the *battle* for the mind. Evangelical Christians tend to address new areas with that old sort of militaristic mentality. That is very dangerous! Several years ago I debated the Baptist preacher who was the head of the Moral Majority in a Midwestern state. We were on a secular university campus and were each giving conservative Christian perspectives on various issues in society and politics. He protested loudly against homosexuals as a part of his more general dealings with family and sexual issues. He said a lot of things that were very cruel and misleading about homosexuality. I countered his comments very gently in my presentation. Afterward, I said to him,

> You know there is one thing I have got to say to you. I think that you have to do a lot more thinking and reflection and studying on the whole issue of homosexuality. Theologically you and I are not very far apart; we probably interpret Romans 1 and Leviticus in the same way. I am not making a theological claim at all here, but I have had

students who are gay/lesbian persons who struggle daily with these issues. Many of the things that you said about homosexuals are just misleading and to their ears would be very cruel kinds of statements.

He pointed at me, thumped me in the chest, and said, "That's the problem with you intellectuals. You want to make all kinds of distinctions. You want to distract us from the struggle. We are on a battleground here; we are in open warfare for biblical morality, the old-fashioned morality of the Ten Commandments." He turned around and walked away. I did not get a chance to say this to him, but biblical morality is also a morality that takes truth seriously. It is a morality that tells us that we ought not to bear false witness against our homosexual neighbors. If it is really a battle for the truth, we have to struggle long and hard to hear what the other person is saying.

That has been so typical in our recent dialogue in evangelicalism over the battle for the Bible. We have not really listened to each other very carefully. There has been a lot of distorting of each other's positions, although I must say again that there is an important issue at stake here. Many of us are willing to explore various critical perspectives that might help us better understand the nature and extent of biblical authority. We believe these critical perspectives might help us understand the way in which the Bible is the infallible guide to issues of faith and practice in our lives. As we explore these, we do so with the profound sense that the Bible ultimately is not human beings reaching out to God, but it is a book in which God reaches down to us. In it He provides us with guidance, information, a message, and loving counsel that we could never gain through the highest explorations of the human consciousness. It is God speaking to us in a very profound sense.

Cultural Conscious

Evangelicals have been reflecting upon patterns of cultural pessimism and cultural optimism. There has been a profound shift in our cultural self-consciousness as conservative Protestants in recent years. Evangelicals have had a profound shift from the cultural pessimism of a dispensationalist premillennialism to the cultural optimism that is more compatible with kind of postmillennial theology and cultural perspective. Yet there has been a lot of confusion because evangelicals have not had a well-worked-out political theology. They have not really thought clearly about the theological categories that are necessary for understanding our place in the world.

Relations Between the Personal and the Corporate

Evangelical Christians have been attempting to integrate the personal and the corporate. They have been looking for proper theological categories for analyzing the patterns of corporate life and for understanding our Christian involvement in those patterns. The resources for that integrative concern, that integrative task whereby we understand the relationship between personal and corporate, have not always been on the top of our minds; but evangelical piety has the resources. We have not drawn on them, however. We have often operated with a truncated version of social reality. We have operated with arbitrary boundaries between the personal and the social. Take the hymn that I quoted earlier, "It Is Well with My Soul."[3] That is a marvelous confession; I love it. It is forevermore well with my soul. When I say that as a Christian I am saying that the God who has proclaimed in Jesus Christ that it is forevermore well with my soul is the God who is not yet ready to say it is well with the whole creation. He is the God who grieves over South Africa; He is the God who grieves overs Nicaragua, Haiti, South Korea, and North Korea. He is the God who grieves over the sexism of our society, the sexual infidelity of our society, the superstition of our society, and the false doctrines that we appropriate in our lives. He is the God who grieves over this world that is broken by injustice, oppression, manipulation, prejudice, and stereotype. The God who has said that it is forevermore well with my soul is the God who looks toward the day when He can say "It is now well with the creation; behold, I make all things new; it is done; it is finished; it is well with the whole creation."

That has not happened yet. God calls me to take the confidence I have that He has cleansed my sins through the blood of Calvary, and to appropriate that into a life of discipleship where I participate in those struggles and those projects that long for and anticipate the day when all things will be made new. That is not an excuse for withdrawal from the social, political, and economic struggles of the day, but it is an impulse toward it. It is a base of confidence that I must build on as I involve myself in the world God has made. There is so much that we need to draw upon there with our fellow Christians.

Several years ago I had a call from a pastor of a large, very conservative church. He asked me to come and talk to his congregation for a Lenten series on Jesus and Politics. After I agreed, he said, "OK, now that you have agreed to do it, I have got to tell you about the problems

---

[3] Words: Horatio G. Spafford, 1828-1888. Music: Philip P. Bliss, 1838-1876, *The Baptist Hymnal* (Convention Press, 1991).

we are having in this church. It is a suburban congregation in a large city that has been struggling with the issue of busing for purposes of racial integration. My people are against busing. I tried to preach on that a couple of months ago, and they would have tarred and feathered me if they could have gotten hold of me afterward. Over and over again I heard from my people that Jesus has nothing to do with issues like busing. For them this is not a spiritual issue at all; it is a worldly political issue, and the church had better stay out of politics. They think I am just preaching politics! I want you to come in and straighten them out."

That was one of the scariest invitations I have ever received. He put it this way, "Really stick it to them, but be gentle." Wednesday evening after a nice pot-luck supper, we went into the sanctuary. The place was full. Before I spoke, we sang a hymn, "Oh Worship the King."[4] Just before I spoke (and I could not have paid them to do this) the little children's choir (all white) sang "Jesus loves the little children, All the children of the world, Ev'ry color, ev'ry race, all are covered by his grace; Jesus loves the little children of the world."[5]

I said, "You know I was supposed to come here and convince you that Jesus cares about things like race relations, but you have already made the case. You have established two things in your singing tonight: first, He is a King; second, He loves black kids. Now once you have established those issues, never again can you ask the question, does Jesus have anything to say about race relations? From here on the only question is: What are we going to do about the concern that we have already established? We have proclaimed in our singing that the Son of God came into the world among other reasons because God loves the little children. The resources, sisters and brothers, are there in our piety if we would explore them."

What does it mean for evangelical Christians to hear George Beverly Shea sing, "I'd rather have Jesus than silver or gold, I'd rather have Jesus than riches untold, I'd rather have Jesus than houses or lands, I'd rather be led by His nail-pierced hands."[6] Once you have heard that, you do not need liberation theology to turn you into an economic radical. Liberation theology pales alongside the proclamation that it is better to be true to the nail-pierced hands of Jesus than to own houses or lands or to be the king of a vast domain. That is powerful stuff. What we need to

---

[4] Words: Robert Grant, 1779-1838. Music: Attr. Johann Michael Hayden, 1737-1806, in William Gardiner's Sacred Melodies, 1815, *The Baptist Hymnal*.

[5] Copyright 1991 Broadman Press (SESAC), *The Broadman Hymnal*.

[6] Copyright Renewed 1966, *The Baptist Hymnal*.

do is to get our people to reflect on the piety to which they are already committed in the singing of their hymns and in their theology.

I am a creationist. It does not mean I believe in a literal six-day creation. I am willing to argue with people about that—some of my best friends are six-day creationists. I know how they think, and I do not think they are crazy, but I do not agree with them. It does trouble me that we evangelical Christians have often operated with a narrow view of what the issues are in defending the idea of creation. It bothers me that many evangelical Christians can get so excited about what public school textbooks say about geological records and about biology and cannot get at all excited about how those very same public schools treat little black, brown, white, yellow, and red children who are created in the very image of God who has made them as special creations.

It deeply troubles me that many of my evangelical friends can get excited about whether or not we are descended from a literal man and a literal woman and cannot get concerned about how the daughters of Eve are treated today. The woman in Genesis 1–2 was told she was created in the very image of the divine Maker and along with the man was given the mandate to exercise dominion in the creation.

It troubles me that many of my evangelical and fundamentalist friends can get so excited about theories about creation; yet, they do not worry that every day the United States creates the materials for hundreds of nuclear warheads so that we have now stockpiled the ability to destroy the entire creation.

Something is strange about all that. We need not to deny that we are creationists, but we do need to explore the rich implications of what it means to affirm that doctrine of creation as set forth in that greatest of all biblical creationist texts, Psalm 24:1: "The earth is the Lord's and the fullness thereof; the world and all they that dwell therein" (KJV). The resources are there, and we have to explore them.

Tradition

Evangelical Christians have been engaged in an extensive quest for traditions of theological and ethical discourse. Evangelicals do not always know how to think and talk about issues related to social and economic life because our theology has been deprived of attention to these categories. What has been exciting in the last couple of decades, among the Northern evangelicals at least, has been the extensive quest for new traditions of discourse. The important book *Habits of the Heart* talks about the need for churches to function as communities of memory, as places where we remember the older ways of speaking and thinking about reality, in a culture which is quickly losing the ability to think about those things. They are squeezed out by the rapid individualization of our relationships and our categories for thinking about human relationships. Evangelical Christians have been a people in search of memories in recent years.

So you get many younger evangelicals who have been exploring the Anabaptist tradition, others looking at the Reformed tradition, others looking at the Lutheran tradition via Bonhoeffer. People have been looking more closely at the social teachings of the Roman Catholic tradition, not only the teachings of various Vatican documents but also of the Franciscan tradition of identification with the poor.

Others have turned to the riches of the African-American tradition of slave-spirituality found in books such as James Cone's *The Spirituals and the Blues*, where he discusses the profound ideological explorations of the African-American slave community. Others have looked at the Wesleyan tradition. Evangelicals have explored traditions of ethical discourse extensively, realizing that in the twentieth-century fundamentalist and evangelical Christianity has been a deprived community when it comes to its ability to think theologically about the issues of ethical life.

Even the new right has been doing that. The interesting book that Jerry Falwell edited along with Ed Hinson and Ed Dobson, *The Fundamentalist Phenomenon*, talks about the influence of the English descending tradition and the Puritan tradition on their own thought. These are important issues. We have to search the past for dimensions and perspectives on social, political, and economic life. Southern Baptists are dealing with many of these same issues.

Conclusion

In conclusion as I look at Baptist thought today, it seems to me that Baptists need to do some exploring of traditions together. I see many people in the American and Southern Baptist churches exploring the contemporary applicability of the Rhode Island perspective or the Roger Williams perspective with a strong emphasis on the issues of church and state. One of the real problems with that today is that it needs a lot of recontextualizing. If you talk like Roger Williams today, you sound like the American Civil Liberties Union. That is not always the right way to talk because Roger Williams was struggling against Anglicans, Roman Catholics, and Calvinist Puritans, but he was not struggling against the kind of secular humanism that is running rampant in our society today. Roger Williams' perspective updated will require a real struggle with the radically different cultural and religious context that we face today as we think about issues of church and state.

People like that in the Baptist community have begun to explore the Anabaptist traditions, especially as it comes to us through the Mennonite community. Others have become cryptocontinental Calvinists while others, and especially on the new right, have become Puritan theocrats, looking to various Puritan and Scottish Calvinist patterns of thought that go far beyond anything Baptists have ever contemplated in the past.

This is a rich discussion. We, those of us who represent the Northern Evangelical community, desperately need dialogue with the Southern Baptist community. My impression is that you need dialogue with us. We must overcome the polarization that so easily sets upon us and has so obviously afflicted your Southern Baptist community. We must reconsider those old questions that evangelicals love to raise: "What happened at the cross?" "Where are we to look for the authority that guides our lives?" How do we take that perspective on what Jesus Christ has done according to the Scripture and apply it in living, vibrant, faithful, prophetic, and priestly ways to the complexities of a world that desperately needs to hear that God was in Christ, reconciling the world to God's own self? That remains the challenge for both Southern Baptists and the American evangelical community.

10

Theology and Piety
—————— Among ——————
Baptists and Evangelicals

Stanley J. Grenz

Introduction

Allow me to begin autobiographically. I grew up in what I imagined to have been typical evangelical churches that boasted typical Sunday Schools and youth groups. I attended what I thought were typical church camps, listened to my father's sermons which I assumed were typically evangelical, and attended typical evangelistic meetings, where I made what I thought was a typical decision for Christ. While a philosophy major in university, I held what I believed to be typical evangelical answers to important intellectual questions. As a result, when I attended a typical evangelical seminary, I assumed that apart from whether the rapture was pre-or post-tribulational, theology would be noncontroversial and that the battle lines were easily drawn between sound biblical positions (concerning which there was broad consensus) and liberal thought.

I was wrong.

Since those years in seminary, I have discovered that theology is much more complicated than a simple "them/us" approach will allow. Theological differences do not only divide "them" from "us," but even the "us" camp encompasses diversity. For this reason it is as difficult to pin down "what evangelicals believe" as it is to say definitively what constitutes *the* Southern Baptist belief system. Nor, I have discovered, is theological agreement necessarily the best way to separate "them" from "us." Nevertheless, the task remains—to offer some comment on the question, What do evangelicals believe?

The Evangelical Movement and the American Theological Landscape

For me the best way to come to terms with the theological orientation of evangelicalism is by seeking to place it within the spectrum of the American theological landscape. In this way one may perhaps see the theology of the movement as it stands out of, and within, the context in which it is articulated.

Like any actual landscape, the theological lay of the land flows in three, not two directions. I find it helpful to orient myself to these by appeal to what constitutes for me the three reference points of systematic theology. A theological system, I maintain, moves among three points or three pillars, each of which contributes to the working out of the theological task.

The task of theology, as I understand it, is to assist the church by reflecting on the articulation of, and on the significance for life in the presence of, the Christian affirmation, "Jesus is Lord." In the completion of this task, the theologian must look in three directions: the biblical documents as expressions of the *kerygma*; the heritage of the believing community which is expressed in, but not limited to, the confessions of the church; and the contemporary situation in which the church is to minister and to be the people of God. Systematic theology then moves among the pillars of Bible, heritage, and culture.

Fundamentalism

With this understanding in view, one can speak of three basic orientations within the American theological landscape. The first, which I call fundamentalism, may be pictured as hugging the first pillar of the theological discipline, the Bible. The chief concern of fundamentalism, understood in this context, is to remain true to the biblical message. As a result fundamentalist theologians are careful to employ biblical terminology in their theologizing and are suspicious of those who use language introduced from other disciplines, especially from the modern sciences.

Fundamentalism serves as a reminder of an important dimension of the theological task, namely, fidelity to the biblical *kerygma*. Its concern, however, disposes fundamentalism to certain problems. The stringent use of biblical categories can result in articulations of the faith that are not understandable to the contemporary world. Further, fundamentalism's mistrust of contemporary culture disposes it toward sectarianism. Fundamentalists are prone to a separationism that can cut them off from other expressions of both the historical and contemporary church.

Progressivism

A second orientation may be termed progressivism, or in its extreme form, liberalism. Progressivism may be pictured as hugging the pillar of culture. Its goal is quite different from that of fundamentalism. Progressives view the task of theology above all as that of speaking in terms the present culture can understand. As a result, biblical categories are often replaced or reinterpreted by the thought forms of the contemporary world. Progressivism and liberalism are important reminders of the necessity that theology speak to culture. This concern can also lead to a loss of the biblical witness or of the heritage of church doctrine.

Confessionalism

Confessionalism, the third theological orientation, may be seen as hugging the pillar of heritage. Confessionalists attempt to ensure fidelity to the doctrinal or ecclesiological tradition of the group. In so doing they witness to the importance that contemporary theologians remain cognizant of the historical trajectory of the church as a whole and the specific expression of the church that they are to serve. The confessionalist concern can become both deaf to the biblical critique of every confessional heritage and irrelevant to the contemporary setting of the church.

The characterization of the landscape indicates that the ideal theological model maintains a balance among all three concerns. Theology must articulate the biblical *kerygma* in a way understandable by contemporary culture while maintaining unity with the one people of God throughout history.

The delineation of these three pillars also indicates that the term *conservative* may have several connotations. Most generally it is used to refer to those who are concerned with maintaining fidelity to biblical doctrine (hence, fundamentalism). Yet conservative may be applied to those who hug the other two pillars as well. Confessionalists may be conservative, for their interest lies in insuring fidelity to the heritage of a specific confessional body. And "conservative liberal" is not a contradiction, when used to refer to those who seek to maintain loyalty to the cultural expressions of an earlier era which are now no longer understandable or relevant.

Evangelicalism

Although it has often wandered from the mark, the evangelical movement, seen in its best light, attempts to work toward this ideal. In fact, I would maintain that evangelicalism offers the best context in which to accomplish theological balance, for it reflects the concerns of the three basic types of theology and allows for the interplay of the three pillars of theology.

Biblical Authority

A truly evangelical theology incorporates the first pillar, the Bible. The desire to take the Bible seriously as the book of the people of God has consistently been at the heart of the evangelical movement in the church throughout its history. Commitment to the Bible as the final authority in all matters of faith and practice has been a hallmark of all participants in the evangelical tradition. As a result, contemporary evangelicals share with the older fundamentalists the desire to develop biblical theology and to defend biblical doctrine. In fact, evangelicals maintain that not only at its core but at every juncture systematic theology must remain true to the doctrine of the apostles and prophets. The Bible must be the standard for doctrine, and sound doctrine must be applied to life.

The Historic Church

In addition to the emphasis on biblical authority, evangelicalism provides occasion for the attempt to remain faithful to the second pillar. Evangelicals desire to stand within the historic tradition of the church. Like their turn-of-the-century fundamentalist forebears, contemporary evangelical theologians often chastise their progressive and liberal opponents, claiming that what to them are innovative stands are merely a rejection of, or a forsaking of, what have been the teachings of the church for almost twenty centuries.

Evangelicals generally elevate one expression of the heritage of the church—the Reformation—above all others. This brings both danger and advantage. Attempted fidelity to the Reformation has meant that evangelicals have tended to find little value in other traditions, specifically those of the Roman Catholic and Eastern Orthodox Churches. The Roman Catholic Church has consistently been the object of evangelical polemic. This has often served to keep alive the controversies of the sixteenth century. Even in the post-Vatican-II times, some evangelicals have remained blatantly anti-Catholic.

There are signs of change, however. Charismatic evangelicals, for example, have enjoyed fellowship with like-minded Catholics. Activist evangelicals have found themselves marching with Catholics on behalf of several causes, especially in abortion protests. Some noted evangelicals have left their denominations to find a new home in Roman Catholic or Orthodox Churches.

While all evangelicals view the Reformation as of great consequence for theology today, diversity appears in their ranks as to which aspect of the Reformation heritage ought to claim highest loyalty. As a result, there are, for example, Lutheran, Calvinist, and even Arminian or Wesleyan evangelicals. There are evangelicals who appeal to the free church tradition of the so-called Anabaptists on the continent or to the Puritan radicals in England who gave birth to the early Baptist movement.

This diversity of heritage makes for diversity in thought within the agreed attempt to be broadly Reformation in outlook. This provides an important positive opportunity for evangelical theologians. The interdenominational character of the movement can offer a broader prospective for the theological enterprise than what may be gained by remaining fixated on the heritage of a single denomination. Thus, within the context of the movement, Baptists, Pentecostals, and Presbyterians have opportunity to learn from each other in a climate both of fidelity to one's own confessional heritage and of mutual affirmation and respect. In this way they are spurred on to develop theologies that are denominational and yet reflect the broader heritage of the church as a whole.

Culture

Finally, evangelicalism provides a context in which to take seriously the pillar of culture. Evangelicals have tended to be more open to dialogue with contemporary culture than fundamentalists. In fact, many historians suggest that this more open spirit, and not doctrine—for both groups share most points of doctrine in common—constitutes the most telling difference between contemporary evangelicalism and fundamentalism. Despite their openness, evangelicals remain cautious in this dialogue with culture lest the uniqueness of the gospel message be offered on the altar of "being current."

Critics to their right and to their left are not always convinced, however, that evangelicals are sufficiently cautious in their approach to American culture. The growing popularity and growth of evangelical churches have, at times, come at the expense of a new cultural captivity to the American way of life and to the policies of the United States government. This tendency has been augmented by the basically conservative theological orientation of evangelicalism, an orientation that easily spills over into political conservatism.

The Foundational Theological
Outlook of Evangelicalism

This description of the self-understanding of the task of evangelical theology forms a context for addressing the question concerning the foundational theological outlook of the movement.

History of Evangelicalism

At this point a helpful perspective is offered by the history of evangelicalism. The theological orientation of the movement finds its genesis in three important events in, or phases of, the movement's history. The first event, the Reformation, bequeathed to the evangelicals of the Reformation churches the great *solas*—*sola scriptura*, *sola Christi*, *sola gratia*, and *sola fide*. As a result the emphases on the sole authority of the Bible and the sole salvific work of Christ leading to salvation by grace through faith alone have characterized evangelicals throughout the world since the sixteenth century.

Whereas the Reformation transpired in Europe and took root on American soil through the coming of the Puritans, a second significant phase of evangelical history was largely an American phenomenon. As was noted earlier, American religious life in the eighteenth and nineteenth centuries was given definitive shape by the Great Awakening and the revivalist movement that followed. Revivalism, occurring as it did in the context of the earlier Puritan quest for certainty of personal election, pressed a concern for personal conversion in the developing evangelical movement. In addition to the necessity of holding forth the heritage of Reformation doctrine, evangelical theology is oriented around the practical task of reflecting on and delineating the nature of the conversion experience, which all evangelicals supposedly share. This gives added importance to issues related to the interplay of the divine and the human in conversion, the marks of salvation, the relationship of conversion to sanctification, and the certainty of one's saved status.

Third, evangelical theology has been shaped by yet another event of American evangelical history, the modernist-fundamentalist controversy. The older fundamentalist movement, which formed the immediate genesis for the new evangelicalism, produced what has come to be called "the Five Fundamentals." The first of the five relates to the doctrine of Scripture—the inspiration of the Bible—whereas the other four are Christological: Jesus' virgin birth, substitutionary atonement, bodily resurrection, and literal second coming. In the face of the challenge of liberalism, the fundamentalists maintained that these doctrines formed a consistent whole, in that the loss of any one of the five led quite necessarily to the rejection of the others.

The codification of the fundamentals of the faith had three important results for the orientation of evangelicalism. First, it gave specific formulation to the emphasis on biblical authority inherited from the Reformation. This paved the way for the emphasis on inerrancy that has come to be elevated by some as the *conditio siae qua non* for a truly evangelical theology. Second, it changed the focus of theological debate away from the question of personal salvation, which lay behind the *solas* of the Reformation response to Roman Catholicism, to the more intellectually oriented discussion of naturalism versus supernaturalism, which lay at the genesis of the struggle with liberalism and came to the fore in the dogmas relating to Christology in the fundamentals. Finally, this event served to orient evangelical theology to questions of propositional truth in contrast to the interest in the person's relationship with God characteristic of the nineteenth century.

The Belief System of Evangelicalism

With these historical considerations in view, the belief system of evangelicalism can now be summarized. Because of the diversity of the movement, this is perhaps best indicated by means of citing as examples the topics discussed in two recent evangelical writings.

Given the orientation of evangelical theology to the quest for propositional truth about God, the topics chosen for delineation in *Evangelical Essentials: A Liberal-Evangelical Dialogue*, featuring two Anglicans, David L. Edwards and the noted evangelical John Stott, are instructive as a reflection of current evangelical thinking.[1] The essays by Edwards and the responses by Stott focus on five issues: biblical authority, the atonement, miracles, morality, and evangelism.

A second paradigm is offered by a prolific evangelical theologian with a Reformed heritage, Donald Bloesch. In his 1973 publication, *The Evangelical Renaissance*, he delineated what he saw as the hallmarks of evangelicalism.[2] Bloesch's list includes the sovereignty of God, the divine authority of Scripture, total depravity, Christ's substitutionary atonement, salvation by grace, salvation through faith alone, the primacy of proclamation, scriptural holiness, the spiritual mission of the church, and the personal return of Christ.

These doctrines form the core of the expanded discussion in Bloesch's subsequent two-volume offering, *Essentials of Evangelical Theology*. In this work, however, he moves beyond a purely doctrinal description of the essence of evangelicalism, claiming instead that the movement's genius lies in both doctrine and experience: "My contention is that to be evangelical means to hold to a definite doctrine as well as to

---

[1] David L. Edwards and John R. W. Stott, *Evangelical Essentials: A Liberal-Evangelical Dialogue* (Downers Grove: InterVarsity, 1988).

[2] Donald G. Bloesch, *The Evangelical Renaissance* (Grand Rapids: Eerdmans, 1973).

participate in a special kind of experience."[3] As a result, he finds in modern evangelicalism a tension between Reformation theology and pietism.[4] At the same time in keeping with his Reformation roots, Bloesch elevates one doctrine above the others, claiming that the doctrine of salvation by grace "is the heart and soul of evangelicalism."[5]

Bloesch is basically correct in his thesis that the essence of evangelicalism lies in both doctrine and experience. However, I would place the two in the opposite order. To be evangelical, I maintain, is to participate in a special experience which is cradled by a specific doctrinal or theological outlook.

Evangelicalism, I think, is more a particular piety than a distinctive theology. "Evangelical" refers to a specific vision of what it means to be Christian, which is less described than "felt." It entails a specific way of being Christian, which includes a fervent desire to make the Bible alive in personal and community life, an understanding of the church as a fellowship of believers, a way of praying, a sense that faith is to be vibrant and central to life, and a specific approach to the telling of one's life story. Of course, all of this presupposes a certain theological outlook which serves as the context for the specifically evangelical piety. The way of experiencing the Christian life, which all evangelicals share with each other and the experience of belonging to this group because of this shared piety—this more so than the theological outlook itself, I believe—gets at the heart of the evangelical ethos.

The Central Theological Issue Within
Contemporary Evangelicalism: Biblical Authority

Although the ethos of evangelicalism, I maintain, is a piety cradled in a theology, the tensions within the movement in recent years have focused on theology, not piety. More specifically, the discussion, often heated and schismatic, has been given over to a debate concerning the proper formulation of the traditional evangelical hallmark of adherence to biblical authority.

It ought to be acknowledged that this debate is not without consequence. The evangelical commitment to biblical authority is crucial, for it forms the foundation for the evangelical ethos. If a common vision of the nature of being Christian lies at the heart of evangelicalism and if this common vision is articulated through the shared nature of the stories of

---

[3] Donald G. Bloesch, *Essentials of Evangelical Theology*, 2 vols. (San Francisco: Harper and Row, 1978-79), 1:ix.

[4] Ibid., 1:5.

[5] Ibid., 2:276.

our "experience with the Lord," then the Bible is significant, for it provides the categories for understanding ourselves and for organizing our narratives. Nevertheless, in many ways the debate has shown itself to be problematic.

For example, despite their shared piety, evangelicals have not been able to devise one agreed-on approach to the Bible. This reality has been evidenced in several recent evangelical publications. In the introduction to a volume of essays arising out of the 1982 evangelical theology consultation of the American Academy of Religion, Robert K. Johnston pinpoints a unity among evangelicals in their common commitment to the Bible's inherent authority.[6] Yet he acknowledges that there is no single evangelical theological methodology. Three examples from the book illustrate this situation.

In his essay James I. Packer proposes a "canonical interpretation" of the Bible. This approach assumes that the Word of God is God's message conveyed by God's messenger by means of language so that by entering into the mind of the biblical writer the exegete enters into the mind of God. Packer further assumes the unity of Scripture, thereby giving to theology the task of "making clear the links" between the materials of the Bible.

Donald Bloesch, in contrast, claims to follow a Reformation model in which the Word of God is received "in a commitment of faith" and then exegeted via a Christological hermeneutic, in which Scripture is to be read in the light of the cross. William Dyrness offers yet another opinion. He employs insights from contemporary narrative theology to offer an approach that focuses on a threefold movement of the Bible in Christian life: the reader tells his or her own story; Scripture allows him or her to hear God's story; and the Bible brings a merging of the reader's story with God's.

In addition to the quest for a shared evangelical approach to the Bible, attempts have been made to encapsulize commitment to biblical authority under the term *inerrancy* and to employ philosophical categories as a means of giving precise definition to the term.

One important impetus in this inerrancy movement has been the understandable desire of some to bring evangelicals to speak with a united voice on the crucial social issues of the day. The current paralysis of the church in speaking to such questions, some maintain, is the result of the erosion of biblical authority among the people of God. This is, in

---

[6] See Robert K. Johnston, ed., *The Use of the Bible in Theology: Evangelical Options* (Atlanta: John Knox, 1985).

part, an accurate assessment. It must be noted that commitment to any one pattern of biblical authority does not guarantee unanimity on the proper response to current issues. Evangelicals who uphold the doctrine of inerrancy often find their ranks divided whenever contemporary social questions are posed. The various gatherings and conferences designed to foster *the* evangelical voice in our society are vivid reminders of the lack of unanimity within the movement. For example, even the International Council on Biblical Inerrancy, meeting in Chicago in December 1986, could not produce a document on social issues that all 300 participants could sign.

This situation suggests that all the attempts to devise an intricate definition of biblical authority under the rubric term *inerrancy* cannot fulfill their intent. Again at this juncture, a view toward the genesis and development of the evangelical movement offers a point of orientation in seeking to understand the present reality.

The Protestant Reformation set into motion a new and powerful way of approaching the Bible. Luther's *sola scriptura* principle entailed a commitment to looking first and foremost to the Scriptures for divine instruction for human life. To this principle was added a related emphasis, the presupposition that the Bible speaks clearly. Early Protestants were convinced that each text of the Bible has but one meaning, in contrast to the fourfold use of the Bible developed in medieval hermeneutics, and that this one meaning could be determined by application of proper exegetical methods. It was expected that in time agreement would be reached concerning the one right understanding of the revelation mediated to humanity by the Scriptures. Protestant history, however, has not fulfilled the dream of the early reformers. Unanimity has proven to be an illusive goal, not merely on the finer and more obscure points of exegesis, but also on certain major doctrinal issues, including the doctrine of Scripture itself.

Yet, the quest continues, and the evangelical movement is an heir to this quest. In the intervening centuries Protestant orthodoxy has augmented the Reformation commitment to *sola scriptura* with a developed theology of the Bible. Significant words in this theology include *inspiration*—verbal and plenary—as well as *infallibility* and, more recently, *inerrancy*.

In spite of this attempt to define carefully the nature of biblical authority and even to reach agreement on proper exegetical methodology, Christians continue to approach the Scriptures in differing ways. Some view the Bible as a storehouse of "propositional truth." For them God's revelation is rational. It appeals to the mind and is designed to being about right beliefs. Such persons enter into debates concerning the objective truthfulness of doctrinal formulations.

Others emphasize the "life-changing" significance of the Bible. The Scriptures are given, they assert, in order that hearts may be opened to receive the gift of God's presence within. God's revelation is seen less in terms of propositions for the mind to accept and more as the good news of available power to live in newness of life.

Another group finds in the Bible the story of God's work in the world. The Scriptures, they maintain, are given in order that the reader may change direction and link one's own story with that of God. Revelation, then, lies with the narratives of the Bible. As the "old, old story" is proclaimed, the Holy Spirit calls the hearer into the family of God.

Yet others emphasize the Bible as the declaration of God's intention for the world. It offers a vision of a future or ideal order, in which human beings live in harmony with each other, with God, and with the entire created order. God's revelation lies in this vision, mediated by the prophets and Jesus and present in the stories of the great acts of God, such as the Exodus and the resurrection of Christ.

Given so many understandings of the nature of the Bible, it is no wonder that evangelicals differ on the proper response to contemporary issues. Obviously one's opinion concerning the application of the Bible to current situations will be affected by one's approach to the biblical material. Those who emphasize the Bible as propositions will look therein for applicable propositional statements. Those who see in the Bible a clear vision for an ideal order, on the other hand, will look to what they find in Scripture concerning that vision for guidance in the present.

The situation is compounded when it is realized that the Bible is a multifaceted work. One simply cannot press the Scriptures totally into one mold. Nor may revelation be limited to one understanding. The intent of the Bible is many-sided, encompassing all the proposals cited above, and others as well. Which emphasis is to take precedence when dealing with a specific issue is, in the final analysis, a value judgment. Actually, all the various approaches to the Bible may have significance for any problem under consideration. The Spirit may be at work seeking to bring insight from the various approaches vying for attention.

This suggests that an eclectic understanding of the nature of the Bible may be the most beneficial. The insights offered by many quarters of the church ought to be listened to and valued, for the Spirit seeks in many ways to speak from the pages of the Bible.

This means, however, that unanimity may never be attained. One specifically Christian answer to each of the grave issues of the day may never be formulated. An "evangelical declaration" that articulates the position of all may be impossible. Yet, this situation is, in the final analysis, healthy. Life consists of specific situations, and in each of them one must listen for and obey the voice of God. This fact, however, does not mean that the Christian voice is to be silenced. Rather, believers must continually struggle to understand how Christian theological commitments, which center on God as the sovereign Lord of creation, are to be lived out and applied to life's issues. In the end it is in the specific situations of life that the Christian voice is most effective. Christians are called to minister to specific persons who are struggling to cope with specific situations. Prayer, the gospel word of encouragement, and action on behalf of others is most effective.

The on-going experience of the evangelical movement would indicate, therefore, that the focus on the term such as "inerrancy" is not sufficient. Commitment to the Bible as our authority is foundational, but formulations as to how the Bible is authoritative, although helpful and important, will not lead to unanimity. This side of the eschaton, Christians will not be spared the difficult task of living in faith, groping together as the diverse people of God who even approach the Bible differently. Together they can hear the voice of the Spirit speaking from the pages of the Bible.

Fortunately, many evangelical church people have not been caught up in the wrangling of the theologians in this matter. For them, "inerrancy" often functions in practice not as a precise scientific assertion but merely as a convenient code word for "biblical authority." To uphold inerrancy, then, is often understood as desiring to take the Bible seriously, to struggle with its meaning for life, and to place oneself under the guidance of the Bible. The question of inerrancy in reality is a way of formulating the more germane question, Do you acknowledge biblical authority? In this matter, the evangelical Christian simply follows the Reformation, declaring with Luther that the final court of appeal is the Bible from which alone a compelling case for belief can be developed, and siding with the Westminster Confession that the final authority in the church is the Holy Spirit speaking through the Scriptures.

The Future of the Discussion

The understanding of the ethos of evangelicalism outlined here may serve to offer a vantage point to mention briefly the perceptions of the SBC that evangelicals may have. These perceptions are both positive and negative.

Rightly or wrongly, the SBC is sometimes perceived as provincial and paternalistic. Southern Baptists have been known to copy the programs of various evangelical groups, while remaining reticent to join with others in their programs. Southern Baptists have been seen as being culturally captive, as is evidenced by the presence of a bit of Dixie in every SBC congregation. Southern Baptists have at times displayed what has been interpreted as an elder brother complex: "Everything is bigger and better in the SBC." Or, "Unless the SBC is doing it, it ain't being done." Finally, evangelical theologians, at times, are prone to the impression that their colleagues in the SBC are only interested in publishing for their own theological sake.

Despite these negative impressions, however, many evangelicals readily claim their Southern Baptist brothers and sisters as being "a part of us." This tendency was noted in the mid-1970s by Foy Valentine, who responded with a firm denial: "Southern Baptists are not evangelicals. They want to claim us because we are big and successful and growing every year." However, I would differ with his assessment. Many of us would want to claim the Southern Baptists because we sense we are kindred spirits who share the same basic piety.

The question remains as to how Southern Baptists will view other expressions of the body of Christ, including not only the broader evangelical coalition but also their coreligionists in other Baptist bodies. Pertinent to the decision concerning the relationship that any group forges with other traditions, however, is a dimension that is more crucial than the debate currently central to evangelicalism (the formulation of the commitment to biblical authority), namely, the issue of ecclesiology. In this matter the overarching question is that of the relationship of denominational loyalty and preservation of denominational distinctives and distinctiveness to involvement in a pandenominational coalition of Christians. For Baptists, involvement in the evangelical movement raises above all two issues of theology: the importance of baptism and the nature of church government. These dimensions, I believe, and not the question of inerrancy, must command our attention and shape the discussion in the future.

Conclusion

As a context for some concluding remarks, allow me to interject my own pilgrimage one more time. I was raised in a small Baptist group (56,000 scattered throughout the USA and Canada) whose genesis lies with the various waves of German immigration to the USA and Canada. This group was supported in its infancy by Northern Baptists, Southern Baptists, and even Canadian Baptists.

I was always cognizant of the fact that we were but a small part of a larger body of Christ that moved beyond denominational and political boundaries. I knew, as well, that we needed the resources of the larger group to fulfill the mandate given to us. We used Sunday School materials from Gospel Light, Broadman, David C. Cook, and Scripture Press. We showed films in church from Billy Graham and Moody Bible Institute. We cooperated with Youth for Christ and other youth organizations. Yet all along, in the midst of this cooperation, I saw myself as a Baptist, more specifically, a North American Baptist (NAB).

The NAB Conference never participated in the modernist-fundamentalist controversy. In fact, we have always been somewhat nontheological in orientation. Our concern has been to promote piety, a family spirit, and missions. Therefore, we have never been fundamentalists in the historical sense. We have always been evangelical in orientation (even though we have not joined the National Association of Evangelicals).

As an outworking of my heritage, I cannot claim to be a "card-carrying evangelical" in Marsden's sense. Nevertheless, I am evangelical in spirit, if the spirit of evangelicalism focuses on the vision of what it means to be Christian I outlined earlier. For me, being evangelical can never come at the cost of being Baptist. Rather, it is as a Baptist that I sense my affinity with the evangelical movement, for my piety as a Baptist coalesces with evangelical piety as I understand it and which I see as comprising the heart of evangelicalism.

Southern Baptists now stand at a crossroad in their history. With the move beyond the boundaries of Dixie, the previous glue shows signs of wear. At the same time, the size and wealth God has graciously bestowed on them entails a grave responsibility before God and on behalf of the church as a whole. The changing internal situation and the special responsibility they bear constitute a call to Southern Baptists to raise anew the questions of their relationship to other Christians. Perhaps the events of the last few years are a part of God's way of challenging this great body of the people of God to rethink who they are in relation to the greater reality of the body of Christ.

11

Southern Baptist
——————— Confessions: ———————
Dogmatic Ambiguity

Bill J. Leonard

In a book published in 1983 Baptist professors James E. Tull, E. Glenn Hinson, and James Leo Garrett responded to the question, *Are Southern Baptists "Evangelicals"?* Their answers—yes (Garrett), no (Hinson), maybe (Tull)—provide an insightful analysis to the history of theology in the SBC. Given his particular approach to the source materials, each scholar seems equally convincing, a fact which illustrates the eclectic nature of Southern Baptist theology.[1] That such a question would be asked is evidence that Southern Baptist theology does not lend itself to systematic uniformity. This theological "elasticity" is one of the denomination's greatest strengths and one of its most significant weaknesses.

From the beginning Southern Baptists understood themselves as bound by certain doctrines which were at once distinctly Christian and discernably Baptist. Yet within that general doctrinal framework existed surprising theological diversity, sometimes even contradiction. Religious statements often combined dogma, piety, and rhetoric in such a way as to make theological precision extremely difficult to maintain. This allowed the Convention to incorporate multiple regional and doctrinal traditions—Calvinist, modified Calvinist, Arminian, modified Arminian, fundamentalist, Landmark, social gospel, even liberal—without major schism. Establishing a consensus as to what "all Southern Baptists believe" was a formidable task, particularly the more precise such definitions became. This theological diversity was often a matter of some public pride for the individualistic Baptists. Journalists and preachers alike often joked that to put four Southern Baptists in a room meant at least

---

[1] James Leo Garrett, Jr., E. Glenn Hinson, and James E. Tull, *Are Southern Baptists "Evangelicals"?* (Macon, GA: Mercer, 1983).

163

five opinions on a given subject. All would agree, however, on the need to win souls and send out missionaries in some form or another. Such diversity also meant that the entire Convention was always at the mercy of those restless subgroups—Landmarkers, fundamentalists, inerrantists, premillennialists, or others—who claimed a divine mandate to impose their specific doctrinal definitions on the entire convention.

Theology was a primary factor in most of the controversies that Southern Baptists confronted throughout their history. Given the fragile coalition around which the SBC was formed, however, theological debate was inseparable from denominational control and influence. No Southern Baptist controversy is ever completely theological or political. Ideology and politics were present from the first. The SBC itself incorporated a wide range of theological traditions within its denominational organization. Most early Southern Baptist churches maintained a strong appreciation for the Reformed theology, yet Regular Baptist Calvinism was modified significantly by Separate Baptist revivalism. Indeed, revivalism in the SBC, as in many evangelical denominations, served to "Arminianize" the churches toward greater emphasis on free will, individual choice, and salvation for "whosoever will believe." Those Southern Baptists who mourn the decline of Reformed theology in SBC life might well blame evangelists, revivals, and statisticians—not neo-orthodox liberals—for the Arminian orientation of popular theology.

Arminianism, though publicly renounced in classrooms and pulpits throughout the Convention, particularly its doctrine of falling from grace, has had far greater popular impact on SBC evangelism than most analysts admit. Those who describe Southern Baptists as modified Calvinists could just as easily classify them as modified Arminians so strong is the emphasis on free will and general atonement. The old acronym TULIP (Total depravity, Unconditional election, Limited atonement, Irresistible grace, Perseverance of the saints) is used to identify Calvinists and four-point Arminians. Retaining perseverance of the saints and rejecting falling from grace, they otherwise reflect Arminian understanding of election, atonement, and free will.

Likewise, Landmarkism, though unsuccessful in imposing its successionist ecclesiology on the entire denomination, remained a powerful influence in the SBC. Varying degrees of social and theological liberalism were also evident in support for such issues as the social gospel, the Civil Rights Movement, peace movements, Christian feminism, and biblical criticism.[2] Southern Baptist "liberals," however, often seem conservative

---

[2] John Lee Eighmy, *Churches in Cultural Captivity* (Knoxville: University of Tennessee Press, 1976), 57-80, 124-30, 147-50; and David Whitlock, *Southern Baptists and Southern Culture: Three Visions of a Christian America* (Ph.D. diss., 1988), The Southern Baptist Theological Seminary.

when compared to liberals outside the denomination. In spite of their apparent cultural and theological homogeneity, Southern Baptists demonstrated surprising diversity of thought and practice. Nowhere is that more evident than in the way Southern Baptists used confessions of faith.

Since 1845 the Southern Baptist Convention has approved only three documents delineating specific theological positions affirmed by the denomination and its churches. The first doctrinal statement was the Abstract of Principles, approved in 1859, not for the entire Convention, but as a guide for faculty members at The Southern Baptist Theological Seminary. The other two statements are contained in *The Baptist Faith and Message*, the denomination's official confession of faith, ratified in 1925 and revised in 1963. These documents place Southern Baptists solidly within the Baptist tradition. They are grounded in two earlier Baptist documents, The Philadelphia Confession of 1742, and the New Hampshire Confession of 1833. They contain statements on Holy Scripture, Trinity, church, ordinances, salvation, baptism, judgment, and Christian ethics. The confessions are specific enough to identify the SBC as a theologically conservative, distinctly Baptist denomination. They are general enough to allow for a variety of diverse interpretations among the autonomous congregations that compose the Convention. No doubt the early Convention builders took some unspoken theological consensus for granted. They also hesitated to define dogma too narrowly lest they alienate large segments of the constituency, thereby increasing the possibility of fragmentation or schism.

The existence of varied theological and regional traditions in SBC life illustrates the great diversity in the Convention from the very beginning. In surveying this diversity, Walter Shurden concluded that "the synthesis of the convention was missionary, not doctrinal, in nature."[3] Given his approach to the issue, Shurden's thesis was an appropriate method for understanding the SBC's unity in diversity. Yet there is another way of approaching the question of synthesis; that is, Southern Baptists have perceived themselves as doctrinally united and theologically homogeneous. In the minds of most Southern Baptists, the Convention's "synthesis" was both missionary and doctrinal. In popular perception, the denomination was united around the great theological truths of the Baptist/biblical tradition. How was it possible for so diverse a constituency composed of so many traditions to perceive themselves as

---

[3] Walter B. Shurden, "Southern Baptist Responses to their Confessional Statements," *Review and Expositor*, 76 (Winter 1979), 2, 82.

doctrinally unified? One explanation is found in an often overlooked article written in 1874 by James P. Boyce, faculty member and first president of The Southern Baptist Theological Seminary.

Boyce wrote in response to an editorial published in *The Baptist* (Tennessee) which objected to the fact that certain ideas promoted at the seminary contradicted doctrinal positions advocated by "four or five state (Baptist) conventions."[4] The writer, a Landmarker, insisted that Southern Baptists should not be asked to support professors whose doctrines were contrary to those preached in Baptist churches. He concluded that the seminary was hopelessly adrift from its theological moorings, "too far removed from the people to ever recover from its embarrassment."[5]

Boyce responded by reminding readers that every seminary professor was required to sign a doctrinal statement, or Abstract of Principles, approved in 1859. They were to teach "in accordance with and not contrary to" the document. He noted that neither the Philadelphia (1742) nor New Hampshire Baptist Confessions of Faith (1833) were used exclusively in preparing the Abstract since various factions of the Convention objected to articles within each of those early Baptist documents. As the Convention sought to develop a doctrinal statement for its seminary, three basic principles were followed. First, it was to provide a clear expression of the "fundamental doctrines of grace." That is, it would incorporate the great evangelical doctrines of the Christian faith. Second, the Abstract should delineate those basic principles which were "universally prevalent" among the people called Baptists. The seminary was identifiably Baptist in its distinctive doctrines. Third, Boyce concluded, "upon no point, upon which the denomination is divided, should the Convention, and through it the Seminary, take a position."[6] Boyce, a Calvinist, recognized that there were differences among nineteenth-century Southern Baptists which should not be allowed to undermine denominational unity.

As it was with the seminary, so it was with the denomination as a whole. Clearly, Southern Baptists understood themselves in terms of both a missionary and doctrinal identity. Yet the doctrines were articulated in such a way as to make room for those churches that reflected a variety of diverse theological traditions. Each could believe that their way was the Baptist way. There was less a synthesis than a grand compromise based on an unspoken agreement that the Convention would resist all attempts to define basic doctrines in ways that excluded one tradition or another,

---

[4] Elder M. P. Lowery, *The Baptist* (February 18, 1874).

[5] Ibid.

[6] James P. Boyce, "Two Objections to the Seminary Part V," *Western Recorder* (June 20, 1874).

thereby destroying denominational unity and undermining the missionary imperative. They were willing to maintain a kind of dogmatic ambiguity. Doctrinal positions were articulated in terms general enough to unite as many Southern Baptists as possible in fulfilling the missionary task.

Boyce refused to make questions of double predestination, alien immersion, or closed communion a test of fellowship at the seminary. He did, however, accept the resignation of Professor Crawford Toy, concluding that Toy's views on Scripture were outside the bounds of the Abstract. How Boyce would respond to contemporary doctrinal debates in the SBC is at best speculative. His vision of the way in which the seminary would respond to Convention divisions does inform the denominationalizing process.

Modifications in theology continued in Southern Baptist denominational life. When the convention finally did approve an official doctrinal statement—*The Baptist Faith and Message* (1925)—it chose to follow the more moderate New Hampshire Confession over the more explicitly Calvinist Philadelphia Confession. This approach to dogma represents one of the major strengths of the SBC in its efforts to avoid schism. It permitted those who affirmed certain "universally prevalent" Baptist beliefs to unite in missionary action. It allowed room for a variety of interpretations and traditions among churches and individuals who considered themselves Baptists, permitting a kind of dogmatic ambiguity in confessional matters. These diverse approaches helped expand Southern Baptist ministries and numbers. It also forced church leaders to look to denominational programs to provide a source of uniformity and solidarity rather than elaborate doctrinal conformity among Southern Baptist people and churches.

The grand compromise was also the denomination's weakness. It meant that the SBC always lived on the edge of controversy and potential schism as representatives of one particular theological viewpoint sought to impose their interpretation on the entire body. That explains why the history of the denomination is characterized by unending controversy and political struggle. Denominationalism, therefore, not only served to provide a sense of unity and identity; it was also a means of dealing with efforts to narrow doctrine and divide the Convention. Denominationalists learned how to allow dissident groups enough power or doctrinal specificity to keep them within the Convention but not enough power or doctrinal conformity to impinge on the beliefs and practices of other traditions present in the SBC. Ideologues were not permitted to distract the Convention from its larger programmatic agenda. Such a procedure kept the SBC theologically conservative and historically Baptist while allowing for surprising diversity in the churches. A survey of the Abstract of Principles and *The Baptist Faith and Message* illustrates that dogmatic ambiguity. The Abstract contains twenty articles which reflect basic Christian and Baptist beliefs, each strongly shaped by Reformed theology. With surprising consistency, the articles avoid specific theories or potentially divisive issues.

Article I asserts that the Scriptures "are given by inspiration of God, and are the only sufficient, certain and authoritative rule of all saving knowledge, faith and obedience." It affirms the authority of Scripture but offers no specific theory of biblical inspiration.[7] Article VII, "The Mediator," acknowledges Christ's role as "mediator between God and man" but does not delineate a particular theory of atonement—ransom, substitution, federal, or example.[8] Article XIV on the church declares that Christ is "Head of the Church" but gives no theory of ecclesiology—although nineteenth-century Landmarkers would have desired a more specific definition.[9] Article XVI on the Lord's Supper declares that "it is in no sense a sacrifice," but "is designed to commemorate" Christ's death. Yet the article does not require acquiescence to an open or closed communion policy. Likewise, the final article (XX) on "The Judgment" acknowledges that God will ultimately "judge the world by Jesus Christ," but no theory of eschatology—premillennial, postmillennial, or amillennial—is set forth.[10] Is this because nineteenth-century Southern Baptists took it for granted that they held the same specific interpretations of these general dogmas? Hardly. The Abstract illustrates James P. Boyce's idea that "upon no point, upon which the denomination is divided, should the Convention, and through it the Seminary, take a position."[11]

The denomination's official confession, *The Baptist Faith and Message*, was a response to specific theological controversies in the Convention. The first confession was a reaction to the fundamentalist/modernist debate which swept American Protestantism in the 1920s. The later revision occurred as a result of a controversy involving seminary professor Ralph Elliott's book on Genesis and the use of higher criticism in biblical studies. Though born of controversy, these documents also indicate the effort of Southern Baptists to define doctrine in terms general enough to incorporate diverse segments of the Convention. Arti-

---

7 *Catalog*, 1987-89, The Southern Baptist Theological Seminary, 2.

8 Ibid.

9 Ibid.

10 Ibid., 3.

11 Boyce, "Two Objections to the Seminary," 2.

cle I states that Holy Scripture is "without any mixture of error, for its matter," a phrase taken directly from the New Hampshire Confession.

The interpretation of that phrase lies at the heart of the current debate over biblical inerrancy. Inerrantists believe that the statement requires adherence to the doctrine of inerrancy. They view it as an affirmation that Scripture is without error in all "matter(s)" whether doctrine, history, theology, or science. Noninerrantists, however, suggest that the phrase speaks to the trustworthiness and absolute authoritative nature of the Bible in "matter(s)" of faith—the essential issue Scripture addresses. In addition, persons in each of the two camps often disagree among themselves as to the specific meaning of *inerrancy* or *authority*. Numerous studies have explored that debate and its implications.[12] The important issue here involves the way in which contemporary Southern Baptists seek to define what seems a less specific statement than many currently desire. It is also evident that both sides in the current debate adhere to a high view of Scripture as an authoritative guide for the church and the individual.

The Baptist Faith and Message also illustrates the influence of modified Calvinism/Arminianism on the SBC. Between the approval of the Abstract of Principles in 1859 and *The Baptist Faith and Message* in 1925, considerable modification in Reformed theology occurred. In fact, the articles on election in the Abstract and *The Baptist Faith and Message* reflect considerable diversity, if not downright contradiction.

Concerning the doctrine of election, the Abstract states: "Election is God's eternal choice of some persons unto everlasting life—not because of foreseen merit in them, but of His mere mercy in Christ—in consequence of which choice they are called, justified and glorified."[13] The words "God's eternal choice of some persons" clearly indicate the influence of the Reformed doctrine of single predestination. *The Baptist Faith and Message*, on the other hand, taken almost verbatim from the earlier New Hampshire Confession, states that "Election is the gracious purpose of God, according to which He regenerates, sanctifies, and glorifies sinners. It is consistent with the free agency of man, and comprehends all the means in connection with the end. It is a glorious display of

---

[12] Robison B. James, ed., *The Unfettered Word* (Waco: Word Books, 1987); Russ Bush and Tom Nettles, *Baptists and the Bible* (Chicago: Moody Press, 1980); Duane A. Garrett and Richard R. Melick, Jr., ed., *Authority and Interpretation* (Grand Rapids: Baker Book House, 1987); Gordon James, *Inerrancy and the Southern Baptist Convention* (Dallas: Southern Heritage Press, 1986) and Joe Edward Barnhart, *The Southern Baptist Holy War* (Austin: Texas Monthly Press, 1986).

[13] *Catalog*, 1987-89, The Southern Baptist Theological Seminary, 12.

God's sovereign goodness . . ."[14] The idea of "free agency" in human beings is less evident in the more Calvinist Abstract. While prevailing popular interpretation no doubt understands election within the context of the general atonement, the Convention has long included many persons who hold varying opinions—Calvinist, modified Calvinist, Arminian—regarding the doctrine.

The use of these confessions also demonstrates the determination of denominational leaders to avoid schism over doctrine whenever possible. When theological disputes threatened denominational unity, the Convention acted, usually leaning toward the right. Yet this rightward tilt alleviated enough pressure to allow the denomination to drift back toward the "conservative middle" without a wholesale purge or debilitating schism. This could not last forever, however. Ultimately, confessions became increasingly creedal.

"Baptists are not a creedal people," Southern Baptist patriarch Herschel Hobbs once wrote.[15] A cursory look at Baptist history might lead one to respond, "Well, sort of." During the twentieth century, Southern Baptists have moved steadily, if not reluctantly, toward creedalism, all the time insisting that it was not really happening. They often attempt to clarify their growing use of doctrinal statements with the phrase, "confessional, not creedal." In one sense, this was an appropriate qualification. In another, such a distinction was essentially academic.

Confessions of faith, originally used by denominationalists to preserve unity and avoid schism, have become a source of division as groups debate the definition of specific dogmas. When cultural and denominational ties were intact, intricate doctrinal definitions were less essential. As those sources of stability collapsed, many Southern Baptists turned to dogma to reinforce diminishing identity, offer security, and lay claim to orthodoxy. Confessions also became tools for wielding power and provided a means for resolving negative or potentially negative relationships. The more corporate the relationship, the more necessary the creed.

From their beginnings in the seventeenth century Baptist groups have not hesitated to use confessions of faith to delineate basic doctrines, provide a source of unity, and establish a basis for membership.

---

[14] "Baptist Faith and Message," in Bill J. Leonard, *Baptist Ideals: Distinctives of our Faith* (Nashville: The Sunday School Board of the Southern Baptist Convention, 1988), 53.

[15] Herschel Hobbs, "Southern Baptists and Confessionalism: A Comparison of the Origins and Contents of the 1925 and 1963 Confessions," *Review and Expositor* 76 (Winter 1979), 55.

English Baptists, both General (Arminian) and Particular (Calvinist), made extensive use of confessions. William Estep suggests that these documents were confessional but not creedal. Creeds he defines as:

> authoritative and often viewed as final, unalterable, and binding statements of faith . . . For Baptists, confessions of faith have never constituted ultimate authority. All major confessions from 1610 to 1963 were considered abstracts of biblical truth as the group formulating the confession perceived it. These confessions have often been uneven and incomplete expressions of the Christian faith. Thus the nature of a particular confession was largely shaped by the purpose for which it was conceived at the time.[16]

Confessions had a derivative authority drawn from Scripture and the community of faith. William Lumpkin, one of the best-known authorities on Baptist confessionalism, notes that most seventeenth-century Protestant groups in Europe and Britain identified themselves through the publication of confessions of faith. Baptist confessions were distinctive in four specific areas. First, their ecclesiology placed emphasis on local communities of believers. Second, they defined the ordinances of baptism and the Lord's Supper in identifiably Baptist ways. Third, they gave strong emphasis to evangelism and missions. Fourth, they stressed freedom of conscience and the separation of church and state. He writes, "There was little fear of the confessions' dominating the groups owning them and even less of their usurping the place of the scriptures."[17] Confessions were never placed above or even alongside biblical authority.

Among Southern Baptists, however, a strong anticreedal, even anticonfessional, sentiment flourished from the beginning. The organizers of the SBC declared in 1845 that "We have constructed for our basis no new creed; acting in this matter upon a Baptist aversion to all creeds but the Bible."[18] This aversion to creedalism was due to several factors. Separate Baptists, strong in the South, opposed confessions as detrimental to personal religious experience. They feared that mental assent to dogma would undermine both radical conversion and biblical authority. The Campbellite movement of the mid-nineteenth century was militantly anticonfessional, rejecting creeds as "authoritative symbols" which

---

[16] William R. Estep, "Baptists and Authority: The Bible, Confessions and Conscience in the Development of Baptist Identity," *Review and Expositor* 84 (1987), 600-601.

[17] William L. Lumpkin, "The Nature and Authority of Baptist Confessions of Faith," *Review and Expositor* 76 (Winter 1979), 24.

[18] *Annual*, SBC, 1845, p. 19; and Walter B. Shurden, "Southern Baptist Responses to their Confessional Statements," *Review and Expositor* 76 (Winter 1979), 69.

threatened biblical faith. Baptists, in a competitive struggle with Disciples, did not want to be cast as creedalists.[19]

When the fundamentalist/modernist controversy finally forced the SBC to produce its first official confession of faith in 1925, the document was introduced with an elaborate disclaimer, qualifying the way in which such a confession was to be used. Southern Baptists are the only Baptist denomination to include such a qualification as a guide for interpreting confessions. These statements concluded that confessions:

> (1) Constitute a consensus of opinion of some Baptist body, large or small, for the general instruction and guidance of our own people and others concerning those articles of the Christian faith which are most surely held among us. They are not intended to add anything to the simple conditions of salvation revealed in the New Testament . . .
>
> (2) That we do not regard them as complete statements of our faith, having any quality of finality or infallibility. As in the past so in the future Baptists should hold themselves free to revise their statements as may seem to them wise and expedient at any time.
>
> (3) That any group of Baptists, large or small, have the inherent right to draw up for themselves and publish to the world a confession of their faith whenever they think it advisable to do so.
>
> (4) That the sole authority for faith and practice among Baptists is the Scriptures of the Old and New Testaments. Confessions are only guides in interpretation, having no authority over the conscience.
>
> (5) That they are statements of religious convictions, drawn from the Scriptures, and are not to be used to hamper freedom of thought or investigation in other realms of life.[20]

These disclaimers support the prevailing idea that Southern Baptists were always confessional but not creedal. Yet they also illustrate once again the Southern Baptist genius for compromise. The 1925 *The Baptist Faith and Message*, plus its introductory disclaimer, satisfied those who wished to define basic Southern Baptist dogma while placating those who were wary of creedal entanglements. Again, Southern Baptists sought to have it both ways, to be creedal and noncreedal at the same time, temporarily forestalling a decision on the use and meaning of confessions. They approved a basic and rather general statement of Baptist beliefs but added an escape clause. Those who differed with the statements on the basis of conscience might still remain Southern Baptists.

Perhaps it was less that denominationalists feared creeds than that they wanted to retain unity among those both for or against the use of

---

[19] Lumpkin, "The Nature and Authority of Baptist Confessions of Faith," 25.
[20] Ibid., 26.

confessions in Baptist life. Once a confession was written down and officially approved, however, the scene was set for its more arbitrary use in defining doctrinal parameters of the SBC. The line between a confession and a creed is thin indeed. In fact, Southern Baptists were naive in their effort to distinguish between confessionalism and creedalism. Since 1979 it has become a particularly academic distinction.

William Lumpkin concludes that "the fear of creeds is, largely, an irrational fear," and that all religious traditions subscribe to creeds—a consensus of belief—written or not.[21] Lumpkin himself uses the terms creed and confession interchangeably to refer to documents which "state facts," but do not necessarily provide interpretation of facts.[22] He believes these confessions/creeds were "recommendations" extended to churches and individuals but "never as decrees."[23]

In the current denominational controversy, many conservative leaders would agree with Lumpkins' idea that creeds are inevitably theological guides for every religious group. They disagree as to the application of such statements to the constituency. Since 1979 they have gone to great lengths to ensure that the statement on Holy Scripture included in *The Baptist Faith and Message*—without any mixture of error, for its matter—be interpreted in light of the doctrine of biblical inerrancy. Others have sought to establish their own list of nonnegotiables as the basis for Southern Baptist theological unity. Still others have attempted to clarify the meaning of *The Baptist Faith and Message* by using other creedal documents such as the Chicago Statement on Inerrancy, a document with no official relationship to the SBC but which is being promoted as a guide for faculties at denominational seminaries.

Actions taken at The Southern Baptist Theological Seminary, Louisville, Kentucky, illustrate the way in which selective creedalism is spreading throughout the denomination. Since 1859 faculty members have been required to sign the Abstract of Principles as a prerequisite for teaching at the school. As noted earlier, they are required to teach "in accordance with, and not contrary to" the articles. With the conservative resurgence, however, new documents have been unofficially added to the list of confessional guides. New faculty members are asked to concur with the statements of *The Baptist Faith and Message* although they are not asked to sign the document. In 1988 the faculty of the school unanimously approved "A Resolution of Recommitment and Renewal" by which they renewed commitment to "our cherished Baptist heritage"

---

[21] Lumpkin, 26.
[22] Ibid.
[23] Ibid., 26-27.

and the school's Abstract of Principles. They also renewed commitment to the "seminary president's intention to work toward reconciliation of the conflict in the convention," pleading faithful cooperation in the "action plan for reconciliation."[24] New faculty members report that the Chicago Statement was discussed as part of their trustee interview prior to being hired by the seminary. The increase in confessional qualifiers illustrates the changing nature of creedalism in the SBC.

These developments support Walter Shurden's contention that Southern Baptist creedalism has increased steadily throughout the twentieth century as both "strict-confessionalists" (fundamentalists) and "mainstream denominationalists" (moderates) have "unwittingly" (or perhaps 'wittingly'!) given prominence to the Confession by indirectly using it as a call for denominational unity."[25] In Shurden's view, confessionalism and centralization combined to make Southern Baptists a creedal denomination. He cites a prophetic observation made by historian William W. Barnes regarding the 1925 confession. Barnes wrote:

> The reception that creed has received, or perhaps one should say, has not received, seems to suggest that Southern Baptists are not yet ready for doctrinal centralization, but the first step has been taken. It may be another century, but if and when the doctrinal question again arises, succeeding generations can point to 1925 and say that the Southern Baptist Convention, having once adopted a creed, can do so again. Perhaps by that time other centralizing forces will have been developed and the convention may have the means and the method of compelling congregations to take notice of the creed adopted.[26]

Barnes recognized that once a confession was written its use would prove divisive. If Southern Baptists ever really were a noncreedal people, they are not any longer.

Conclusions are tentative at best. First, theology has been an important concern of Southern Baptists from the beginning of the Convention. Theological issues were at the heart of most Convention controversies throughout its history.

Second, basic theological positions regarding the great doctrines of the church were interpreted from a distinctly Baptist perspective. Southern Baptists were aware of theological boundaries from the time the Convention was founded.

---

[24] "A Resolution of Recommitment and Renewal," The Southern Baptist Theological Seminary, 1988.

[25] Shurden, "Southern Baptist Responses to their Confessional Statements," 82.

[26] Shurden, "The Problem of Authority in the Southern Baptist Convention," 230.

Third, doctrines were defined in terms broad enough to encompass the diverse theological traditions and subgroups which composed the SBC. Until 1979 attempts to define dogma in ways that would alienate large segments of the constituency were resisted by the Convention with amazing success.

Fourth, certain Baptist distinctives were held in an uneasy tension. Individual distinctives existed in tension with other ideals. For years denominationalists sought to maintain a balance that fostered compromise and inhibited the possibility of schism.

Fifth, within this delicate balance existed a wide variety of theological attitudes and interpretations with roots in Calvinist, modified Calvinist, modified Arminian, Arminian, Landmarkers, Fundamentalist, neo-orthodox, evangelical, charismatic, and social gospel interpretations of Christianity.

Recent efforts have narrowed the theological parameters of the SBC considerably and upset the delicate balance which the denomination struggled, with amazing success, to maintain. By 1990 the real question was: How narrowly can the denomination define itself and still remain intact?

In what may be the latter days of the Southern Baptist Convention, therefore, permit me to make a futile and frivolous proposal which began a year ago at the Futsukaichi Baptist Church in Fukuoka, Japan. The church meets in a rented room over a bar—a good place for a church, I think. Forty to sixty people crowd into that room each Sunday and squeeze around an organ, a piano, and a koto, the thirteen string traditional Japanese harp. In the middle of worship everybody stands and sings the Apostles' Creed (in Japanese, of course). That experience was as close to the early church as I have ever felt. Hearing that, I decided this: Christians should never sign a creed they cannot sing. Creeds, like faith, must begin in the heart, not the head. If we must have a creed—and it appears we must—we should use the Apostles' Creed, something we can confess at worship in the community of faith. The Southern Baptist Convention is collapsing all around us. Perhaps the people who survive are those who can confess toward Golgotha:

> I believe in God the Father Almighty, Maker of Heaven and earth; and in Jesus Christ His only Son our Lord; who was conceived by the Holy Spirit, born of the Virgin Mary, suffered under Pontius Pilate, was crucified, dead and buried; he descended into hell; the third day he rose again from the dead; he ascended into heaven, and sitteth on the right hand of God the Father Almighty; from thence he shall come to judge the quick and the dead.

> I believe in the Holy Spirit; the holy Catholic church; the communion of saints; the forgiveness of sins; the resurrection of the body; and the life everlasting. Amen.

12

Southern Baptists

——————— & ———————

American Evangelicals:
A Common Salvation?

Daniel L. Akin

Introduction

"This chapter is obviously unnecessary," may well be the reaction of most readers. The average evangelical and the mainstream Southern Baptist would quickly and without hesitation affirm, "Why of course we hold to and teach a common salvation." Some might even argue that the two groups are identical in their theology of salvation, if not also in their methodology of evangelism. As we move into the 1990s and toward a new millennium, is this actually the case? Certainly dissenting voices are raised against the general consensus, but their numbers appear small.[1] Perhaps we have assumed a commonality of soteriology that on closer inspection will prove to be a reality. However, a closer look might reveal, if not key theological differences, at least significant methodological and ecclesiological differences.

There are several ways to approach our particular question, make analyses, and draw conclusions. One is to investigate various representatives of American evangelicals and Southern Baptists. This approach is problematic due to (1) space constraints in this volume, and (2) determining which particular individuals and how many to consider. A second approach and one I consider more profitable and representative is a confessional analysis. Confessions are the general consensus of a particular body, large or small, and go beyond the beliefs of particular theologians to include or reflect the people in the pews as well. The report of the

———————————

[1] See James L. Garrett, E. Glenn Hinson, and James E. Tull, *Are Southern Baptists "Evangelical"?* (Macon, GA: Mercer, 1983).

committee on *The Baptist Faith and Message* said in 1963 that confessions:

> constitute a consensus of opinion of some Baptist body, large or small, for the general instruction and guidance of our own people and others concerning those articles of the Christian faith which are most surely held among us.[2]

The committee goes on to affirm that such confessions are not final or infallible statements. They are guides for interpretation, statements of spiritual conviction drawn from the Scripture, capable of revision, and not to be used to infringe upon liberty of conscience in religious matters.[3]

I propose to inspect and analyze the most recent confessions of American evangelicals and Southern Baptists. For Southern Baptists this is the *1963 Baptist Faith and Message*. For American evangelicals I will examine the recent *Evangelical Affirmations* statement of 1989.[4] Evangelicals convened at Trinity Evangelical Divinity School on May 14-17, 1989, and though some evangelicals attended from outside the United States, the conference was dominated by Americans. The statements on salvation by both will be investigated, interpreted, and then compared. Our observations will then be summarized in a concluding statement.

1963 Baptist Faith and Message

Built upon the *1925 Baptist Faith and Message*, that was based upon the 1833 *New Hampshire Confession*, the 1963 statement contains sections on the Scriptures, God, humankind, salvation, God's purpose of grace and the church, baptism and the Lord's Supper, the Lord's day, the Kingdom, last things, evangelism, and missions. Scripture appears at the end of each article to support the biblical nature of the statements.

Article IV on salvation has an introductory paragraph that is expanded into more detailed statements on regeneration, sanctification, and glorification. It is worthwhile to reprint the statement in full.

---

[2] *1963 Baptist Faith and Message*, 4. Henceforth referred to as *BFM*.

[3] Ibid., 4-5.

[4] The final statement of the conference was actually formulated by a committee after the conference had dismissed. Though some modifications were made, the statement overall is reflective of the view of the Conference as a whole and of contemporary evangelicals. We will refer to the *Evangelical Affirmations statement as E.A.*

IV. SALVATION

Salvation involves the redemption of the whole man, and is offered freely to all who accept Jesus Christ as Lord and Saviour, who by His own blood obtained eternal redemption for the believer. In its broadest sense salvation includes regeneration, sanctification, and glorification.

A. Regeneration, or the new birth, is a work of God's grace whereby believers become new creatures in Christ Jesus. It is a change of heart wrought by the Holy Spirit through conviction of sin, to which the sinner responds in repentance toward God and faith in the Lord Jesus Christ.

Repentance and faith are inseparable experiences of grace. Repentance is a genuine turning from sin toward God. Faith is the acceptance of Jesus Christ and commitment of the entire personality to Him as Lord and Saviour. Justification is God's gracious and full acquittal upon principles of His righteousness of all sinners who repent and believe in Christ. Justification brings the believer into a relationship of peace and favor with God.

B. Sanctification is the experience, beginning in regeneration, by which the believer is set apart to God's purposes, and is enabled to progress toward moral and spiritual perfection through the presence and power of the Holy Spirit dwelling in him. Growth in grace should continue throughout the regenerate person's life.

C. Glorification is the culmination of salvation and is the final blessed and abiding state of the redeemed.

Gen. 3:15; Ex. 3:14-17; 6:2-8; Matt. 1:21; 4:17; 16:21-26; 27:22-28:6; Luke 1:68-69; 2:28-32; John 1:11-14, 29; 3:3-21, 36; 5:24; 10:9, 28-29; 15:1-16; 17:17; Acts 2:21; 4:12; 15:11; 16:30-31; 17:30-31; 20:32; Rom. 1:16-18; 2:4; 3:23-25; 4:3 ff.; 5:8-10; 6:1-23; 8:1-18, 29-39; 10:9-10, 13; 13:11-14; 1 Cor. 1:18, 30; 6:19-20; 15:10; 2 Cor. 5:17-20; Gal. 2:20; 3:13; 5:22-25; 6:15; Eph. 1:7; 2:8-22; 4:11-16; Phil. 2:12-13; Col. 1:9-22; 3:1 ff.; 1 Thess. 5:23-24; 2 Tim. 1:12; Titus 2:11-14; Heb. 2:1-3; 5:8-9; 9:24-28; 11:1-12:8, 14; James 2:14-26; 1 Peter 1:2-23; 1 John 1:6-2:11; Rev. 3:20; 21:1-22:5.

The statement is permeated by biblical terms and phraseology. The work of Christ is briefly summarized in terms of "eternal redemption," being more fully expanded in article II, section B on "God the Son." People are said to come into a right relationship with God by accepting Jesus Christ as Lord and Savior, which is further clarified as consisting of repentance and faith. Both are identified as works of grace. Repentance is defined as "a genuine turning from sin toward God." Faith is explained as "the acceptance of Jesus Christ and commitment of the entire personality to Him as Lord and Saviour." Christ can be both Lord and Saviour because He is the eternal Son of God: He was incarnate, born of a virgin, lived without sin, and made provision for the redemption of humankind from sin through His death and resurrection (article II). When people exercise repentance and faith, they are justified before God, entering into "a relationship of peace and favor with God."

Article V on "God's Purpose of Grace" further expounds the doctrine of salvation. Its importance lies in emphases on God's sovereignty and grace and humanity's perseverance in Christ through the sanctifying work of the Holy Spirit of God. The statement reads as follows:

V. GOD'S PURPOSE OF GRACE

Election is the gracious purpose of God, according to which He regenerates, sanctifies, and glorifies sinners. It is consistent with the free agency of man, and comprehends all the means in connection with the end. It is a glorious display of God's sovereign goodness, and is infinitely wise, holy, and unchangeable. It excludes boasting and promotes humility.

All true believers endure to the end. Those whom God has accepted in Christ, and sanctified by His Spirit, will never fall away from the state of grace, but shall persevere to the end. Believers may fall into sin through neglect and temptation, whereby they grieve the Spirit, impair their graces and comforts, bring reproach on the cause of Christ, and temporal judgments on themselves, yet they shall be kept by the power of God through faith unto salvation.

Gen. 12:1-3; Ex. 19:5-8; 1 Sam. 8:4-7, 19-22; Isa. 5:1-7; Jer. 31:31 ff.; Matt. 16:18-19; 21:28-45; 24:22, 31; 25:34; Luke 1:68-79; 2:20-32; 19:41-44; 24:44-48; John 1:12-14; 3:16; 5:24; 6:44-45, 65; 10:27-29; 15:16; 17:6, 12, 17-18; Acts 20:32; Rom. 5:9-10; 8:28-39,10:12-15; 11:5-7, 26-36; 1 Cor. 1:1-2; 15:24-28; Eph. 1:4-23; 2:1-10; 3:1-11; Col. 1:12-14; 2 Thess. 2:13-14; 2 Tim. 1:12; 2:10, 19; Heb. 11:39-12:2; 1 Peter 1:2-5, 13; 2:4-10, 1 John 1:7-9; 2:19; 3:2.

This statement is in some sense so general that it is capable of being affirmed by hyper-Calvinist, modified Calvinist, and even those closer to, but not identified with, Arminianism or semi-Pelagianism. The emphasis on the biblical doctrine of perseverance or, as it is more popularly called, "the security of the believer," makes this clear. Though a few Southern Baptists have deviated from the doctrine of the security of the believer,[5] most Southern Baptists affirm it as a cherished and rightly honored truth of Scripture.

Though often discussed under the category of ecclesiology, the ordinances of baptism and the Lord's Supper do appear mysteriously in the arena of soteriology in the writings of some evangelicals. For Southern Baptists, any appearance of the ordinances is always welcome, but they are clearly out of place in the doctrine of salvation. The 1963 *BFM* in article VII says, "Christian baptism is the immersion of a *believer*. . . . It is an *act of obedience symbolizing* the believer's faith. . . . It is a *testimony to his faith* . . ." With reference to the Lord's Supper it states "The Lord's Supper is a *symbolic act* of obedience whereby members of the church, . . . *memorialize* the death of the Redeemer and anticipate His second coming" (emphasis mine). There is nothing of paedo-baptism, nothing of a salvific note in either ordinance.

Southern Baptists affirm salvation to be *sola gratia* and *sola fide*. As Herschel Hobbs simply but accurately says, "Salvation is by grace through faith in Jesus Christ. When man would not, could not be saved by the law, God provided salvation by grace through faith."[6] Indeed article III states that men "transgressed the command of God, . . . and are under condemnation. Only the grace of God can bring man into His holy fellowship and enable man to fulfill the creative purpose of God."

One last area should be noted before examining the *Evangelical Affirmations* statement. Article X deals with last things. The statement clearly denies two popular theological concepts which are related but not identical in our day: universalism and annihilationism. The statement contains the affirmation:

> Christ will judge all men in righteousness. The unrighteous will be *consigned to Hell*, the *place of everlasting punishment*. The righteous in their resurrected and glorified bodies will receive their reward and will dwell forever in Heaven with the Lord. (Emphasis mine.)

Hell as a literal place of conscious punishment is the only meaning a natural reading of the statement will allow. Though we do not rejoice in such a destiny for anyone, Southern Baptists have in all their confessions always adopted this understanding of eschatological judgment.

---

[5] For example, see Dale Moody, *The Word of Truth* (Grand Rapids: Eerdmans, 1981).

[6] Herschel Hobbs, *The Baptist Faith and Message* (Nashville: Convention Press, 1971), 58.

Evangelical Affirmations Statement of 1989

Evangelicals of varied denominations converged on Chicago in May 1989 to reaffirm and express essentials of the evangelical faith in the face of numerous challenges and charges from modern secularism, Eastern pantheism, practical agnosticism, and religious indiscretions.[7] With respect to soteriology the conference affirmed the following in its published statement that may be listed as follows:

(1) The gospel is the good news that the Son of God became incarnate "to offer himself for sinners and to give them everlasting life."

(2) Jesus Christ is fully God and fully man.

(3) "The incarnation, substitutionary death and bodily resurrection of Jesus Christ are essential to the gospel. Through these events a *gracious God* has acted in *time and history* to reach out to humanity and save *all who believe in Him*" (emphasis mine).

(4) "Without Christ and the biblical gospel, sinful humanity is without salvation . . . Any 'gospel' without the Christ of the Bible cannot be the saving gospel and leaves sinners estranged from God and under his wrath."

(5) "As a result of the fall of the race into sin, human beings must be born again to new life in Christ. They can be pardoned and redeemed by faith in Christ alone."

(6) "Faith and practice go hand in hand. Genuine faith and a changed heart will result in a changed life evidenced by good works."

(7) "We affirm that only through the work of Christ can any person be saved and be resurrected to live with God forever. Unbelievers will be *separated eternally* from God. Concern for evangelism should not be compromised by any illusion that all will finally be saved (universalism) (emphasis mine).

The confession has a final summary section titled *Conclusion: Evangelical Identity*. The first two paragraphs summarize the soteriological affirmations and are therefore appropriately reprinted.

Evangelicals believe, first of all, the gospel as it is set forth in the Bible. The word evangelical is derived from the biblical term *euangelion* meaning "good news." It is the Good News that God became man in Jesus Christ to live and die and rise again from the dead in order to save us from our sins and all its consequences. The Saviour's benefits and His salvation are received through personal faith in Christ. They are not conditioned on our merit or personal goodness but are based wholly on the mercy of God.

---

[7] *E. A.*, 1-3.

Evangelicals are also to be identified by what is sometimes called the material or content principle of evangelicalism. They hold to all of the most basic doctrines of the Bible: For example, the triuneness of God the Father, God the Son, and God the Holy Spirit; the pre-existence, incarnation, full deity and humanity of teaching; His substitutionary atonement; His bodily resurrection from the dead, His second coming to judge the living and the dead; the necessity of holy living; the imperative of witnessing to others about the gospel . . . These doctrines emerge from the Bible and are summarized in the Apostles' Creed and the historic confessions of evangelical churches.

Comparing Southern Baptists and Current Day American Evangelicals

Many Southern Baptists are comfortable with American evangelicals. At the Evangelicals Affirmation Conference this was quite evident by the number of Southern Baptists present and by those who participated as speakers and seminar leaders. Southern Baptists were represented by Southern Seminary, Beeson Divinity School of Samford University, Southwestern Seminary, Baylor University, Southeastern Seminary, and Criswell College. Theologians, pastors, and laity of Southern Baptist heritage were present. Most Southern Baptists and American evangelicals are in substantial agreement soteriologically because they are in agreement about the Bible. Millard Erickson well states the case regarding something Southern Baptists and American evangelicals by and large agree upon, saying:

The inerrancy of scripture assures us that the salvation accomplished by Jesus Christ is of exclusive and universal value and applicability. When Peter said in Acts 4:12, "Salvation is found in no one else . . ." we can believe that this is indeed what God wanted to convey to those hearers and to us as well. Jesus' statement, "I am the way, and the truth and the life. No one comes to the Father except through me" (John 14:6), is also an authoritative word to us that Jesus and Jesus alone is the means by which we find salvation. We need not wonder whether there is some other possibility by which these people can obtain forgiveness of the sinfulness of which they, like all other humans, are guilty. There is only one way, and we must proclaim it. The inerrant word teaches us that there is universal need but that there is also a universal solution to that need.[8]

---

[8] Millard Erickson, "Implications of Biblical Inerrancy for the Christian Mission" in *The Proceedings of the Conference on Biblical Inerrancy 1987* (Nashville: Broadman Press, 1987), 230.

The essence of an evangelical theology of salvation affirms that salvation from sin is obtained through the grace of God, not that it is earned by good works or given because of merit on the part of men and women. To expand this definition and to provide a larger context for understanding evangelicalism we can note the following special emphases or characteristics as summarized from R. V. Pierard in the *Evangelical Dictionary of* Theology.

> (1) "Man is born totally depraved and sinful. He is completely unable to merit a right standing before a personal God who is holy, righteous and just."
>
> (2) "God Himself has provided a solution for man's sin problem by sending His Son, Jesus Christ, into the world to pay the penalty for sin in man's stead. He accomplished this by His death on the cross. His bodily resurrection from the dead is the vindication of the success, completion and acceptance by God of His work. Christ's death was substitutionary, a ransom for sin, a fatal blow to the prince (Satan) and powers of darkness and a satisfaction of God's righteous justice."
>
> (3) "Salvation is by divine grace alone. It is received personally through faith in the risen Christ (cf. Ephesians 2:8-10). Good works are not the basis of salvation, but are the natural outgrowth of salvation as the Holy Spirit who is received at salvation works out that salvation in the inner man. The beginning of the Christian life from God's perspective is called regeneration or the new birth (cf. John 3). From man's perspective it is called conversion.[9]

Southern Baptist and American evangelical confessions are in substantial agreement as our investigation has shown. Though phraseology and form vary, the content agreement of the two confessions is clearly evident. Humans are fallen and sinful apart from God. In grace God sent His eternal Son who was born of a virgin. He lived a sinless life, died vicariously as an atonement for sin, was raised bodily, and is now glorified in heaven. As individuals trust or place faith in Christ, they are justified before God and receive salvation. To refuse Christ is to remain under God's wrath and await eschatological judgment of an eternal nature. On these confessional statements both groups heartily agree. However, they are not necessarily identical. Several differences in emphasis, if not content, should be pointed out. These differences can be listed briefly and commented upon by way of summary and conclu-

---

[9] R. V. Pierard, "Evangelicalism," in the *Evangelical Dictionary of Theology*, ed. Walter A. Elwell (Grand Rapids: Baker, 1984), 374-382. Also see Charles M. Horne, *The Doctrine of Salvation* (Chicago: Moody Press, 1971, 1984).

sion. Soteriologically, it is my observation that at a number of points Southern Baptists are actually more consistently biblical.

First, Southern Baptists are more biblical than some other evangelicals in their emphasis on repentance. Though the E.A. affirms a changed life as a result of salvation, the word *repentance* is unfortunately absent. Some contemporary evangelicals in light of a prosperous American society and unwarranted theological and exegetical conclusions have almost dismissed repentance as a valid and necessary element in the gospel proclamation and salvation. I have in mind here the lordship salvation debate, an issue on the hot burner in contemporary evangelicalism. Southern Baptists' basic "biblicism" causes them rightly to affirm repentance and its proper importance in salvation.

Second, Southern Baptists are more biblical than some others in their teaching on the ordinances or sacraments. The E.A. has no statement on the ordinances. This omission is not accidental. In the plenary sessions it was stated that the writing committee could not even agree on whether to use the word "sacraments" or "ordinances." Southern Baptists are clear at a number of points here, and in my opinion, more consistent soteriologically and accurate biblically than some evangelicals. For example: (1) There is nothing salvific in the ordinances. When undergirded by faith they (the ordinances) are certainly aids to community worship and personal sanctification. They are, however, to repeat for emphasis, not salvation. (2) Baptism is by immersion and only for believers. Paedo-baptism groups, while welcomed in the larger community of evangelicals, are on less solid ground biblically. When one examines the New Testament, it appears to me that baptism by immersion for believers only is the scriptural model. Infant baptism is an extrabiblical, really a nonbiblical, creation which throughout history has confused and clouded the simple message of the gospel. At this point Southern Baptists proclaim the proper role of baptism in a biblical/evangelical theology.

Third, Southern Baptists are more biblical than some others in their affirmation of the doctrine of the perseverance of the believer. The doctrine of perseverance is also absent from the E.A. because certain participants could not affirm such a doctrine. While not ignorant of all the theological discussions historically of this doctrine, and also of its denial by some Southern Baptists, I would still affirm as a valid theological principle the doctrine of perseverance and its evangelical heritage. Biblically it has solid support (see *BFM* article VI); and theologically it is the most reasonable deduction from the belief in (a) a sovereign God and (b) *sola gratia*. Southern Baptists believe that what God begins He completes, what He holds He will not let go. We affirm with Paul: "For I know whom I have believed and I am convinced that He is able to guard what I have entrusted to Him until that day" (2 Tim. 1:12, NAS).

Finally, Southern Baptists are more biblical than some others in their belief in a conscious eternal punishment for the unbeliever in a place the Bible calls "the lake of fire" or "Hell." Universalism is clearly inconsistent with evangelical/biblical soteriology. Conditional immortality or annihilationism has also been historically inconsistent with evangelical/biblical soteriology. However, in our day the winds of theological change are blowing in a new direction. Now, it is not only cults like Jehovah's Witnesses who teach this doctrine, but several within evangelical circles as well.[10] Some of these prominent spokespersons no doubt played a significant part in (1) rather heated and prolonged debate over the inclusion of the traditional understanding of hell in the evangelical statement, (2) a split vote in the final plenary session whether to include such a statement, and (3) the omission of such a statement in the E.A. The only affirmation given is a general statement about eschatological judgment that is sufficiently vague to include both perspectives.

Southern Baptists historically have rejected this approach. Though some on the fringes of Southern Baptist life might hold to conditional immortality or annihilationism, the vast majority would reject such a position as unscriptural and evangelistically dangerous. It is my hope Southern Baptists will be at the forefront in maintaining biblical integrity and orthodox consistency at this crucial point. We do not rejoice in the reality of a conscious place of eternal separation from God called Hell, but we believe Scripture affirms it.

Conclusion

Do American evangelicals and Southern Baptists proclaim a common salvation? The answer I believe is that generally they do. On the essentials and basics they agree. Methodologically and on some secondary issues, they differ. Where these differences appear, Southern Baptists appear in a number of instances to be more consistent and faithful to the historic confessions than some particular groups or individuals within the greater evangelical community. Our commonality, however, is the basis for our continued cooperation, and our differences are opportunities for gracious and respectful debate and dialogue. It is my prayer as we move toward the year 2000, American evangelicals, of which Southern Baptists comprise a large percentage, will make it their primary task to share this message of good news on a global scale until our Saviour comes again.

---

[10] See for example the statement to this effect of John R. W. Stott in David L. Edwards with a response from John Stott, *Evangelical Essentials* (Downers Grove, IL: InterVarsity, 1988), 312-329.

13

Southern Baptists

—————— & ——————

American Evangelicals: A Common Mission?

David F. D'Amico

Southern Baptists and American evangelicals have sailed the seas of missionary responsibility guided by different but comparable vessels during their common history. The core of their beliefs is the gospel. The motivating force of their institutionalizing has been missions. The demonstrations of contemporary church life are overwhelmingly missionary and evangelistic. The contents of the rest of this book deal at length with historical, theological, and cultural similarities and differences between Southern Baptists and American evangelicals. I will address, in this chapter, evangelistic and missiological issues, describing and analyzing converging interests between Southern Baptists and American evangelicals during the last decade.

I propose the following *thesis*: the task of world evangelization and missions is overwhelming, urgent, and unfulfilled. Different Christian groups have attempted to make plans for worldwide evangelization, especially during the twentieth century. Recent data demonstrates the fallacy of each denomination's making and executing plans on its own. Cooperation, attempted at different levels with guarded agendas, must continue. The results of recent events provide hope for a climate in which the common mission can be better accomplished, perhaps by the year 2000.

I will survey recent developments in cooperative missions and world evangelization endeavors, seeking to demonstrate that, for the cause of missions and world evangelization, Southern Baptists and American evangelicals are willing to dialogue, pray, discuss, cooperate, and dream together as they face the dawn of the twenty-first century.

A Common Mission?

I approach this subject with assumptions closely related to my convictions, ministry experience, and persuasion. They include my involvement in ecumenical seminars dealing with the development of early Christianity held in Texas while I was a professor of church history at Southwestern Baptist Theological Seminary in Fort Worth. While in ministry at the South Main Baptist Church in Houston, I was a member of the Central Planning Committee for "Houston '85." We organized the Convocation for Evangelizing Ethnic America held at South Main church. While ministering in New York, I represented Southern Baptists in the Committee of Denominational Executives and in a Baptist/Catholic dialogue extending for three years and discussing significant theological and ecclesiological issues of common concern.

Major Southern Baptist-Evangelical Mission and Evangelism Cooperative Efforts, Houston '85 (April 15-18, 1985)

Under the umbrellas of the Lausanne movement Southern Baptists and evangelicals find themselves comfortably thinking, planning, and strategizing for world evangelization. The National Convocation on Evangelizing Ethnic America, held in Houston on April 15-18, 1985, was a demonstration of significant cooperation between Southern Baptists and evangelicals.

The convocation was conceived as an event to be sponsored by the North American Lausanne Committee for World Evangelization. Mission executives from different denominations and parachurch groups were approached to implement the dream. An *ad hoc* steering committee initiated the proceedings, naming as a continuation body a central planning committee. Oscar Romo, director of the Language Missions Division of the Home Mission Board, SBC, became the chairperson of the convocation.[1] J. Paul Landrey, at that time director of World Vision U. S. Ministry, and now president of the Latin American Mission, became the coordinator of the convocation. The membership of the Central Planning Committee represented major evangelical mission agencies (denominational and parachurch) who were concerned and committed to evangelize ethnic America, including such notable evangelical leaders as Billy Melvin, executive director of the National Association of Evangeli-

---

[1] Randy Frame, "Church Leaders Challenge the Notion that America is a Melting Pot," *Christianity Today* (May 17, 1985), 40, reported: "The Southern Baptist Convention's successful model was the main reason the Lausanne Committee chose Oscar Romo to serve as Houston '85 conference chairman."

cals, and Thomas Zimmerman, general superintendent of the Assemblies of God.

The genesis of the convocation began informally when C. Peter Wagner, professor of missions of the School of World Missions of Fuller Theological Seminary, and I, as minister to internationals of the South Main Baptist Church of Houston, discussed our common dreams and goals. Wagner had written several books on church growth, upholding the homogeneous unit principle. I had been practicing ethnic evangelistic strategy with the multiethnic congregations of the Houston church. Our desire was to extend the vision other evangelicals had of the significant opportunities to evangelize peoples of different ethnic backgrounds living in the United States. Wagner had been and continues to be an admirer and advocate of the evangelistic and church-planting strategy of Southern Baptists among ethnics.[2]

The purpose of the convocation was to call together the key leadership of American churches and Christian organizations for the specific purpose of uniting in prayer, researching the current ethnic realties in the United States, sharing lessons learned from successes and failures, and mobilizing all churches in the exciting task of ethnic evangelization.[3]

The participants paid for their travel, lodging, and registration, demonstrating high commitment by attending the meeting. The South Main Baptist Church, under the leadership of Pastor Kenneth Chafin, provided free use of its facilities and contributed resources in equipment and volunteers.

The program of the convocation included plenary addresses, ten major workshop tracks, Bible studies, and fellowship. Participation was optimum. "It was the first major consultation of its kind to be held in the United States. More than 47 Protestant denominations and organizations were represented, with nearly 700 registrants representing 63 language/culture groups."[4]

Participants represented a diverse group, including top ranking denominational and organizational leaders, along with hundreds of pastors and lay people involved in ethnic evangelism at the grassroots. The results of the convocation focused different avenues of cooperation between Southern Baptists and evangelicals. Leighton Ford, chairperson of the Lausanne Committee for World Evangelization, addressing the

---

[2] See especially, C. Peter Wagner, *Church Growth and the Whole Gospel* (San Francisco: Harper & Row, 1981), 180.

[3] "Hearing and Obeying His Voice," *The Mandate* (September 1984), 1.

[4] Randy Frame, "Church Leaders Challenge," 40.

closing session "stated that the convocation had broadened the vision for world evangelization among North American evangelicals."[5]

The missiological benefits of the convocation for those interested in the evangelization of ethnics in the U. S. are available in the resources developed from the workshops and addresses, including data gathered by the Home Mission Board, SBC. In addition, the planning committee approached a representative of the Billy Graham Center in Wheaton, Illinois, to provide a continuation of the concerns and networking begun in Houston. The center has done so in facilitating its personnel and resources to different ethnic groups during the last five years.[6] Southern Baptist missiologists have also served as resource persons to evangelical mission agencies requesting their expertise in ethnic evangelism and church planting.[7]

Evangelicals participating in the meeting became better acquainted with Southern Baptists. The fact that a local church hosted the meeting corrected misconceptions some persons had.

> As the conclusion of the convocation approached, attention turned heavily to the sharing of strategies and experiences, and to laying a foundation for greatly increased networking among those involved in ethnic evangelism. Dr. Romo commented that he believed the expanded contacts and friendships growing from the convocation would be among Houston '85's most significant results.[8]

The Dallas I Meeting
(September 17-18, 1987)

The mover and prompter for this meeting was R. Keith Parks, president of the Foreign Mission Board of the Southern Baptist Convention. Parks had been impressed by the openness and enthusiasm of the two Third World leaders who had met in Ridgecrest, North Carolina, during the summer of 1985. At that time leaders representing national Baptist conventions in countries where Southern Baptists have missionaries expressed their concerns and desire to work in closer cooperation and asked for a larger involvement in the development of missionary strategy. Parks corresponded with thirty-six chief executives of the largest groups doing missions around the world, inviting them to attend a

---

[5] Michael Tutterow, "Reaching the Real America," *The Mandate* (October 1985), 3.

[6] Interview with James Kraakevik, director of the Billy Graham Center, Wheaton, Illinois, June 16, 1989.

[7] Interview with Oscar Romo, January 11, 1990.

[8] Tutterow, "Reaching," 3.

meeting. He received thirty-five responses. Thus, the Dallas I meeting became a reality.

During the meeting, labeled by the Foreign Mission Board press release as an "interdenominational Global Missions Conference" and by others as "ad hoc meeting of mission agencies,"[9] twenty mission agencies were represented, some by their chief executives. "The leaders represented groups with about 20,000 missions personnel overseas and annual budgets totaling more than $510 million."[10] Much of the time was spent in prayer and dialogue.

Dallas I was beneficial because it brought together evangelicals committed to world evangelization. The opportunity of seeing one another face to face, praying, sharing common concerns, and attempting to seek future contacts was by itself a significant breakthrough. Moreover, they reached significant agreements. The accords included joint prayer efforts, approval of holding another meeting focusing on the exchange of information about reaching the unreached, and exploring the possibilities of sharing research data in the field of world evangelization.

Leaders expressed their optimism about the possibilities of sharing the gospel with everyone in the world. H. Eddie Fox, representing the Methodist General Board of Discipleship and the World Methodist Council, succinctly expressed the convictions of most participants when he declared: "The tasks of world evangelization are too big for us alone. Without any doubt, the Spirit of the Lord is moving across the church around the world to move out in mission and evangelizing now."[11]

The Dallas II Meeting
(February 9-11, 1988)

If the Dallas I meeting was a dream-dialogue-prayer-get-acquainted conference in which mission executives agreed to cooperate in the common task of world evangelization, the Dallas II meeting was a middle-management-executed, research-interest, focused meeting attempting to investigate whether cooperation in essential areas was possible.

---

[9] Ed Dayton, comp., *Inter-Agency Consultation for Resources and Information for Reaching the Unreached* (Monrovia, CA: MARC, 1988), 2.

[10] "Top Mission Leaders Seek Ways to Accelerate Spread of the Gospel," Baptist Press release, September 22, 1987. The press release includes the names of executives and the mission organizations they represented in Dallas I. Denominations and parachurch groups are included.

[11] Ibid.

Ed Dayton, a recognized and affirmed evangelical leader of World Vision International, convened the convocation. The stated purpose of the assembly was "to bring together a variety of American mission agencies particularly concerned with identifying and reaching unreached peoples and peoples groups, and to explore ways of identifying and exchanging information that will enhance the task."[12]

The three-day consultation allowed representatives of the mission agencies to disclose the capabilities of their expertise in world evangelization research, including specific aspects of computer data base and software that can be accessed by other agencies.[13] The restricted focus of Dallas II may explain why two Lutheran and one Presbyterian mission agencies did not participate. Still, it was a profitable meeting. Of the fifty-one agencies invited, twenty-eight sent representatives, and some who were unable to send representatives demonstrated interest for future cooperation. The objectives of the consultation were achieved and agreements were reached for future cooperation.

A pattern developed in this consultation demonstrating the active role of the Southern Baptist Foreign Mission Board in seeking cooperation, sharing data about world evangelization, and perhaps convincing certain skeptics of the evangelical world that Southern Baptists are serious in their commitment to cooperation in the world evangelization task. Outlining the participants' future commitments and work, Ed Dayton reported:

> (1) There was a unanimous *commitment to cooperate* amongst ourselves and other agencies around the world in the task of world evangelization.
> (2) Each agency provided the name of a *contact person for future work*, and for keeping abreast of what others are doing.
> (3) *There was a complete willingness to contribute* to an ongoing network in its particular areas of expertise by each agency present.
> (4) *There was a unanimous willingness* to stay informed about what others are doing, and an openness to sharing.
> (5) There was a warm response to SBC initiatives to make available to those agencies concerned with world evangelization on an initial experiment in providing global data.[14]

---

[12] *Inter-Agency Consultation*, 2.

[13] Ibid. Attachments 6-17 contain forty pages of detailed missiological information from selected mission agencies, including type of computer equipment used. The description of the data demonstrates the openness of the agencies to inform others as to what they are doing.

[14] Ibid., 9-10.

Logically, the mission agencies with larger resources were better able to demonstrate their willingness to cooperate with other denominational and parachurch agencies. The Foreign Mission Board, SBC; MARC, of World Vision International; and Global Mapping International possess extensive and valuable data. Two years after these agreements were reached, A. Clark Scanlon, director of the Research Planning Office of the Foreign Mission Board, reported that about thirty-five mission agencies have used information from its data base. The retrieval and use of the World Evangelization database from the Foreign Mission Board *is provided free of charge* to other mission agencies. This is done for two reasons. Use of data becomes an incentive for and must be exclusively related to world evangelization.[15]

The Global Consultation on World Evangelization by A.D. 2000 and Beyond—GCOWE (Singapore, January 5-8, 1989)

The development of this consultation followed the same pattern of preparation of previous meetings (agreement, naming of committees, assignment of tasks to specific staff for planning and program, and related matters). GCOWE became the culmination of the cooperative efforts started by Keith Parks in 1987. The Southern Baptist Foreign Mission Board played a significant role in its success. After Dallas II a group of leaders interested in the Two-Thirds World aspects of world evangelization, including Thomas Wang and Luis Bush, reflected about their role. The Steering committee of GCOWE included, therefore, Western and Two-Thirds World leaders. Thomas Wang represented Asia; Panya Baba, Africa; Luis Bush, Latin America; Floyd McClung, Europe; William O'Brien, the United States.

Historians, missiologists, and world-evangelization proponents can determine the magnitude of the consultation with greater accuracy than that of previous conferences. The momentum gathered in Singapore was transferred to Lausanne II, the International Congress for World Evangelization, held in Manila in July 1989 and remains very active at the present. At least two books have been published describing the historical background and effects of GCOWE.[16]

---

[15] Telephone interview, A. Clark Scanlon, January 4, 1990.

[16] Jay and Olgy Gary, eds., *The Countdown Has Begun: The Story of the Global Consultation on A.D. 2000* (Rockville, Va: A.D. 2000 Global Service Office, 1989); Thomas Wang, ed., *Countdown to A.D. 2000* (Pasadena, Calif.: The A.D. 2000 Movement, 1989).

What are the significant features of the consultation? In the area of *participation* previous patterns continued. The participants committee invited world leaders to seek greater inclusiveness. The rationale for participation was interest and commitment to world evangelization, ownership of some evangelization plan, and ability to defray expenses. The steering committee dealt forthrightly with the utmost limits of ecumenism. They invited Roman Catholics dedicated to world evangelization plans, and six participated. The process was informal. Seven hundred persons were invited by letter and 314 attended, representing fifty nations.[17]

The *content* of the consultation dealt with plans for world evangelization. At this juncture the research expertise and work of David B. Barrett became essential. He and others prepared the working documents that would serve as bases for discussion and distributed them to the participants for input and comments. These documents became a lightning rod during the proceedings. Some interpreted the thorough preparation as a sign of a preconceived agenda from the American participants.[18] In addition, representatives of different denominational, parachurch, and catholic mission agencies delineated their respective evangelization plans to those present. The enthusiasm with which each group described their world evangelization plans galvanized the interest of those more intimately committed to long range planning.

The steering committee reported at the end of the consultation that they had completed their task and were ready to dissolve. Some leaders desired a continuation task team. About one third of the participants decided to continue the efforts by organizing an office commissioned to network with other movements and to disseminate information about world evangelization plans. The office, operating under the direction of Jay and Olgy Gary, is called the A.D. 2000 Information Office and is located in Pasadena, California.

---

[17] Gary, *The Countdown Has Begun*, 238.

[18] Telephone interview, William O'Brien, January 5, 1990. See also Gary, *The Countdown Has Begun*, 46-48. The documents prepared included, *Two Thousand Plans Toward A.D. 2000: A Kaleidoscopic Global Plan to See the World Evangelized by A.D. 2000 and Beyond*, drafted by David B. Barrett et. al. (GCOWE, 1989); *A.D. 2000 Global Goals: A Selection of 168 Proposed Great Commission Goals*, comp. David B. Barrett et. al. (GCOWE, 1989); David B. Barrett and James W. Reapsome, *Seven Hundred Plans to Evangelize the World: The Rise of a Global Evangelization Movement* (New Hope Publishers, 1988); Todd M. Johnson, *Countdown to 1900: World Evangelization at the End of the Nineteenth Century* (New Hope Publishers, 1988); and Luis Bush, Jay Gary, and Mike Roberts, ed. *Towards A.D. 2000 and Beyond: A Reader* (GCOWE, 1989).

The *effects* of GCOWE are significant. As a culminating covenant, the participants approved the "Great Commission Manifesto." This short declaration included a theological paragraph containing affirmations of a Trinitarian stance, salvation by faith in Christ, and orthodox stances on the nature of Christ, authority of the Scriptures, and holiness of life. After a confession of sin in the form of pride, prejudice, and competition that has hindered the work of world evangelization, the manifesto upholds cooperation and partnership, empowerment and compassion, and presents an outline of steps needed to fulfill the Great Commission. The section on cooperation and partnership is cited here to illustrate the new environment prevalent these days in evangelical circles.

> We have listened to each other and rejoice at what God is doing through many plans for world evangelization.
>
> We learned that there are over 2000 separate plans relating to world evangelization.
>
> We see afresh that cooperation and partnership are absolute necessities if the Great Commission is going to be fulfilled by the Year 2000. For the sake of those who are lost and eternally separated from God, we have dared to pray and dream of what might happen if appropriate autonomy of churches and ministries could be balanced with significant partnership.[19]

The leaders responsible for organizing and executing GCOWE evaluated the results of the meeting positively. It legitimized from missiological perspectives the study and promotion of evangelization plans with A.D. 2000 as the target date. Jay Gary declared that the assembly moved the cause of world evangelization to a higher plateau by giving "tremendous impetus to regional and national A.D. 2000 consultations," allowing "for good interaction between participants on the principles and presuppositions of A.D. 2000 thinking," and by fostering "an international identity for the A.D. 2000 vision."[20] It provided considerable content to the program of the next major event, Lausanne II.

---

[19] Wang, *Countdown to A.D. 2000*, xi-xiii.

[20] *The Countdown Has Begun*, 64. For more candid assessment of organizers Gary and O'Brien, see ibid., 62-65, 237-240. For personal reflections about the results of GCOWE by selected parachurch leaders see, Wang, *Countdown to A.D. 2000*, 159-173.

Lausanne II: International Congress on World Evangelization (Manila, July 10-22, 1989)

The congress drew 3,586 participants representing 186 nations and many denominations and parachurch organizations. Planners attempted to have a larger participation from Christians of the Two-Thirds World, where the majority of the membership of the universal church resides. The implicit purpose of the congress was to rally diverse Christians from all over the world to meet, pray, study, discuss, and affirm the common cause of world evangelization. The major issues included the uniqueness of Christ, the primacy of the local church, the role of the laity as primary agents of evangelization, the role of the poor, urbanization, and modernity.

A considerable number of Southern Baptists participated, some of whom were prominent in the organizational developments, program content, and communications. William O'Brien's major address discussing cooperation was well received. He challenged evangelical Christians to join hands "no matter what their race, gender or economic status and pour out the resources they have—material, physical and spiritual—to the end that all persons may hear of Jesus Christ."[21]

The spirit of Lausanne II can be gauged by the contents of the Lausanne Covenant developed in 1974 and reaffirmed with the "Manila Manifesto." The latter extols the reality of inclusiveness, the sincere attempts towards cooperation, the high commitment to the underprivileged of the world, the concern for reaching persons in urban centers of the world for Christ, and the stressing of the role of women and laypersons in church life.

> Its most distinctive features are a strong assertion of the uniqueness of Jesus Christ as the only way to salvation in our pluralistic world, a forceful and far-reaching commitment to social action as part of preaching the kingdom of God, insistence on the necessity for all members of Christ's body to be involved in witness (including women and the laity), an emphasis on cooperation in evangelism even with those communions that are not part of the evangelical movement, and a stress on deliberate strategies to reach those people in the modern world in difficult situations who have not yet heard the message of Christ.[22]

---

[21] William O'Brien and Michael Chute, "Evangelization Said to Need Cooperation, Not Competition," *Florida Baptist Witness*, August 3, 1989, 15.

[22] Richard V. Pierard, "Lausanne II: Reshaping World Evangelicalism," *The Christian Century* (August 16-23, 1989), 742.

Commentators reflected positively and negatively on the effectiveness of the Congress, the domination of Western control in the planning process, the significant place given to charismatics in the program, and the continuation of the Lausanne movement after Billy Graham passes the mantle to others.[23]

After providing data attempting to substantiate energetic efforts of Southern Baptists for cooperating with evangelicals in the common cause of world evangelization, it is appropriate to discuss some aspects of Southern Baptist cooperation in other areas.

The Realities of Cooperation

Southern Baptists demonstrate varied degrees of cooperation in foreign and home mission fields. Generally, they have been reluctant to cooperate with other evangelicals in a structured manner for various reasons. Some have limited exposure by living in a protected environment where Southern Baptists are a majority.

In foreign fields some may find themselves for the first time contemplating the possibilities of partnership. Southern Baptists deploy missionaries in countries where some national Baptist Conventions have had unfortunate experiences with other evangelicals. These negative experiences led to mistrust and decreased the desire to cooperate.[24]

Some evangelicals and parachurch groups resent and sometimes envy the financial level of support Southern Baptist missionaries receive from the Foreign Mission Board. In addition, many sincere and open-minded evangelicals interpret the lack of Southern Baptist cooperation as a sign of arrogance, provincialism, or limited perception about the urgency of the world evangelization task.

In foreign fields Southern Baptists and other evangelicals have cooperated specifically to defend religious freedom. They joined efforts in Argentina during the first Peron regime and in Colombia during the period of violence beginning in 1948. In places such as Asia and Africa, cooperation is easier on account of the environment, the type of leader-

---

[23] See Ray Bakke, "Lausanne II in Manila: Some Reflections," *International Urban Associates Newsletter* (Fall 1989), 1; "Global Camp Meeting," *Christianity Today* (August 18, 1989), 39-40; and Lyn Cryderman, "Manila Manifesto to Undergo Further Study," *Christianity Today* (September 8, 1989), 62-63. Some observers indicated their concern that the Lausanne committee became too closely identified with the A.D. 2000 Movement. Leighton Ford replied: "We support any effort to reach the world with the gospel, but Lausanne does not endorse particular movements."

[24] In Brazil and Chile many Baptist churches have experienced divisions caused by the impact of charismatic groups who proselyte their members.

ship, and sometimes the fact that Southern Baptists are latecomers to the mission scene.

The Southern Baptist Foreign Mission Board does not have an official policy regarding cooperation. It encourages missionary personnel to make decisions according to the situations faced. During the last ten years, Southern Baptists have attempted to cultivate relations with other evangelicals, as demonstrated above, but fear prevents some evangelicals from accepting these gestures of friendliness.[25] The official statement of the Foreign Mission Board for cooperation with other Christians in the mission field encourages friendship and many kinds of cooperation with other Christian groups.

> One of the implementing guidelines in the staff strategy statement adopted in 1982 is, "Southern Baptist mission work is carried on in the context of the larger Christian family and in cordial relationship and increasing correlation with the work of other denominations." The central principle of such relationships is fellowship and cooperation without entanglement or diversion from the mission task.[26]

Winston Crawley listed significant issues to consider in dealing with other Christians in the mission field. These include, positively, joint efforts in education and evangelistic campaigns; and, negatively, membership in the council of churches and the freedom national Conventions exercise to join councils, the complication of cleavage between "conciliar" and "evangelical" ecumenism, and relations with parachurch organizations. The relations with parachurch organizations are more intricate because they include Southern Baptists as well as non-Southern Baptist parachurch organizations.

> The Foreign Mission Board and its missionaries seek to stay on friendly terms with parachurch organizations, while making as much use as possible of the contributions they might offer to the work, provided there can be enough clarity of relationship to avoid misunderstanding and problems.[27]

During the recent political turmoil experienced by agencies of the Southern Baptist Convention, it is encouraging to conclude that all the initiatives taken by executives of the Foreign Mission Board regarding cooperation with evangelicals have been heartily endorsed by the Board of Trustees. The endorsement has been both implicit and explicit. Implic-

---

[25] Telephone interview, Winston Crawley, January 3, 1990.

[26] Winston Crawley, *Global Mission* (Nashville: Broadman, 1989), 227.

[27] Ibid., 230.

itly the support is seen in the involvement of personnel, resources, and materials deployed in the events held from 1987 to the present.

The enlarged task of the Research and Planning Office under the direction of A. Clark Scanlon includes studies in church growth and church planting. Missionary researchers James Slack and Jim Maroney seek to exchange information with other evangelicals, including the Assemblies of God, the Christian and Missionary Alliance, and the Church of God.

The work of mission strategist David Barrett, a consultant of the Research and Planning Office, has lately shaped considerably the policy of the Foreign Mission Board, especially as it relates to innovative approaches to deploying missionary personnel.

Analysis and Implications for the Future

Theologians and historians seem to be absorbed by the desire to be labeled correctly under certain rubrics, some of which are quite indefinite (evangelical, fundamentalist, right-wing evangelical, inerrantist, and so forth). On the other hand, practitioners of missions and evangelism are sincerely absorbed in attempting to achieve world evangelization. I submit that fulfilling *the Great Commission has been the common mission of Southern Baptists and American evangelicals.*[28] The efforts toward cooperation exemplified in the developments surveyed in this article must continue to multiply.

The best vehicle for fermenting the common cause is, with all its limitations, the Lausanne movement. It started with the Lausanne I Congress in 1974 and has continued as an informal movement. It receives cohesiveness through the resolution and concerns of individuals and organizations interested in the task of global evangelization. The structure is simple. It functions through committees and commissions and relies on individuals and organizations for financial support. The movement allows persons from varied doctrinal and ecclesiological persuasions to gather together to dream, learn, and devise plans which can be implemented through the channels of denominational entities and parachurch groups.

The gathering of the harvest of lost persons across the world (see John 4:35-38) will glorify God while diminishing our theological pride and provincialism. An extraordinary example of evangelical-Baptist-

---

[28] The label "Great Commission Christian" has been used recently by many in publications and conferences and has a positive value to blend cooperation and to identify people.

Catholic cooperation took place in Budapest in July of 1989. In that historic meeting Billy Graham preached, and thousands responded to the evangelistic invitation, including many Roman Catholics. That event can serve as a paradigm for the future.

As we anticipate the dawning of the twenty-first century, we must be strong in our resolve to fulfill the task of world evangelization. This we must do with a clear theological conscience and believing that Jesus Christ, the Lord of the church, in the day of judgment, will call us His children—not Southern Baptists or American evangelicals.

PART IV

Further
———————— Reflections ————————

14

One Baptist's Dream: A Denomination Truly ——— Evangelical, ——— Truly Catholic, Truly Baptist

E. Glenn Hinson

I have a dream for the Southern Baptist Convention. My dream is a denomination *truly* evangelical, *truly* catholic, and *truly* Baptist. In each case I have emphasized the word *truly*. In doing so, I am implying as forcefully as I can that the Southern Baptist Convention falls short of these three goals. Indeed, if Southern Baptists are not careful, we will have at best a caricature and at worst an antithesis of each of these. Instead of Christians and churches faithful to the evangel with its demands of costly grace, we will have culture and civil religion, Americanism at its worst. Instead of a "catholic" Christ in whom "there is neither Jew nor Greek, bond nor free, male nor female" (Gal. 3:28), we will have a "parochial" Christ in whom there is room only for confessors of a narrow creed submissive to infallible and inerrant interpreters of the divine will. Instead of churches, agencies, and institutions in which the Holy Spirit is allowed to effect obedience by voluntary means, the essence of the Baptist tradition, we will have those in which contrived and artificial hoopla are substituted for the Spirit.

I speak here as if these were future dangers. Surely they are. However, you know, as I know, that they are already upon us. Perhaps that is as it should be, for we Christians and churches are always striving to achieve a goal we can never achieve on earth. We are confronted with the harsh reality that, here and now, we will be less than faithful. Too easily we substitute success for faithfulness. We go with *our* plans and *our* program as if God depended on them. We forget that our successes are often our greatest failures and our failures are often God's successes.

To paraphrase Mother Teresa of Calcutta, "God did not call us to be successful. God called us to be faithful."

We cannot rest content with our present level of faithfulness. The goal we must set before us is to be *truly* evangelical, *truly* catholic, *truly* Baptist. We must strive to achieve the *essence* of these traditions, not the caricatures our present circumstances have drawn. Let me now elaborate by speaking in each instance of the goal and its caricature now threatening to impose itself upon us.

Truly Evangelical

First, I dream of a denomination that is truly evangelical. Some will probably wonder whether I have slipped a cog here or, perhaps, seen the light when I speak of a hope that we will be "truly evangelical." In an earlier writing I have questioned the "evangelical" tag as applied to Southern Baptists.[1] Contrary to the way some have construed what I said, however, I did not say, "Baptists are *not* evangelicals." What I said was, "Baptists are *other than* evangelicals (thinking here of the hodge-podge bearing that label in the United States) and they had better know the difference." Am I now contradicting myself?

Certainly not intentionally. I am here using the word *evangelical* in its proper etymological sense and not in one of the myriad applications in Europe, North America, Latin America, or elsewhere. Leo Garrett has catalogued dozens of these in an effort to establish the "parallels" between evangelicals and Southern Baptists.[2] The meaning of the word I am interested in here, however, is the one drawn from *evangelion*, the Greek word for *gospel*. So defined, the evangelical goal is nothing more and nothing less than being faithful to the gospel.

Recognizing the problem of interpreting the Scriptures, the New Testament as well as the Old, we can admit that it is difficult to say what the gospel is and still more difficult to say what it *means* when applied to our life situations. As much as anything, the battle in which we are engaged in the Southern Baptist Convention is over this point. In all modesty we can admit that we may misinterpret and misapply just as others, however progressive or reactionary, do. If we are to stand on any more secure turf than they, we must be dead sure we frame and use the

---

[1] E. Glenn Hinson, "Baptists and Evangelicals: What Is the Difference?" *Baptist History and Heritage* 16 (April 1981): 20-32.

[2] James Leo Garrett, Jr., E. Glenn Hinson, and James E. Tull, *Are Southern Baptists "Evangelicals"?* (Macon, GA: Mercer University Press, 1983).

best hermeneutic we can. The end product alone will verify which hermeneutic is best.

What is the end product of the caricature of the gospel propounded by the group controlling the SBC? Make no mistake about it; this movement is not primarily concerned about a defense of the Bible, as Harold Lindsell and a number of spokespersons for this group argue. True, they use the words *inerrancy* or *infallibility* with great effectiveness to put their opponents on the defensive. Since none of the fundamentalists, save those who regard the *King James Version* as inerrant and infallible, however, claims to have an inerrant or infallible autograph, the real concern is to establish a few pastors of jumbo-size churches as inerrant and infallible interpreters—Baptist popes, if you please. The main criteria are not biblical or theological but pragmatic—the size of their churches, the number of baptisms per year, the amount of church building, and so forth. Thus caricatured, *evangelical* becomes synonymous with the success motif of American business.

All denominations in America, even such conservative ones as the Roman Catholic Church,[3] have experienced a baptism in the corporation motif, our prevailing social model. None, however, has come closer to complete accommodation to it than the Southern Baptist Convention. Since I have traced the stages by which this happened elsewhere,[4] I need only indicate the end result. Evangelism, meaning the winning and baptizing of converts, has become a business. Nothing is wrong, of course, with employing corporation structures and methods if we are really talking about genuine conversion to God through Jesus Christ—denying self, taking up one's cross, and following Him. Yet that is precisely where the question arises. *To what have we been converting people?*

Members of upper-middle-class or upper-class congregations cannot be smug here. We, too, are doing poorly in issuing the call to conversion.[5] We, too, make people feel good about doing what they have already decided they are going to do anyway. Maybe there is a greater measure of faithfulness to the gospel in some area than is true for the caricatures of evangelical, but how much greater?

---

[3] For the Roman Catholic Church's experience, see Charles Dahm, *Power and Authority in the Catholic Church* (Notre Dame, IN: Notre Dame University Press, 1981), a study of Cardinal Cody's reign in Chicago.

[4] See Garrett, Hinson, and Tull, *Are Southern Baptists "Evangelicals"?*, 160-64.

[5] See Jim Wallis, *Call to Conversion* (New York: Harper & Row, 1981).

Having given modesty its due, however, let me return to the caricature. The high priest of the New Right is Jerry Falwell. Falwell's influence is not as far-reaching as he assumes, as Jeffrey K. Hadden and Charles E. Swann have proven in *Prime Time Preachers*.[6] As recent political and economic tides have risen and fallen, moreover, so has his popularity and influence. Be assured, he does have influence, most notably in the Southern Baptist Convention and among Southern Baptist ministers.

Item One—A survey of Southern Baptists undertaken for Southern Seminary by Albert McClellan in the early eighties indicated that Falwell was the single most influential person in shaping the perceptions of Southern Baptist ministers. Those interviewed hardly mentioned the name even of Billy Graham when asked, "What person most influences you or your pastor?" Most of the time, they named Falwell. A separate study by Furman political science professor James Guth confirmed this.[7]

Item Two—Falwell displayed his impact on the Southern Baptist Convention in New Orleans in 1982. He was present and consulted, not in the Superdome, where he would have been too visible, but in the Hyatt Regency headquarters of Convention leaders. The resolution in support of Israel, which sounded like a blanket approval of Israel's invasion of Lebanon, had a definite Falwellian tang. Ed McAteer reportedly wanted to see this resolution pass more than any other, and he nearly succeeded in ramrodding it through. Keith Parks, president of the Foreign Mission Board, and some other leaders barely managed to get the action tabled by warning of its serious implications for the Southern Baptist Foreign Mission program. Jerry Falwell phoned Menachem Begin to congratulate him on the bombing of the Iraqi nuclear reactor and regularly sends money to Israel. He has traced his keen interest in Israel to the Six-Day War in 1967 which restored Israel to its Davidic boundaries. The next step is to rebuild the temple.[8]

In 1989 Falwell chose the Southern Baptist Convention in Las Vegas to announce the disbanding of Moral Majority. Although financial problems had something to do with this decision, he may have signaled

---

[6] Jeffrey K. Haden and Charles E. Swann, *Prime Time Preachers* (Reading, MA: Addison-Wesley Publishing Co., Inc., 1981), 47-67. Recent polls (1989) have revealed further dramatic drops in listeners in the wake of the scandals involving Jim Bakker and Jimmy Swaggart.

[7] James L. Guth, "The Education of the Christian Right: The Case of the Southern Baptist Clergy," unpublished paper delivered at the Society for the Scientific Study of Religion, Providence, R.I., October 22-24, 1982.

[8] Grace Halsell, *Prophecy and Politics* (Westport, CN: Lawrence Hill & Co., 1986); she gathered data from two tours Falwell led to Israel to meet with Israeli leaders.

by the context for the announcement that he no longer needed Moral Majority because he now has the Southern Baptist Convention! Falwell also addressed Southern Baptist evangelists at Las Vegas.

Item Three—Fundamentalists from all over the United States are linking up with Falwell to effect their vision for a "Christian" America. Falwell knows power and how to use it. In the first issue of the *Fundamentalist Journal* he editorialized:

> The Fundamentalist movement has come of age. Born in the heat of controversy with Liberalism at the turn of the century, Fundamentalism has not only survived—it has now arrived with long-overdue national recognition. The conservative religious movement has become the dynamic spiritual force in America today. Its impact has brought renewed hope to millions of God-fearing Americans.[9]

Although Falwell went on to admit that no fundamentalist could speak for all, he added that "it is our desire to create a forum to encourage Christian leadership and statesmanship to stand for the old-time religion in these critical days."[10]

It is useful to recognize that Falwell is a child in the faith of J. Frank Norris. His Thomas Road Church in Lynchburg, Virginia, is a member of the World Baptist Fellowship founded by Norris. The first issue of the *Fundamentalist Journal*, recently closed down as well after seven years' publication, included Norris among the twelve apostles of fundamentalism it featured on its cover. The others are: R. A. Torrey, Robert Ketcham, Bob Jones, Sr., Oliver B. Greene, John R. Rice, Billy Sunday, W. B. Riley, J. Gresham Machen, G. B. Vick, T. T. Shields, and L. S. Chafer. Ironically, therefore, Norris, the avowed enemy of the Southern Baptist Convention, has come back not merely to haunt it but perhaps to control it.

What is the gospel of Jerry Falwell? It is the fundamentalism of his mentors plus a social, political, and economic fundamentalism which they would have viewed with jaundiced eyes.

Falwell, who proudly accepts the fundamentalist tag, affirms the famous five fundamentals first articulated in 1895 at the Niagara Bible Conference: verbal inspiration of the Bible to the point of inerrancy and infallibility, literal virgin birth, substitutionary atonement, literal bodily resurrection, and second coming. In addition, he affirms the earlier fundamentalist emphasis upon evangelism.

---

[9] *Fundamentalist Journal* 1 (September 1982), 4.
[10] Ibid.

Over against fundamentalists of an earlier day, and even himself, Falwell has become a social and political activist. He criticizes himself for being negative and pessimistic, sitting back and letting the country apostasize, nearly destroying itself by inward decay, and almost totally avoiding the political process and condemning those who attempt to address social issues. The first issue of the *Fundamentalist Journal* included a "Patriot's Survey," which asked readers to state where they "stand on these vital issues." The issues are pornography, crime, drugs, promiscuous sex, legalized abortion, and homosexuality being taught "in the public schools as an alternative life-style." You will know also of Falwell's "Wake Up America" Campaign intended to return us to the days of our forebears, namely, the Puritans.

Lest you think Falwell has forgotten the importance of Baptist connections, he scheduled "Baptist Fundamentalism '84" held in Washington, D. C. Convention Center on April 11-13, 1984. In recent years he has ridden a crest far higher than his mentor, J. Frank Norris, ever rode.

Some would like to think, nay, ardently work to assure, that the Southern Baptist Convention, its churches and its people, represent this kind of evangelicalism. The question is: Is this *true* evangelicalism, a true representation of the gospel? In responding we should not make the mistake of condemning everything people of the right do or say in blanket fashion. Some "liberal" critics, for instance, have censured the religious right's political and social involvement despite the fact that they have chided and derided fundamentalists for years for noninvolvement. Such matters as abortion are legitimate areas of concern. Anyone who has observed what goes on in giant urban hospitals, where a full-term fetus is aborted with no more consideration than an appendix might be removed, cannot help but exercise some caution. We all need to be concerned, too, about the family, the moral fiber of our nation, education, pornography, national security measures, and other issues.

No, not everything Jerry Falwell and his entourage do or say is malign or perverse. The problem lies, rather, with their overall perspective. It is the same problem which has increasingly burdened fundamentalism. Like all ideologies which try to solve complex issues by a few simple and pat solutions, *fundamentalism presents a truncated version of the gospel, and in doing so it is, measured by traditional Christian standards of orthodoxy, thoroughly heretical and blatantly idolatrous.* Early fundamentalism, as I have shown in an earlier paper,[11]

---

[11] E. Glenn Hinson, "Neo-Fundamentalism: An Interpretation and Critique," *Baptist History and Heritage* 16 (April 1981), 33-42, 49.

articulated a fairly well-rounded statement of faith and theology. A confession drafted at Niagara, New York, in 1878 contained fourteen rather than five articles and began with a strong and personal Trinitarian statement. By this time the new fundamentalists hardly bother even with the five articles. Now they put all their chips down on an inerrancy statement or items to test whether one subscribes to inerrancy. About the only item in their confessional statements that falls into the category of personal faith is belief in a personal devil!

More troubling still, however, for here is where heresy lapses into idolatry, is the *burning* concern of the religious right, whatever lip labor they expend on the traditional fundamentalists, for the United States and the conservation of a particular way of life. They speak as Americans from the Puritans on have often spoken in the past, especially in times of war: God has chosen this nation and invested it with a messianic purpose. Alas, a great national apostasy has occurred, and it is that which Christians of the right must combat, first in the churches and then throughout the society.[12]

Caught up in a tide generated by the political right, Falwell and his followers attached many of their hopes to the idol of that movement, Ronald Reagan. In 1980 and 1984 Reagan skillfully manipulated concerns of the religious right about such issues as abortion, prayer in public schools, and tax credits for tuition to garner support for his own election. He and the fundamentalists wedded their ideologies to such an extent that the latter cannot exercise any prophetic judgment about defense measures, support of Israel, ownership of the Panama Canal, or supply-side economic theory. All have to do with God's will. In 1988 George Bush took advantage of similar issues to best his Democratic opponent. Americanism is not the gospel of Jesus Christ!

Truly Catholic

Second, I dream of a denomination that is truly catholic. I have little doubt this statement will raise quite a few eyebrows, first because it implies that Southern Baptists are already or are becoming "catholic" and secondly because it suggests that we should aspire to become more catholic than we are. Are not Baptists, at least in theory, almost the polar opposite of "Catholics"?

The answer to this question may be yes if we mean "Catholic" with a capital C: Roman Catholic, Anglo-Catholic, or Orthodox being the main representatives. If we mean "catholic" with a little c, however, the

---

[12] Jerry Falwell, *Listen America* (Garden City, NY: Doubleday, 1976).

answer may be no, for the Protestant reformers, Baptists included, argued that they were the "truly catholic" church. Rome abandoned the essence of catholicism by its unfaithfulness to the Word of God and by its failure to represent the whole of Christendom. The word *catholic* is a Greek composite meaning "according to the whole." According to our Baptist forebears, the fatal misstep came when Constantine opted for Christianity and thus forcibly imposed a uniform religion upon all persons in the Roman Empire. This "holy alliance," far from healing the divisions among Christians and settling their squabbles, resulted in irreparable breaches.

For our forebears, therefore, a "truly catholic" church would have been one with room voluntarily to be obedient to the Word of God as one discerned such obedience under the direction of the Holy Spirit. It would have let the Spirit guide and direct both individuals and congregations to discern truth and implement it in daily life and manners.

To their perceptions I would add two drawn from early Christianity, one that the early Christian churches intended and the other a caricature. As I have contended in a faculty address delivered at Southern Seminary several years ago,[13] the early churches aspired to be a church that fulfilled the Great Commission, to be "all things to all persons." "Catholic" meant, above all, missionary. Unfortunately, something else happened, too. Rather than going ahead with this task, they let misguided zeal divert then toward hyperorthodoxy and, from there, divisions and persecutions, just as is now happening in the Southern Baptist Convention. When Rudolf Sohm and Adolf Harnack debated the nature and origin of Catholicism, they depicted this caricature of Catholicism extending several centuries beyond the period of the early church to the Vatican Council of 1870 and after. For Sohm Catholicism had to do, above all, with legalism. For Harnack, it had to do with dogmatism. My own conclusion is that true catholicism has to do with the world mission of Christ through the church but that the caricature can easily emerge from it. It *has* emerged in the Southern Baptist Convention, very much as it did in early Christianity.

What are the features of this distorted version of catholicism? One is *narrow creedalism*. In the fourth century Christians battled over one word just as we are. For them the word was *homoousios*, meaning "of the same essence," as applied to Christ in relation to God the Father. Other words—*homoios*, meaning "like," or even *homoiousious*, a sin-

---

[13] See my faculty address at Southern Seminary on "The Nature and Origin of Catholicism," *Review and Expositor* 72 (Winter 1975): 71-89.

gle letter off, meaning "of like essence"—would not suffice. For us it is *inerrancy* as applied to the Scriptures. Judging by inquiries seminary professors regularly receive regarding their orthodoxy, it will *not* do to announce the errancy of Scriptures. You either believe in inerrancy, or you do not. Thus if you do not say so, you do not believe it. This can be tested by asking whether you believe Adam was one man and Eve one woman, that they gave birth to the first human child, etc. Or whether you believe Jonah was a real person swallowed by a real whale and spit up on a literal earth.

No more than the fourth-century fathers, however, have we settled the issue of right belief by reason or persuasion. Thus a second feature of distorted catholicism emerges, namely in a *reliance upon power politics*. Christians of the early centuries after Constantine called on the emperors and the power of the state, sending into exile with conciliar curses those who refused to subscribe to the right word. Which side went into exile depended, of course, on which way the political winds blew. We resort to electioneering in the grand American tradition. Fly 'em, bus 'em, pay their way . . . just get 'em there for that crucial vote for president. Then let the president nominate a Committee on Committees who subscribe to "inerrancy"; let them name a Committee on Nominations who can follow suit; and, finally, let them choose trustees for the boards who can complete the power play. Shades of the Democratic or Republican Conventions!

Southern Baptists can be grateful to God that the separation of church and state in the United States prohibits state interference in church affairs. Or does it? Lest we relax too much on the knowledge of this guarantee, I would interject some cautionary comments. In 1983 Bailey Smith, president of the Convention, appointed Norris Sydnor, a neophyte black Southern Baptist serving as part-time pastor in Maryland, chairman of the Resolutions Committee. Never having attended a Convention in his life, Sydnor had to call on a fellow charter member of the Religious Roundtable, Ed McAteer, to guide him. McAteer consulted with Reagan staff members in Washington who, among other things, wanted a strong resolution in favor of Reagan's proposed prayer amendment and tuition tax credit plan. Vice President George Bush addressed the Pastor's Conference on the eve of the Convention and commended his hearers for support of prayer in public schools and the "Moral Majority."[14]

---

[14] *Western Recorder*, June 23, 1982, 4.

Such connections as these, however, may have less long-range injurious impact than the way everything has become politicized, particularly in the denominational agencies but even in the churches. This has been evident at Southern Seminary. We are constantly looking over our shoulders to see who is listening or watching. A handful of fundamentalist students regularly report what professors say in the classrooms to fundamentalist watchdogs. As a result, some professors will not allow students to tape their lectures and will not give handouts in class. Even chapel worship is politicized. Rather than gathering as a community to give undivided attention to the worship of God, we have to represent the conflicting political currents either within the Convention or within the Seminary itself. Truth is the first casualty in this, as in other wars!

Here is where a third and perhaps the most serious distortion intrudes, that is, in *the identification of the institution or the program with the Holy Spirit*. One thing we in our anti-institutional tradition must learn to acknowledge and to recognize is that the Holy Spirit can and does work through the corporate as well as the individual will. Our forebears accentuated the latter to the extent that they went too far in their efforts to correct an abuse.

Nevertheless, the early Catholic Church went too far in the opposite direction. Reacting out of fear of diversity of thought and practice as represented especially in the early pentecostal Montanist movement, church leaders tried to lock the Holy Spirit into a neat system. No longer was the Spirit seen to "blow where the Spirit wills" but to come only through sacraments administered by properly certified male priests supervised by reliable bishops.

Fundamentalism threatens a similar constriction of the Holy Spirit. It is a caricature but not much of one to say that, according to the dispensationalist view that underlies fundamentalist theology, the Holy Spirit expired about A.D. 100, as soon as the last New Testament writing was composed, or perhaps held out on deathbed until about A.D. 393 when a North African Council presided over by Augustine sealed the Western canon. Now it is a matter of accepting the authorized interpretations of "safe" leaders, notably, the pastors of jumbo-size churches. They will "speak with the voice of God," as ancient bishops often claimed of themselves, and thus secure one and all against unauthorized and unorthodox teaching.

The reaction of fundamentalists to the charismatic movement is but one witness of their efforts to control the Spirit. Fearful lest God make any disclosures apart from the Scriptures, whose interpretation they would fain control, they have taken strong measures against the Spirit and prophesying. Associations in Dallas, Oklahoma City, and others have excluded churches with charismatic pastors or constituencies. Fundamentalist scholars, for example, at Dallas Theological Seminary, have hacked away at post-New Testament evidence for authentic charismatic and reinterpreted New Testament evidence in such a way that glossolalia is viewed either as temporary or as speaking in tongues not learned.[15]

To the dangers of creedalizing, overpoliticizing, and overinstitutionalizing, we must add a fourth: *perverting the missionary spirit by bigotry and parochialism.* For a time after the conversion of Constantine early Christianity retained its missionary fervor and outlook. Indeed, that fervor heightened to the point of bigotry. Fired with zeal to win all to the one true religion, Christians burned synagogues, tore down pagan temples, and pummeled their occupants. By the time of Theodosious I (379-395) Christianity had become the established religion of the Empire, and bigotry had become a virtue. All traces of competing cults, even Christian groups counted unorthodox, had to be eliminated. The tragic sequel to this outlook was persecution of Jews and crusades against Moslems and heretics during the Middle Ages.

Ironically, however, the completeness of Christianity's victory sapped its missionary zeal. The more it established itself, the more it lapsed into the role of maintaining the status quo. Early on, Christians used the term *paroikia* in its original sense of "sojourning" or living temporarily. From about A.D. 400 on, however, they used it to describe their settled state as reflected in a system of dioceses and parishes. By about A.D. 1000 they no longer exhibited the spirit of Abraham willing to go to a land "he knew not whither."

If I do not misread the thrust of fundamentalist thinking at the moment, many would have us fan the flame of religious zeal until all would conform to the comfortable mold shaped by themselves. They would eliminate the diversities of American pluralism. They would take advantage of a position of establishment to see that the whole body politic imbibed of the one "true" expression of Christianity.

There is a subtle seductiveness about this outlook but history warns us that there will be a heavy price to pay for it. In America, for instance, those Puritans, whom fundamentalists admire so much for their zeal, settled into a comfortable conformity which by the third generation produced a near-complete absenting of themselves from the churches. By

---

[15] See E. Glenn Hinson, "The Significance of Glossolalia in the History of Christianity," in *Speaking in Tongues: A Guide to Research on Glossolalia*, ed. Watson E. Mills (Grand Rapids: Eerdmans, 1986), 183-184, 189-193.

1700 only a fraction of the heirs of those first zealots participated actively in the churches.[16] Contrariwise, hardly any other factor explains the vitality of the American churches as well as nearly complete religious freedom which allows room for pluralism.[17]

Truly Baptist

Third, I dream of a denomination that is truly Baptist. By Baptist I do not mean anything identifiable externally in our practice, not even in believers' baptism. Some externals are important, and we would be wise to continue them, but they do not define the essence of the Baptist tradition. The *essence* of our tradition has to do with voluntariness in religious response, what E. Y. Mullins called "soul competency." To be authentic and responsible, our forebears never tired of saying, "Faith must be free." Religious coercion of any kind invalidates faith and nullifies its effectiveness. As a consequence of this central conviction, our forebears rejected the baptism of infants or children, adopted a policy that maximized individual participation, declared the autonomy of congregations, put themselves in the forefront of the battle for religious liberty, penned some of the most eloquent and far-reaching pleas for completeness of freedom in religious matters, and ardently advocated the separation of church and state as a way of safeguarding this priceless possession.

Here, too, a caricature is imposing itself. Out of zeal for souls, some are running pell-mell in the opposite direction from the voluntary principle to embrace a corporatist model in which the church assumes the primary responsibility for the faith of its members, or, as we have seen in looking at early catholicism, it is believed that the Spirit works primarily or exclusively through the corporate. Consider the impact of this shift on the derivative ideas Baptists have cherished.

Item One—Baptism of Believers? The average age of baptism in the Southern Baptist Convention is now eight years or less. The number of preschoolers (ages three to five) baptized has crept steadily upward as baptisms generally have held steady or declined in the past twelve years.

---

[16] See Edwin Scott Gaustad, *The Great Awakening* (New York: Harper & Brothers, 1957), 9ff.

[17] Winthrop S. Hudson, *The Great Tradition of the American Churches* (New York: Harper & Brothers, 1953), has made a strong case for the fact that the voluntary principle accounts for religious vitality.

	Preschool	**Ages 6-8**
1976	2,061	33,501
1977	1,704	33,892
1978	1,826	34,747
1979	2,087	37,307
1980	2,377	40,295
1981	2,519	37,367
1982	2,631	37,690
1983	2,556	36,568
1984	2,541	36,700
1985	2,455	36,764
1986	2,987	37,979
1987	2,938	37,115
1988	2,738	40,591

Some of the preschoolers were three years of age.

I am not as alarmed as some, especially European, Baptists are about decline in the age of baptism. It is due in great part to an improvement in our nurturing process. In frontier days prospects may have attended meetings only a couple of weeks out of the year and thus received little nurture. Today many of our children grow up never knowing a dividing line between non-Christian and Christian; they have "always believed and belonged." Nevertheless, there is cause for alarm. Some churches, notably the jumbo-size, hyperevangelistic type, are letting the seductiveness of numbers lure them into abandonment of our cherished conviction that the Spirit and not human devices must win those who come and that the decisions must be voluntary.

Item Two—Democratic Polity. Whether in local congregations or in other levels of organization, traditional Baptist reliance on highly participatory democracy is taking a beating. The success syndrome of American corporate life and the church growth model, which is success oriented, have convinced some that a hierarchical arrangement will get the best results. In the jumbo churches, which serve as role models of the fundamentalist movement, the pastor has to have the last word in everything. At the Convention in San Antonio, small wonder that a resolution on the priesthood of believers would come out as an affirmation of pastoral authority!

Item Three—Religious Liberty. Fundamentalist leaders in the SBC will affirm their commitment to *individual* liberty just as Jerry Falwell does. They also affirm freedom of local churches. When they come to further application, however, they exercise reservations. Such liberty should not extend to denominational employees. Employees should represent the beliefs of the *majority* in the Convention, who supposedly agree with the fundamentalists. *Unless employees of the denomination represent the mind of the Convention majority*, the reasoning runs, *they cannot effect the program which the Convention prescribes.*

In the graphic phrasing of Adrian Rogers, "If we believe pickles have souls and they (professors in seminaries or other denomination employees) cannot teach it, then they should not take our money." This opinion shows shades of the Roman Catholic reformer Ignatius Loyola's Rule 13 for Thinking with the Church: "If we wish to be sure that we are right in all things, we should always be ready to accept this principle: I will believe that the white that I see is black, if the hierarchical Church so defines it."

You can see the subtle twist of our Baptist tradition here. Freedom for individuals, but denominational employees—professors in the seminaries, missionaries, Sunday School Board personnel—are not individuals. They are not their own. They belong to the corporation, and the corporation will tell them what to do. That, may I point out, has been the reasoning of the Roman Catholic Church through much of its history. It is an exact specimen of the corporatist model.

Item Four—Separation of Church and State. I need hardly point out to you what is implied for our historic Baptist stand for voluntariness in religion in Resolution 9 —"On Prayer in Public Schools"—adopted at New Orleans. This resolution offered support for President Reagan's proposed prayer amendment, which would read: "Nothing in this Constitution shall be construed to prohibit individual or group prayer in public schools or other public institutions. No person shall be required by the United States or by any state to participate in prayer." Resolution 14— "On Scientific Creationism"—should occasion less surprise, for a number of state conventions have issued similar statements since the twenties. President Reagan's proposal concerning tuition tax credit for education also received sufficient support to make us realize how establishment-minded Southern Baptists have become. Here we find ourselves ready to forget the bitter sufferings of our forebears to end public taxation for support of private or parochial schools.

To sum up all of these things in a graphic way, imagine a spectrum extending from voluntarist to corporatist. In our beginnings we Baptists would have occupied the extreme voluntarist end of the scale alongside Quakers; Roman Catholics would have been at the extreme corporatist end. Where do we find ourselves now? While Roman Catholics have been sliding across the spectrum toward the voluntarist end since the Second Vatican Council, we have been zipping toward the corporatist end. Just as zeal for souls caused early Christians to move in that direction when opportunity presented, so too has it done to us. As a result, there is serious question as to whether the Baptist tradition will survive in the Southern Baptist Convention. We may already have passed midpoint here in terms of our corporate self-image. Can we be ever again truly Baptists?[18]

If this means recovery of the extreme voluntarism of our earliest forebears, the answer is surely negative. Let us pray to God, however, that we have not passed the pre-Vatican II Roman Catholic Church going the other way, as some seem to wish. If I properly assess our total situation, we had best strive to find a way of balancing the evangelical and the voluntarist strains by way of a position that is truly catholic.

Where, Then, from Here?

This, then, is the vision—a denomination *truly* evangelical, *truly* catholic, and *truly* Baptist; not the caricature of these. Given the current state of the Southern Baptist Convention, seemingly so far removed from the vision, how do we move toward the vision?

Experience of the past ten years has dampened optimism I once had that the Southern Baptist Convention might actually attain such a goal. The path ahead is by no means clear, but there are hopeful signs. After ten years the new political religious right has expended its best efforts and spent most of its energies with little to show for the effort except control of the Southern Baptist Convention. Pat Robertson suffered a devastating defeat in the Republican primaries in 1988. Jerry Falwell deftly stepped back from the political limelight. Announcing his support for Vice President Bush and claiming victory on all fronts with the latter's election, he announced his withdrawal from political activities. In the summer of 1989 he disbanded Moral Majority. The religious political right, meantime, is losing a bogeyman, as Communism totters. The "Iron Curtain" is being ripped to shreds. Marxists regimes are swaying in Poland, Hungary, Czechoslovakia, and Germany. One million

---

[18] See my essay on "The Future of the Baptist Tradition" in *Are Southern Baptists "Evangelicals?"*, 186-187.

people poured through the Berlin Wall, the symbol of the effort to control.

How these events will affect fundamentalist control of the Southern Baptist Convention cannot be determined at this point, but one can hardly imagine that they will not have an impact. Freedom is a basic human right. It also belongs to the very nature of the gospel of the free grace of God. Can Baptists, who were midwives of liberty in the United States, stand by and witness the liberation of peoples and nations all over the world without once again recalling and recommitting themselves to their heritage? I do not see how they can.

At the same time, absolutist groups, once in power, will not yield or share power readily. Mainline Southern Baptists, therefore, will have to continue to find ways to apply pressure to force power sharing. Several different approaches have emerged: right wing leaders continue to rally messengers to the annual Convention in support of candidates who profess to be inerrantists but also loyalists. For the long run, unfortunately, electing a moderate will not solve the major problem. Although the Southern Baptist Convention has become the "Catholic Church of the South," it uses the polity of a minority group which is subject to immense abuse. Some radical revamping of polity will have to occur before the churches find an effective way to deal with controversies such as the one which now rages.

The state Conventions, meanwhile, have begun to take some steps to counter widespread disfranchisement as a result of fundamentalist control. In 1988 the Baptist General Association of Virginia addressed a "Memorial" to the Southern Baptist Convention in Las Vegas asking the latter to "consider and respond" to five issues: (1) relationship of the SBC to the Baptist Joint Committee on Public Affairs; (2) options for allocating money through the Cooperative Program; (3) theological education characterized by (a) serious academic scholarship, (b) openness of inquiry, (c) balance in theological approach, and (d) responsible freedom "within the bounds of historic Baptist confessions of faith"; (4) appointment of persons nominated by the Baptist General Association of Virginia to membership to the SBC Committee on Committees; and (5) a new style of partnership between the SBC and state Conventions. In 1989 the Association took the further step of delineating some options for disbursement of funds by the churches.[19]

The state Conventions stand in a key position to influence what happens in the Southern Baptist Convention because they channel

---

[19] *1989 Southern Baptist Convention Annual*, 70-71.

Cooperative Program funds to the SBC. If they returned to the original method of disbursing funds directly to the agencies, they could put pressure on fundamentalists to share power. Even if the latter continued to appoint only their own partisans to boards, commissions, and other agencies, they would have to pay attention to funding. Eventually, fundamentalist leaders would realize they would benefit from a balanced representation on all committees and boards.[20]

Other churches have not stood by and allowed foreclosure of options as Southern Baptist institutions have fallen under fundamentalist control one by one. A number have added their names to the list of churches already dually aligned with the American Baptist Churches. The Southern Baptist Alliance has taken steps to promote fellowship among "moderate" churches, to arrange for alternate places of education for ministers, and to support projects threatened by fundamentalist control of the SBC. Several Baptist universities are making plans to open divinity schools during this decade.

At the beginning of the last decade of the twentieth century the Southern Baptist picture is fuzzy. The net effect of ten years of fundamentalist control is downward spiral in many areas. The Cooperative Program has not kept pace with inflation. The Foreign Mission Board appointed the fewest missionaries since 1972. Southeastern Seminary has been threatened with the loss of its accreditation. Seminary enrollments are dropping not merely because the "baby boom" is past but because controversy has created confusion about vocation. A giant corporation running well before a hostile takeover is no longer the nation's most envied religious enterprise. Is there hope?

If there is, it probably lies in the same place as a major part of the problem, that is, in Baptist polity. Autonomy of churches, associations, and conventions assures that Baptists can assert themselves to find an answer to their problems. As people rise up everywhere to call for the Baptist cry for freedom, maybe Southern Baptists will see and hear and act to achieve the vision of a people truly evangelical, truly catholic, and truly Baptist.

---

[20] See further E. Glenn Hinson, "Professor Asks States: 'Refranchise Majority'," *SBC Today* (September 1988), 16.

15

Are Southern
———— Baptists ————
"Evangelicals"?
A Further Reflection

James Leo Garrett, Jr.

It is gratifying to me that many of the issues E. Glenn Hinson and I discussed and vigorously debated prior to 1983 concerning Southern Baptists and evangelicals[1] have been further pursued in the context of the late 1980s and supplemented by other important considerations at The Southern Baptist Theological Seminary's 1989 and 1990 Conferences on Southern Baptists and evangelicals.

Let it be pointed out, for the sake of clarification, that Professor Hinson and I did not commence to write our principal chapters in *Are Southern Baptists "Evangelicals"?* with the thought that we were to be engaged in a debate with one another. Rather, each of us had written some materials reflective of a viewpoint, and Mercer University Press then proposed to publish these materials in a volume in which the later Professor James E. Tull would serve as introducer and referee; Professor Hinson and I would offer rebuttals to each other's viewpoint.

In 1981 and 1983 Professor Hinson and I also offered presentations of our viewpoints in *Baptist History and Heritage*.[2] In 1989 I sought in a popular article to further identify Southern Baptists as "denomination evangelicals" in the context of the Believer's Church Conference

---

[1] James Leo Garrett, Jr., E. Glenn Hinson, and James E. Tull, *Are Southern Baptists "Evangelicals"?* (Macon, GA: Mercer University, 1983).

[2] Hinson, "Baptists and Evangelicals: What is the Difference?" 16 (April 1981): 20-32; Hinson, "Neo-fundamentalism: An Interpretation and Critique," 16 (April 1981): 33-42, 39; Garrett, "Southern Baptists as Evangelicals," 18 (April 1983): 10-20.

held at Southwestern Baptist Theological Seminary and the Evangelical Affirmations Conference held at Trinity Evangelical Divinity School.[3]

The provocative and informative papers and responses presented at the Southern Seminary conferences press further toward a more accurate and fruitful understanding of its theme. I address my comments to these papers and responses.

Defining "American Evangelicals"

Richard Mouw's proposal to use the hymn "It Is Well with My Soul" as the springboard for the delineation of evangelicals is an intriguing one. In a popular setting it can grab the attention of Christians who call themselves or might be denominated "evangelicals." Although the hymn can well delineate the evangelical understanding of salvation, it does not speak to the authority of the Bible or to the mandate of evangelism and missions.

Stanley J. Grenz's proposed delineation of the "ethos" of evangelicalism in terms of "shared piety" has value, especially if one should accept Donald G. Bloesch's view that evangelicalism necessarily embraces the heritage of pietism.[4] Grenz's comment that nonevangelical Christians "say their prayers" and evangelical Christians "have a word of prayer" is insightful. I know post-Vatican Council II Roman Catholics, however, who do not "say their prayers" and Baptist churches in which "read prayers" are increasingly common. At this point John P. Newport's effort to draw in the research and perspective of Donald W. Dayton concerning Holiness and Pentecostal Christians becomes significant. Even if Grenz's desire to define evangelicalism as "shared piety" should be accepted as valid, it should not preclude a recognition that there are varieties of piety, worship, and lifestyles among evangelicals ranging from cognitive to emotive, from rather individualistic to congregation-oriented, and from polemical to irenic. It seems important to recognize, as Richard Mouw has suggested, that F. Ernest Stoeffler's identification[5] of three weaknesses in the heritage of Pietism (anti-intellectualism, otherworldliness, and ecclesiastical separatism) should help us

---

[3] "Who Are Southern Baptists in 1989?" *Baptist Standard*, (July 26, 1989), 12; condensed as "Southern Baptists Called 'Denominational Evangelicals'," *(Word and Way)*, (May 25, 1989), 6.

[4] Donald Bloesch, *Essentials of Evangelical Theology*, 2 vols. (San Francisco: Harper and Row, 1978, 1979), 1:5; *The Evangelical Renaissance* (Grand Rapids: Eerdmans, 1973), 101-157.

[5] F. Ernest Stoeffler, "Epilogue," in Stoeffler, ed., *Continental Pietism and Early American Christianity* (Grand Rapids: Eerdmans, 1976), 270-271.

to understand the older fundamentalism and its present day expressions. Stanley Grenz does not stop, however, with his proposed definition of evangelicalism as "shared piety." He goes on to embrace (and I think rightly) the "doctrine and experience" formula of Donald G. Bloesch[6] but reverses it so as to read "experience and doctrine."

Leon McBeth has previously given an attitudinal, as distinct from theological, definition of fundamentalism.[7] I assume that he has presupposed that definition in dealing with present-day evangelicalism, broadly or narrowly defined. The J. Frank Norris brand of fundamentalism, not the Northern mainstream type of fundamentalism, is McBeth's frame of reference and principal reason "for cringing." Mainstream or Northern/Western evangelicals, however, have undergone change within this century, even as Southern Baptists have undergone change, and I would contend that our present posture must take a realistic view of both movements as they are and as they are becoming.

Joel Carpenter's chapter, replete with important insights both about Southern Baptists and about Northern evangelicals, has helpfully identified the latter as a "diverse transdenominational" parachurch network--those whom George Marsden has called "card-carrying evangelicals", or evangelicals who identify themselves by this label. It should be obvious by now that most Southern Baptists do not reckon themselves or cannot rightly be denominated as "card-carrying evangelicals". Only under Marsden's broad definition of evangelicals can we pursue meaningfully the question of relationships between Southern Baptists and non-SBC evangelicals. Marsden's fivefold theological profile of broadly defined evangelicalism is quite consonant with Richard Quebedeaux's threefold profile,[8] which I favorably cited in 1983.[9] Using the profile, I proceeded to conclude that Southern Baptists were "denominational Evangelicals,"[10] and now David S. Dockery has not only concurred in this conclusion but also clarified it by his distinction, made also by Stanley Grenz in his North American setting, between "Evangelical first" and "Baptist second" (for evangelicals such as Carl F. H. Henry, E. J. Carnell, Billy Graham, Harold Lindsell, Bernard L. Ramm, Vernon Grounds, and

---

[6] Bloesch, *Essentials of Evangelical Theology*, 1:ix.

[7] Leon McBeth, "Fundamentalism in the Southern Baptist Convention in Recent Years," *Review and Expositor* 79 (Winter 1982): 85-86.

[8] Richard Quebedeux, *The Young Evangelicals* (New York: Harper and Row, 1974), 34.

[9] "Who Are the 'Evangelicals'?" in Garrett, Hinson, and Tull, *Are Southern Baptists "Evangelicals"?*, 61.

[10] "Are Southern Baptists Evangelicals?" in Garrett, Hinson, and Tull, *Are Southern Baptists "Evangelicals"?*, 126.

George Ladd) and, by implication, "Baptist first" and "evangelical second" (for Southern Baptists evangelicals serving in SBC seminaries, boards, agencies, and as pastors).

Defining "Southern Baptists"

The task of defining "Southern Baptists" may begin with but does not end with saying that Southern Baptists are members of churches that contribute to the Cooperative Program of the Southern Baptist Convention.[11] Joel Carpenter rightly discerns that denominational loyalty and support of the Cooperative Program have been (whether they still are may be debated) essential characteristics of Southern Baptists.

John P. Newport has described three strands (A, B, C) among twentieth-century Southern Baptists, partly in order to interpret the 1980s as the era of the dominance of strand C in the SBC. Richard R. Melick, Jr., has found that Newport's three strands are not "clear-cut" *theologically* definable strands, since there have been overlapping and movement over the boundaries of the Newport typology.[12] Melick may be correct that Newport's three strands are not precisely definable theological categories, but that alone does not make the strands invalid since culture, regionalism, ethical concerns, and polity have also shaped and diversified Southern Baptists.

Stanley Grenz rightly probes the denominational isolationism of Southern Baptists, asking, for example, why they did not affiliate with the National Association of Evangelicals and offering three reasons.[13] He overstates his rationale when he assumes that responsible Southern Baptists clearly and directly have identified the "body of Christ" with the SBC. I know of no representative Southern Baptist leader who has made such an unqualified assertion. How non-Southern Baptists perceive Southern Baptists' isolation and how Southern Baptists have sought to justify it are two different questions. Grenz does not clearly indicate whether by "body of Christ" he means all the redeemed of

---

[11] Daniel Vestal and Robert A. Baker, *Pulling Together!* (Nashville: Broadman Press, 1987); Cecil Ray and Susan Ray, *Cooperation: The Baptist Way to a Lost World* (Nashville: Stewardship Commission, SBC, 1985).

[12] Melick seems to place George W. Truett under Strand C. That, I would contend, is to misunderstand Truett's ministry, theology, and role in the SBC and the Baptist World Alliance.

[13] Two further clarifications are needed: (1) the possible affiliation with the NAE was on the part of certain individual Southern Baptists who lived in Tennessee and Kentucky, and the issue never came formally before the SBC; (2) the SBC gave considerable formal consideration, in more than one annual session, to the question of possible membership in the World Council of Churches and the National Council of Churches.

humanity or a kind of panaevangelicalism. Furthermore, the SBC's membership and active participation in the Baptist World Alliance from its inception in 1905, unmentioned by Grenz, is a factor that has qualified SBC isolation.

Understanding who Southern Baptists are is an ongoing task, especially as internal diversities increase. David S. Dockery has helpfully referred to different styles among Southern Baptist congregations (the "liturgical," the "teacher-preacher," "the revivalistic," and the "quasicharismatic") and different types of Southern Baptist polity, as practiced but not necessarily as professed (the "congregational," the "dictatorial," the "committee-led," and the "elder-ruled"). Such differences are a fertile field for more intensive research and publication.

What direction should Southern Baptist theology take in the 1990s? David Dockery has implied that SBC theologians ought to publish more and said such theology should be directed to the decade of the 1990s.[14] John Newport has called for a recovered and reapplied multifaceted Baptist theology that gives emphasis to soteriology and ecclesiology, and Stanley Grenz regards ecclesiology, not biblical inerrancy, as the area that "must command our attention and shape the discussion in the future." For Richard Melick the nature of biblical authority looms large, for the "simple biblicism" characterizing Southern Baptists in the past must yield to "a more adequate biblicism." What constitutes the "more adequate" is a crucial question.

Commonalities, Differences, and Relationships Between the Two

Glenn Hinson has espoused the view that Southern Baptists now "have far more in common with Roman Catholics" than they "do with [non-Baptist] 'Evangelicals'." Hinson and I have together participated in the Roman Catholic-Southern Baptist Scholars' Dialogue, he for nine years and I for six. We have shared in the challenging opportunity of dialogue with Roman Catholics in the post-Vatican Council II era and have located our commonalities. We cannot go back to the overarchingly polemical stance that characterized our Baptist predecessors. Still I find Hinson's conclusion untenable. There are Mariological, ecclesiological, sacramental, and sacerdotal differences that still are important. He seems to be upset by the fact that Southern Baptists have become so numerous in the states of the South and the Southwest, where we are so

---

[14] See Timothy George and David S. Dockery, eds., *Baptist Theologians* (Nashville: Broadman Press, 1990).

dominant we cannot think like Baptists, whose identity was established in a minority situation. I, too, do not wish to see Baptists lose their freedoms and Baptist identity but I am not afraid that they will do so through dialogue with non-Baptist evangelicals.

Leon McBeth, who rightly expresses concern about fundamentalist hegemony in the SBC, seems to be reluctant to allow for or point to any significant interchange between Southern Baptists and non-Baptist evangelicals beyond the gesture of an extended hand.

Joel Carpenter has clarified the biases that do exist on both sides of the Southern Baptist-evangelical divide. His computer analogy for the organizational differences is apt. John Newport has called on Southern Baptists to study and relate to non-Baptist evangelicals, even as the two seminary-sponsored Ridgecrest conferences did, and has invited the evangelicals, especially in their scholarly and publishing ventures, to include more Southern Baptists. Richard Melick has concluded from a survey that in the leading non-Baptist evangelical seminaries fewer than 5 percent of the students are Southern Baptists and that few professors in SBC seminaries have studied in specifically evangelical educational institutions.[15]

Mouw, Carpenter, Newport, Dockery, and Melick see a need for more dialogue and significant interchange between Southern Baptists and non-Baptist evangelicals. With this I concur. At the present, deepening personal relationships, study of differing histories, common experience in ministry and in missions, and abandonment of stereotypes would seem to be more important than structure or organization. Such developments could more likely occur if and when there should be depoliticization of the internal processes within the SBC.

---

[15] It would be interesting to determine also what percentage of the professors in non-Baptist evangelical colleges and seminaries have studied in SBC seminaries and SBC-related colleges and universities.

16

A Call for Baptist Evangelicals

&

Evangelical Baptists: Communities of Faith and A Common Quest for Identity

R. Albert Mohler, Jr.

The remarkable shifts that have taken place on the American religious landscape since the midcentury have left three major players on the American Christian scene: the mainline Protestant churches, Protestant evangelicals, and Roman Catholicism. The so-called "seven sisters" which constituted the mainline or "mainstream" front at the midcentury have fallen on hard times, and the mainline has, as some have suggested, become more "sideline" or "oldline." Both their theological witness and their ability to shape culture have been seriously eroded.

A resurgent Roman Catholicism has emerged in what Richard John Neuhaus has termed "the Catholic moment"; and, though American Catholicism is plagued with its own internal conflicts, it will continue to be a major voice in the public square.[1]

Evangelicalism constitutes the third, and probably the most vigorous, cohort amidst American Christianity. The evangelical alliance that emerged in the period just after World War II is largely intact and has an acknowledged place in the public square and the public church. Mainline churches have lost millions of members in the last two decades, and a discernible process of mainline "decline" is now assumed to be a self-evi-

---

[1] See Richard John Neuhaus, *The Catholic Moment: The Paradox of the Church in the Postmodern World* (San Francisco: Harper and Row, 1987). Neuhaus has, of course, now experienced his own "Catholic moment"; converting from Lutheranism to Roman Catholicism in late 1990.

dent pattern in American Protestantism.[2] Those bodies classified as evangelicals have, on the other hand, experienced significant growth and development.

When discussed in the context of American Christianity as a whole, Southern Baptists are almost uniformly classed among the evangelicals. But, are Southern Baptists evangelicals? That issue, suggested James E. Tull, is an "open question."[3] For some Southern Baptists it remains an open question. Others have reached a firm determination. Several contributors to this volume, including both evangelicals and Southern Baptists, have answered with an emphatic "Yes." Others, no less emphatic, insist that Southern Baptists are not evangelicals, as the term is generally applied to a conservative Protestant movement and subculture in the United States.[4]

At the onset we must admit that the issue of whether Southern Baptists are evangelicals, if it actually remains open to question, is but one of several pressing and inescapable "open questions" addressed to both Southern Baptists and the evangelical movement. The open questions concern the basic vision, nature, and character that produced Southern Baptists and the evangelical movement. Both the evangelical movement and the Southern Baptist Convention find themselves embroiled in controversies and conflicts which call into question the future of their respective experiments. In both cases, the most basic and most pressing issue is *identity*.

The issue of identity has been a preoccupation of the church from its inception. The question of what kind of people God has called into being confronts the church in every age. It is an inescapable and

---

[2] See, for example, Milton J. Coulter, John K. Mulder, and Louis B. Weeks, eds., *The Mainstream Protestant "Decline": The Presbyterian Pattern* (Louisville: Westminster/ John Knox, 1991). Recent research indicates that those leaving the mainline churches are not necessarily moving into more evangelical churches. Many, if not most, are probably joining the unchurched. See C. Kirk Hadaway, "Denominational Defection: Recent Research on Religious Disaffiliation in America" in the volume above.

[3] James Leo Garrett, Jr., E. Glenn Hinson, and James E. Tull, *Are Southern Baptists "Evangelicals"?* (Macon, GA: Mercer University Press, 1983).

[4] We should note that the contributors to the present volume include both Southern Baptists and non-Southern Baptist representatives of the evangelical movement. The Southern Baptists were split on the issue, with representatives including Dockery, Garrett, and the present writer identifying Southern Baptists with the evangelical movement; Newport and others uncertain; and Hinson and McBeth insistent that Southern Baptists are not evangelicals in this sense. Note, however, that the evangelical representatives, including Marsden, Carpenter, Johnston, and Grenz, uniformly classified Southern Baptists in some way with the evangelical movement.

unavoidable issue. As John Leith comments: "The Christian community that has survived has always seriously sought the integrity of its own identity."[5] Indeed, the issues of *identity* and *integrity* are indivisible. The absence of a clear and evident identity robs the church of its integrity and witness.[6]

A faltering sense of identity now threatens both the evangelical movement and the Southern Baptist Convention. Both have struggled with these issues throughout the 1980s. Pride indeed comes before a fall. The year 1976 should stand as a reminder that confusion concerning identity is a recipe for ferment. In that year *Newsweek* magazine declared the "Year of the Evangelical," and Southern Baptists gathered to adopt "Bold Mission Thrust." Within three years both groups would be embroiled in soul-searching and conflict.

Southern Baptists are not accustomed to asking questions of identity in terms of internal debate, or, at least this was the case until recent years. External threats and the presence of other religious bodies with competing truth claims and practices had forced Southern Baptists to define themselves over against those claims and practices and to forge an identity as a distinctive denomination. Baptist identity was cast to meet the challenges of other vigorous denominations.

By the turn of the twentieth century, Southern Baptists, though diverse in geography, worship tradition, and certain practices, had developed a consensus of conservative theology (shaped around a modified Calvinism) and cooperative methodology. Southern Baptists generally assumed a common identity based on doctrinal commitments, missionary vision, and distinctive Baptist practices.[7]

By the midcentury, Southern Baptists were forced to confront basic identity issues and what one Southern Baptist historian termed an "identity crisis."[8] With considerable foresight W. R. Estep predicted that

---

[5] John H. Leith, *From Generation to Generation: The Renewal of the Church According to Its Own Theology and Practice* (Louisville: Westminster/John Knox, 1990), 25.

[6] As Samuel S. Hill and Robert G. Torbet suggest, ". . . self-identity is necessary if Baptists are to maintain their integrity in the midst of the varied and often conflicting pressures of our time." See *Baptists North and South* (Valley Forge: Judson, 1964), 14.

[7] Such a consensus is suggested by Bill J. Leonard in his discussion of the "Grand Compromise" which produced the modern Southern Baptist Convention. See his *God's Last and Only Hope: The Fragmentation of the Southern Baptist Convention* (Grand Rapids: Eerdmans, 1990).

[8] William R. Estep, "Southern Baptists in Search of an Identity," in *The Lord's Free People in a Free Land*, ed. W. R. Estep (Fort Worth, TX: Faculty of the School of Theology, Southwestern Baptist Theological Seminary, 1976), 245-270.

Southern Baptists were "entering a crisis of major proportions." As he stated:

> The nature of the problems confronting the denomination are so varied and complex they tend to defy analysis. In the face of bewildering cross currents that now course through an increasingly heterogenous denomination is a problem that, to some extent, encompasses all the others: the question of identity.[9]

Whether prompted by external or internal forces, the issue of identity has shaped every major conflict and controversy in Baptist history. As William H. Brackney comments: "Baptist history is replete with self-doubt and identity crises."[10]

This most recent identity crisis is the underlying dynamic in the current Southern Baptist controversy. Rival visions of Baptist identity now compete for power and majority status within the Convention. Both visions, now organized into opposing political parties claim to represent "real Baptists," and identity-rhetoric is employed generously by both sides in the denominational struggle.

Who are the real Baptists? Are they the Southern Baptists who define themselves primarily by identification with "Baptist distinctives" such as religious freedom, soul competency, and the priesthood of believers?[11] This "liberty party" locates Baptist identity in these affirmations and resists any move toward greater theological and doctrinal specificity. Their presuppositions rule out substantive and enforceable doctrinal parameters. Though historic Baptist confessions are acknowledged, they are treated as merely illustrating what some Baptists believed at one time and serve no regulative function. Proposals for more clearly defined parameters are met with cries of "creedalism" and coercion.

The "truth party," on the other hand, defines Baptist identity in terms of continuity with the conservative theological traditions that shaped and sustained the Southern Baptist Convention, relatively

---

[9] Estep, "Southern Baptists in Search of an Identity," 145.

[10] William H. Brackney, "Commonly (though falsely) Called . . .: Reflections on the Search for Baptist Identity," in *Perspectives in Churchmanship: Essays in Honor of Robert G. Torbet*, ed. David S. Scholer (Macon, GA: Mercer University Press, 1986), 81.

[11] None of these "distinctives" is, of course, unique to Baptists, though Baptists have given these issues a unique emphasis and advocacy. In the current battle these distinctives are themselves issues of debate, as evidenced by the furor over competing understandings of the priesthood of believers.

unthreatened, from its birth until the middle of the twentieth century.[12] Proponents point to the classical orthodoxy of the denomination's founders, the unmolested continuation of that tradition well into the twentieth century, and the conservative doctrinal positions uniformly taken by the Convention itself, including the 1925 and 1963 versions of *The Baptist Faith and Message*. They define themselves over against more revisionist and accommodationist theological positions and resist any theological compromise on core beliefs. Religious liberty and soul competence are affirmed but with the presupposition that these Baptist emphases were developed as a protection against the coercive power of the state and not against the self-determination of a voluntary association.

The Southern Baptist Convention was born in a pre-critical age, that is, before the influence of critical methodologies and theological modernism had reached the South.[13] Yet, by 1859 and the founding of the denomination's first theological seminary, the move toward clearly defined doctrinal parameters was evident. As the founders of The Southern Baptist Theological Seminary made clear, the statement of faith was to have an enforceable regulative authority.[14]

The Southern Baptist Convention has been caught in a tension between *what can be assumed* and *what must be articulated*. The Convention could assume almost universal agreement on the core doctrines of the classical Christian tradition in 1845. By the 1960s this was no longer possible. Modernity now forces the Convention to articulate more clearly the confessional boundaries of convictional cooperation.

---

[12] The use of the terms "liberty party" and "truth party" is borrowed somewhat from Samuel S. Hill's interesting typology of Southern religion, in which he identifies a "truth party," a "conversion party," a "spirituality party," and a "service party." My use of the label he ascribes to his first type differs from Hill's approach in that he identifies the truth party with fundamentalism and an uncooperative stance which does not fit many Southern Baptist churches. See Samuel S. Hill, "Fundamentalism and the South," in *Perspectives on Churchmanship: Essays in Honor of Robert G. Torbet*, 47-65.

[13] Southern Baptists were not alone in this pre-critical condition. Southern Presbyterians did not confront issues of theological revision and the impact of so-called "higher biblical criticism" until well into the twentieth century. See "Pluralism and Policy in Presbyterian Views of Scripture," by Jack B. Rogers and Donald K. McKim, in *The Confessional Mosaic: Presbyterians and Twentieth Century Theology*, ed. Milton J. Coulter, John M. Mulder, and Louis B. Weeks (Louisville: Westminster/John Knox, 1991), 37-58.

[14] The seminary's "Abstract of Principles" is a part of the institution's charter. See R. Albert Mohler, Jr., "Beyond the Impasse: Has Theology a Future in the Southern Baptist Convention?" in *Beyond the Impasse: Scripture, Interpretation, and Theology in Southern Baptist Life*, ed. Robison James and David S. Dockery (Nashville: Broadman Press).

Identity remains the issue. "Card-carrying members" of the Truth Party and their opposites in the Liberty Party are unlikely to coexist side by side indefinitely. The battle for denominational control has been won by the national leadership of the Truth Party, but this has not settled all issues concerning the future of the Convention. Many Southern Baptists have declined to carry either card. The overwhelming electoral support garnered by conservative candidates in SBC elections indicates that a majority of Southern Baptists agree that a process of denominational renewal must include theological recovery and the establishment of articulated and regulative doctrinal parameters. Yet they are also concerned that the denomination not be destroyed in the process.

So the Southern Baptist Convention remains in an identity crisis. Its future will be determined by whether or not it will be able to solve that identity crisis and still remain intact.

American evangelicals find themselves in a similar quandary. Indeed, the story of the evangelical movement in America is, in essence, a narrative of a conservative stratum of American Protestantism in search of an identity which is neither fundamentalist nor liberal.

The essays in this volume demonstrate that the term *evangelical* is itself an issue of debate. Since the root of the word relates to the gospel itself, few Christian groups would eschew the word altogether. As a matter of fact, many who are clearly outside the evangelical movement wish to claim the label.

In its most common usage the term identifies the conservative wing of American Protestantism[15] and is most specifically identified with the movement which emerged out of fundamentalism in the 1940s and 1950s with leaders such as Carl F. H. Henry, Bernard Ramm, E. J. Carnell, Harold J. Ockenga, and Billy Graham.[16] The leaders of this new movement declared their intention to forge a new "third force" that would be fully orthodox and yet fully engaged with the larger context of thought and culture.

---

[15] As Roman Catholicism is embroiled in its own inner conflicts, some conservative Catholics have turned to the evangelical movement for colleagues and common resources. See Keith A. Fournier, *Evangelical Catholics* (Nashville: Thomas Nelson, 1990). Similarly, some evangelicals have found themselves drawn to the more liturgical churches. Examples of this include Robert Weber of Wheaton College, now an Episcopalian and Thomas Howard of Gordon College, who converted to Roman Catholicism. See Robert Weber, *Evangelicals on the Canterbury Trail* (Grand Rapids: Eerdmans, 1985).

[16] See R. Albert Mohler, Jr., "Evangelical Theology and Karl Barth: Representative Models of Response," (Ph.D. diss., The Southern Baptist Theological Seminary, 1989).

The roots of this movement in fundamentalism are apparent and acknowledged, yet it also lays claim to a more comprehensive continuity with the classical tradition of the church. The young leaders, soon labeled the "New Evangelicals," defined themselves against the obscurantism, separatism, and cultural isolation of fundamentalism, but also equally against modernist or liberal theology and the revisionist tendencies already apparent in the mainline churches.[17] The term "new evangelicalism" first coined by Ockenga but popularized by Henry, Carnell, and Ramm, was an attempt to link the new movement with the classical evangelical tradition—a tradition which represented a bold and fulsome orthodoxy without the separatism that had come to characterize American fundamentalism by the 1930s.[18] By the 1960s, the "new" was dropped, and "evangelicalism" came to be identified with the network, movement, and subculture that emerged or reoriented themselves under the leadership of the New Evangelicals.

The present hour finds evangelicals, no less than Southern Baptists, in the grip of a severe identity crisis. The pressures of modernity and the presence of rival claims to the evangelical mantle have forced this identity crisis with a renewed urgency.

Some are ready to dispense with the word altogether. Harold Lindsell, a former editor of *Christianity Today* and one of the early faculty members at Fuller Theological Seminary, has suggested that the accommodationist tendencies of modern evangelicalism should prompt the genuinely orthodox to reclaim the fundamentalist label.[19] From a different perspective, Donald W. Dayton and William Abraham suggest that *evangelical* is "an essentially contested concept";[20] that is, a term or

---

[17] See Harold J. Ockenga, "From Fundamentalism, Through New Evangelicalism, to Evangelicalism," in *Evangelical Roots*, ed. Kenneth Kantzer (Nashville: Thomas Nelson, 1978), 35-48; and George M. Marsden, "From Fundamentalism to Evangelicalism," in *The Evangelicals: What They Believe, Who They Are, Where They Are Changing*, ed. David Wells and John Woodbridge (Nashville: Abingdon, 1977), 142-162.

[18] George Marsden's essay in the volume and his recent *Understanding Fundamentalism and Evangelicalism* (Grand Rapids: Eerdmans, 1991), are perhaps the most concise survey of this historical development.

[19] Harold Lindsell, *The New Paganism* (San Francisco: Harper and Row, 1987). A similar judgment came from Francis Schaeffer in his *The Great Evangelical Disaster* (Westchester, IL: Crossway, 1984).

[20] The term "essentially contested concept" is a technical device developed by W. B. Gallie to identify concepts "the proper use of which inevitably involves endless disputes about their proper uses on the part of their users." See his *Philosophy and Historical Understanding* (London: Chatto and Windus, 1964), chapter 8.

concept which produces more confusion than clarity. Speaking of "evangelical" Abraham comments:

> The term is generally used in a mode of appraisal; it is rarely a purely neutral or descriptive form. It is employed to accredit some kind of achievement generally valued by those who apply the term to themselves. The achievement in mind is internally complex. There is no single essence or one particular condition that captures the achievement concerned or will be agreed upon by all evangelicals.[21]

Those ready to jettison the term tend to represent the fringes of the evangelical movement; either those on the evangelical right who were never quite ready to abandon fundamentalist separatism or those on the left whose revisionist tendencies cannot be accommodated in the evangelical tent. For the most part, the term continues to function with a sufficient, if incomplete, clarity of usage.

The essays by Carpenter, Marsden, and Johnston reveal the diversity represented within the contemporary evangelical tent. Marsden cites Johns Hopkins University historian Timothy Smith's use of the terms "evangelical mosaic" and "evangelical kaleidoscope" to reflect this diversity. Johnston attempts to define evangelicalism in terms of "family resemblance." Such attempts are potentially helpful, but they are of limited assistance in the struggle to solve the identity crisis.

The central issue in the identity quest is what constitutes the *essence* of evangelical faith and the unity that produced the evangelical movement. If *Who Are the Genuine Southern Baptists?* is an issue of debate, so is *Who Are the Authentic Evangelicals?* With parallels to the Southern Baptist dynamic, many evangelicals are divided between what might be termed an "Experience Party" and a "Doctrine Party."

The Experience Party seeks to define evangelicalism in terms of a common experience of conversion and the Christian life. Wesleyan, holiness, Pentecostal, and charismatic strains of the evangelical movement often claim this as the central ingredient to evangelical definition. To those strains must be added others whose image of evangelicalism was formed by revivalism.[22]

---

[21] William J. Abraham, *The Coming Great Revival: Recovering the Full Evangelical Tradition* (San Francisco: Harper and Row, 1984), 73-74.

[22] Many Southern Baptists have been similarly influenced by revivalism (at the expense of more substantive doctrinal formation) and locate religious experience as the defining mark of Southern Baptist identity. This would include persons included in both moderate and conservative camps in the SBC and explains why some Southern Baptists are relatively apathetic toward doctrinal issues.

The Doctrine Party identifies evangelicalism with a bold advocacy of the orthodox tradition, including the unblemished authority of Holy Scripture. While also insistent on the necessity of personal experience and conversion, the Doctrine Party seeks to defend "the faith once received" and to witness to classical orthodoxy while surrounded by a culture of compromise.[23]

The essays in this volume demonstrates the conflict between these two rival interpretations of evangelical identity. When placed alongside the Southern Baptist context, striking similarities appear. Southern Baptists and American evangelicals now find themselves debating common issues, if in different contexts.

The Issue of Historical Roots

A people caught in an identity crisis will naturally look to their historical roots for guidance. Divided as they are by so many issues, Southern Baptists cannot agree on the essence of their historical roots and development. Torn in previous generations by battles over Baptist successionism (Landmarkism), the current division falls along different lines. Southern Baptists are confronted with rival historiographies. The Liberty Party holds a libertarian historiography which treats Baptist history largely in terms of a people born in dissent who became the advocates of religious liberty and unfettered freedom of conscience. The *sine qua non* of Baptist identity is liberty. As the title of a recent book published by the Southern Baptist Alliance suggests, *Being Baptist Means Freedom*.[24]

Other Baptists contend for a historical perspective that includes a much greater attention to the orthodox faith of early Baptists and their heirs. Baptist advocacy of religious liberty and the freedom of conscience has not, they remind, prevented Baptist churches, associations, and Conventions from drawing tangible doctrinal parameters and confessing their common faith in straightforward terms.

Evangelicals are likewise divided. Advocates of the Wesleyan/Pentecostal traditions charge that the traditional evangelical historiography

---

[23] David Wells, a representative of the Doctrine Party, states clearly this concern: "Evangelicals by definition affirm the formal and material principles, but these are transmuted, in practice, simply into a way of looking at life. What now defines an evangelical is more often than not merely a private, interior quality that he or she has, rather than very specific doctrinal beliefs. Who is and not an evangelical therefore becomes a slippery and awkward question." "No Offense: I Am an Evangelical," in *A Time to Speak: The Evangelical-Jewish Encounter* (Grand Rapids: Eerdmans, 1987), 37-38.

[24] Alan Neely, ed., *Being Baptist Means Freedom* (Charlotte, NC: The Southern Baptist Alliance, 1988).

identifies the movement, in the main, with what they term the "Reformed/Presbyterian/Baptist" strain that was most formative in the New Evangelicalism. These conflicting versions of evangelical history shape the debate over evangelical identity.[25]

The Issue of Doctrinal Parameters

What theological limits conscribe Baptist and evangelical identity? As has already been stated, some Baptists resist the notion of any regulative theological parameters. No authority external to the individual should, they argue, coerce or lay claim upon the individual conscience. Others argue that this is not the point. Coercion is not the issue, these Baptists say, but the right and responsibility of a denominational body to set limits upon acceptable doctrinal diversities.

The SBC Peace Committee, established at the 1985 Southern Baptist Convention in Dallas, Texas, became a battleground for these two competing positions, thus mirroring the conflict in the denomination at large.[26] Conservatives, frustrated that their quest for some enforceable doctrinal specificity had been met with great resistance, were successful in detailing four very specific theological determinations, but were unsuccessful in their effort to move the issues from the "findings" section to "recommendations."

The course of the Southern Baptist conflict has revealed the fault line between those who believe that greater doctrinal specificity (and a more regulative status for Baptist confessional documents among denominational employees) is a necessary corrective to a process of doctrinal accommodation and those who feel that such a move is antithetical to the Baptist spirit.

The same issue plagues evangelicalism. In both contexts the key issues of debate have been the authority and interpretation of the Bible. Biblical inerrancy, which emerged as a key issue of evangelical debate in the 1970s, continues to divide evangelical from evangelical and Southern Baptist from Southern Baptist, though studies indicate that a majority of both evangelicals and Southern Baptists affirm the doctrine.[27]

---

[25] See Donald W. Dayton, *Discovering An Evangelical Heritage* (New York: Harper and Row, 1976).

[26] See Herschel H. Hobbs, "The Status Quo: An Analysis," *The Christian Index*, January 24, 1991, 6, 13.

Likewise, exegetical issues and current hermeneutical movements have produced varied responses. What are the limits of legitimate evangelical biblical interpretation? Redaction criticism, questions of historicity, the influence of feminist hermeneutics, and other issues divide both evangelical and Southern Baptist ranks.

The central issue is this: How can a denomination such as the Southern Baptist Convention, or a transdenominational movement such as 'American evangelicalism, maintain either identity or integrity without careful attention to the acceptable limits of doctrinal diversity? Furthermore, when do issues of doctrinal diversity finally reach the limits of belief and disbelief?[28]

Rampant theological pluralism is the natural, and probably unavoidable, product of a parameter-free theological environment.[29] The theological confusion that marks the mainline churches provides abundant evidence of what an ideology of pluralism produces. Mirroring Anglican claims to "comprehensiveness," mainline churches have attempted to open themselves to any and all theological positions and have become, in large part, a discordant mass of confusion.

As Leonard I. Sweet commented, theological pluralism "became the fairy godmother of modernist Protestantism, non-inclusivism its wicked stepfather."[30] Furthermore, denominations committed to pluralism had become "a veritable flea market of faiths."[31]

At least one mainline body has an "Office of Pluralism," acknowledging the status of the inclusivist agenda.[32] Reflecting on the progress of the pluralist agenda, one inside observer acknowledged that "such a

---

[27] See, for example, the research conducted among SBC pastors by Professor Nancy Ammerman of Emory University in her recent volume, *Baptist Battles: Social Change and Religious Conflict in the Southern Baptist Convention* (New Brunswick: Rutgers University Press, 1990), see especially 74ff.

[28] See my discussion of boundaried and centered groups, the necessity of doctrinal parameters, and the issue of theological triage in "Beyond the Impasse: Has Theology a Future in the Southern Baptist Convention?," cited above.

[29] An advancing pluralism can be observed in both evangelical and Southern Baptist ranks. Evangelicals, given their transdenominational organization and lack of a deliberative process, generally rely on parameters established by individual institutions, voluntary Evangelicals, and the Evangelical Theological Society. Southern Baptists have no effective Conventionwide doctrinal parameters for local churches, though all six SBC seminaries have statements of faith which must be signed by all permanent faculty. Much of the debate in the Southern Baptist conflict, and a considerable part of the traumatic controversy related to the seminaries, concerns the extent to which these statements of faith exercise a *regulative* function.

[30] Leonard I. Sweet, "The Modernization of Protestant Religion in America," in *Altered Landscapes: Christianity in America 1935-1985*, ed. David W. Lotz (Grand Rapids: Eerdmans, 1989), 36.

[31] Ibid., 37.

church is destined to capitulate within its own life the divisions of the culture and that its theology will enjoy no sanctuary from the painful process.[33]

What doctrinal standards apply? Or are such standards considered to be hopelessly noninclusive and coercive? Richard G. Hutcheson comments:

> While doctrinal standards establish general parameters, they are seldom applied in a way excluding anyone. Even candidates for the clergy, in mainline denominations, are more likely to be rejected for excessive narrowness than for violation of confessional standards. As for the laity, one can hardly conceive a belief, idiosyncracy, or variance which would disqualify a layperson conscientiously and sincerely seeking membership in a mainline church.[34]

Evangelicals and Southern Baptists have much to learn by observing this process in other communions.[35] The issues of doctrinal standards and parameters and the determination of a proper mode of confessionalism will determine whether or not Southern Baptists and evangelical bodies are willing to follow the mainline model.

The Issue of Higher Education

Southern Baptists and evangelicals have established and supported a remarkable network of colleges, universities, and theological seminaries. Southern Baptist colleges and universities range from small liberal-arts colleges to major regional universities such as Baylor, Wake Forest, Samford, Mercer, Furman, and the University of Richmond. Evangelicals have a similar, and no less impressive, network of colleges such as Wheaton, Gordon, Trinity, Taylor, Seattle Pacific, and Eastern. Southern Baptists boast six of the largest theological seminaries in the world, and evangelicals can boast of institutions such as Fuller Theological Seminary, Trinity Evangelical Divinity School, and Gordon-Conwell Theologi-

---

[32] An office of Pluralism was established within the Theology and Worship Ministry Unit of the Presbyterian Church U.S.A. in its reorganization conducted in the late 1980s. See Jack B. Rogers and Donald K. McKim, "Pluralism and Policy in Presbyterian Views of Scripture," in *The Confessional Mosaic: Presbyterians and Twentieth-Century Theology*, 55.

[33] James H. Moorhead, "Redefining Confessionalism: American Presbyterians in the Twentieth Century," in *The Confessional Mosaic*, 83.

[34] Richard G. Hutcheson, *Mainline Churches and the Evangelicals* (Atlanta: John Knox, 1981), 31.

[35] Many evangelicals are, of course, members of mainline churches and thus can observe the process close at hand.

cal Seminary. The Beeson Divinity School of Samford University was launched in 1988 with a publicly announced design to bridge Southern Baptists and evangelicals.

One of the most vexing issues confronting both evangelicals and Southern Baptists is the nature of a genuinely *Christian* higher education.[36] The shift of many institutions from an evangelical base to more accommodationist and inclusivist postures—with little attention given to a Christian world view—brings into question the distinctively Christian character of some denominational and supposedly evangelical institutions.[37]

These concerns have been refocused by the research of sociologist James Davison Hunter, whose extensive project on the evangelical engagement with modernity and the future of the evangelical movement will shape discussions for years to come. Hunter describes a process of "cognitive bargaining" in which Christian scholars concede truth claims in order to meet the expectations of the larger academic culture. That is, Christian scholars (and their students) are pressured to surrender truth claims and "downplay supernaturalism."[38]

The effect of this process, and other patterns, have shaped higher education—and the theological disciplines—and will shape the future of evangelicalism and the Southern Baptist Convention. Because of this fact, higher education and the education of ministers will remain the most critical battleground in denominational and parachurch battles.

Are Southern Baptists "Evangelicals"?

Like so many issues of debate in the Southern Baptist conflict, this question must be clarified before any answer can be offered. A historical perspective reveals that Southern Baptists were most certainly considered a part of the "evangelical alliance" of the nineteenth century. Similarly, Southern Baptists largely accepted the label "fundamentalist" before the term took on militant, separatist, and uncooperative connotations in the 1930s.[39] The essays contained in this volume demonstrate

---

[36] See the insightful treatment of this issue by George M. Marsden in "The Soul of the University," *First Things*, 9, (January 1991).

[37] See the interesting discussion of these issues in William C. Ringenberg, "The Christian College," *A History of Protestant Higher Education In America* (Grand Rapids: Eerdmans, 1984).

[38] James Davison Hunter, *American Evangelicalism: Conservative Religion and the Quandary of Modernity* (New Brunswick: Rutgers University Press, 1983), and *Evangelicalism: The Coming Generation* (Chicago: University of Chicago Press, 1987).

that the question must be posed differently at the end of the twentieth century.

Here, again, the issue of Baptist identity is crucial. Those who define Southern Baptist identity in terms of a libertarian experiential tradition are prone to see the Baptist tradition and contemporary evangelical movements at odds. Glenn Hinson has suggested that the name Baptist "refers to that version of the Christian faith which places the priority of voluntary and uncoerced faith or response to the Word and Act of God over any supposed 'objective' Word and Act of God."[40] With this definition of Baptist identity as presupposition, Hinson sees the evangelical movement as a threat to Baptist voluntarism. In fact, he suggests that Southern Baptists and evangelicals "come from different wombs."[41] Evangelicals, Hinson laments, are "preoccupied with orthodoxy" and, with missionary zeal, "are infusing their outlook deeper and deeper into Southern Baptist life."[42] Hinson's essay in the present volume continues and extends this argument, revealing a heightened concern that Southern Baptists will succumb to what he sees as an inherently authoritarian and coercive movement.

Leon McBeth's essay reveals a similar concern, as he sees evangelicals as "militant, anti-denominational, [and] anti-ecclesiastical." "I do not want to be either an evangelical or a fundamentalist, at least as I understand the terms," he avers. Both Hinson and McBeth read evangelicalism through "fundamentalist-colored glasses." They seem unable to distinguish between separatistic and militant fundamentalism (such as that modeled by J. Frank Norris and Bob Jones, Sr.) and the evangelical movement of the late-twentieth century.[43] Just how *un*preoccupied with orthodoxy should a Baptist denomination be? we might ask.

Baptists who limit their vision of evangelical identity to militant fundamentalism and who base their vision of Baptist identity on a spiritual voluntarism that will abide no doctrinal parameters will naturally attempt to put distance between the Baptist heritage and the evangelical movement.

Others see the issue in different terms. Seeing the Baptist heritage as a wedding of uncoerced experiential faith with classical orthodoxy,

---

[39] Compare the use of the term in the Southern Baptist Convention before and after the rise of J. Frank Norris and independent Baptist fundamentalism in the South.

[40] Garrett, Hinson, and Tull, 172.

[41] Ibid., 166.

[42] Ibid.

[43] Clark Pinnock's distinction between evangelicals in army boots and those in running shoes is a helpful corrective at this point.

these Southern Baptists see American evangelicals as esteemed allies with many shared concerns and an overarching common commitment to the gospel. Thus, maintaining that Southern Baptists have a unique contribution to make to the evangelical movement, James Leo Garrett suggests the label of "denomination Evangelicals."[44]

If Southern Baptists are not evangelicals, just how should they be classified? The fact of the matter is that Southern Baptists will *increasingly* be seen as evangelicals, whether they intend to be so identified or not. A case can be made that Southern Baptists were, until the late 1970s, following a trajectory in keeping with the pattern of mainline Protestantism. That trajectory has now been slowed, but the future course of the Southern Baptist experiment is not yet clear.

In terms of core beliefs, Southern Baptists are, with very few exceptions, clearly evangelical. Participants in the recent "Evangelical Affirmations" conference organized by Carl F.H. Henry and Kenneth Kantzer adopted a statement which listed "three marks" of evangelical identity. These were: (1) belief in the gospel as set forth in Scripture (salvation through grace by faith); (2) commitment to the basic doctrines of the Bible as found in the Apostle's creed and other historic confessions (the "material or content principle"); and (3) an acknowledgment of the Bible as the authoritative and final source of all doctrines (the "formative or forming principle").[45]

A Call for Evangelical Baptists and Baptist Evangelicals

The best hope for the recovery of the Southern Baptist Convention lies in the rediscovery and reclamation of an authentic and distinctive Southern Baptist evangelicalism—*genuinely Baptist*, and *genuinely evangelical*. This Baptist evangelicalism would protect the distinctive Baptist emphasis on religious liberty and uncoerced faith, but it would

---

[44] This is also a helpful corrective to George Marsden's definition of "card-carrying evangelicals," who see themselves primarily as "part of a transdenominational evangelical movement." There are also "card-carrying evangelicals" who function in what we might term a "denomination mode" and do not see their strong and undiluted denominational identity in conflict with their common identity with the larger evangelical community.

[45] Carl F.H. Henry and Kenneth Kantzer, eds. *Evangelical Affirmations* (Grand Rapids: Zondervan, 1990), 37. The statement continues: "These then are the three distinguishing marks of all evangelicals. Without constant fidelity to all three marks, evangelicals will be unable to meet the demands of the future and interact effectively with the internal and external challenges noted in these affirmations. Evangelical churches also hold various distinctive doctrines that are important to them; but nonetheless, they share this common evangelical faith" (38).

also contend for the integrity of orthodox doctrine and the necessity of confessional parameters. It would reaffirm Southern Baptist commitment to the Great Commission and, at the same time, realize that the gospel itself is threatened by the acids of modernity.

Southern Baptists have much to learn from the evangelical movement and much to teach in return. Evangelicals have traversed much of the ground Southern Baptists are not contesting, and the Southern Baptist conflict has taken place within the context of a major cultural and ideological shift in the life of the Western world—a shift which adds great urgency to the development of evangelical solidarity.

As Robert Wuthnow and others observe, American religious life is now marked by an unmistakable faultline that divides religious liberals from conservatives. This divide is more firmly established and plays a far more pivotal role than divisions between denominational traditions, geographical regions, or congregational styles. The vast majority of Southern Baptists and American evangelicals stand unashamedly on the same side of the divide.

Let me state clearly: The greatest danger is that Southern Baptists will not meet the challenge of the present hour and recover an authentic Baptist evangelicalism. Southern Baptists are now in a period of reconstruction. The future shape of the Convention must avoid the twin dangers of obscurantist, angry, and separatist fundamentalism on the right and revisionist compromise on the left. In between lies the evangelical option—an irenic, bold, and convictional posture which combines concern for orthodox doctrine with a spirit of engagement with the larger world and a missionary mandate.

Without abandoning that which is distinctive to the Baptist heritage, we should link arms in a common witness to the truth of the gospel, to the full truthfulness and authority of Holy Scripture, to the necessity of redemption through Christ's atoning work and the gift of faith, to the uniqueness of Jesus the Christ and salvation through Him alone. We must recommit ourselves to the missionary mandate of the Great Commission and to the nature of the church as a "peculiar people"—willing to bear the scandal of the cross for the high calling of giving witness to the gospel for Christ's sake.

In so doing, Southern Baptists—and American evangelicals—must claim continuity with those who, from the first century onward, have been *evangels* of the gospel. For, as darkness falls and unbelief gains, we are called to hold forth a light the world cannot dim.

Bibliography

American Evangelicals

Bloesch, Donald G. *The Evangelical Renaissance*. Grand Rapids: Eerdmans, 1973.

_____. *The Future of Evangelical Christianity: A Call for Unity Amid Diversity*. Garden City, NY: Doubleday, 1983.

Dayton, Donald W. *Discovering an Evangelical Heritage*. New York: Harper and Row, 1976.

_____ and Robert K. Johnston. *The Variety of American Evangelicalism*. Downers Grove: InterVarsity, 1991.

Ellingsen, Mark. *The Evangelical Movement: Growth, Impact, Controversy, Dialogue*. Minneapolis: Augsburg, 1988.

Erickson, Millard J. *The New Evangelical Theory*. Westwood, NJ: Revell, 1968.

Frank, Douglas W. *Less Than Conquerors: How Evangelicals Entered the Twentieth Century*. Grand Rapids: Eerdmans, 1986.

Hatch, Nathan O. and Mark O. Noll. *The Bible in America*. New York: Oxford, 1982.

Henry, Carl F.H. *Evangelicals in Search of Identity*. Waco: Word, 1976.

Hunter, James Davison. *American Evangelicalism*. New Brunswick, NJ: Rutgers University Press, 1983.

_____. *Evangelicalism: The Coming Generation*. Chicago: University Press, 1987.

Marsden, George M. *Fundamentalism and American Culture : The Shaping of Twentieth Century Evangelicalism 1870-1925*. New York: Oxford, 1980.

Nelson, Rudolph. *The Making and Unmaking of an Evangelical Mind: The Case of Edward Carnell*. Cambridge: University Press, 1987.

Noll, Mark A. *Between Faith and Criticism: Evangelicals, Scholarship, and the Bible in America*. San Francisco: Harper and Row, 1986.

Padilla, C. Rene, ed. *The New Face of Evangelicalism*. Downers Grove: InterVarsity, 1976.

Quebedeaux, Richard. *The Worldly Evangelicals*. San Francisco: Harper and Row, 1978.

_____. *The Young Evangelicals*. San Francisco: Harper and Row, 1974.

Ramm, Bernard L. *The Evangelical Heritage*. Waco: Word, 1973.

Shelley, Bruce. *Evangelicalism in America*. Grand Rapids: Eerdmans, 1967.

Woodbridge, John D., Mark A. Noll, and Nathan O. Hatch. *The Gospel in America*. Grand Rapids: Zondervan, 1979.

Southern Baptists

Ammerman, Nancy T. *Baptist Battles*. New Brunswick, NJ: Rutgers University Press, 1990.

Armstrong, O. K. and Marjorie Moore Armstrong. *The Indomitable Baptists*. Garden City, NY: Doubleday, 1967.

Baker, Robert A. *Tell the Generations Following: A History of Southwestern Baptist Theological Seminary*. Nashville: Broadman, 1983.

_____. *The Southern Baptist Convention and Its People, 1607-1972*. Nashville: Broadman, 1974.

Basden, Paul and David S. Dockery, eds. *People of God: Essays on the Believers' Church*. Nashville: Broadman, 1991.

Brackney, William H. *The Baptists*. New York: Greenwood, 1988.

Cox, Norman and Lynn May, eds. *Encyclopedia of Southern Baptists*. 4 vols. Nashville: Broadman, 1958-82.

Ellis, William E. *A Man of Books and a Man of the People: E. Y. Mullins and the Crisis of Moderate Southern Baptist Leadership*. Macon, GA: Mercer University Press, 1985.

Garrett, Duane and Richard R. Melick, Jr. *Authority and Interpretation: A Baptist Perspective*. Grand Rapids: Baker, 1986.

Garrett, James Leo, Jr., ed. *Baptist Relations with Other Christians*. Valley Forge: Judson, 1974.

Garrett, James Leo, Jr., E. Glenn Hinson, and James E. Tull. *Are Southern Baptists "Evangelicals"?* Macon, GA: Mercer University Press, 1983.

George, Timothy and David S. Dockery. *Baptist Theologians*. Broadman: Nashville, 1990.

Hill, Samuel S. *Encyclopedia of Religion in the South*. Macon, GA: Mercer University Press, 1984.

Leonard, Bill J. *God's Last and Only Hope: The Fragmentation of the Southern Baptist Convention*. Grand Rapids: Eerdmans, 1990.

Lumpkin, W. L., ed. *Baptist Confessions of Faith*. Valley Forge: Judson, 1959.

McBeth, H. Leon. *A Sourcebook for Baptist Heritage*. Nashville: Broadman, 1990.

_____. *The Baptist Heritage*. Nashville: Broadman, 1987.

Nettles, Thomas J. *By His Grace and for His Glory: A Historical, Theological, and Practical Study of the Doctrines of Grace in Baptist Life*. Grand Rapids: Baker, 1986.

Rosenberg, Ellen M. *The Southern Baptists*. Knoxville: University of Tennessee Press, 1989.

Shurden, Walter B. *Not a Silent People: Controversies that Have Shaped Southern Baptists*. Nashville: Broadman, 1972.

Torbet, Robert G. *A History of the Baptists*. Valley Forge: Judson, 1963.

Tull, James E. *Shapers of Baptist Thought*. Valley Forge: Judson, 1972.